Contents

Preface

The process of financial management takes place at two levels. At the individual level financial management involves tailoring expenses according to the financial resources of an individual. Individuals with surplus cash or access to funding invest their money to make up for the impact of taxation and inflation. The present book takes into consideration the different academic aspects of financial and investment management for undergraduate students studying financial and investment management in universities and management institutes. This work opens up a new dimension in the era of modern management. This work would be of great help to managerial practitioners at any organisational level who are responsible for a function, department or set of responsibilities. Investment is one of the important segment of capital formation. Investment management encourages investor to participate in the security market. The mechanism of the security market is relatively technical and dealing in the market requires skill.

Finance is the science of funds management. The general areas of finance are *business finance*, *personal finance*, and *public finance*. Finance includes saving money and often includes lending money. The field of finance deals with the concepts of time, money, risk and how they are interrelated. It also deals with how money is spent and budgeted. One facet of finance is through individuals and business organizations, which deposit money in a bank. The bank then lends the money out to other individuals or corporations for consumption or investment and charges interest on the loans.

Financial management entails planning for the future of a person or a business enterprise to ensure a positive cash flow. It includes the administration and maintenance of financial assets. Besides, financial management covers the process of identifying and managing risks. The primary concern of financial management is the assessment rather than the techniques of financial quantification. A financial manager looks at the available data to judge the performance of enterprises. Managerial finance is an interdisciplinary approach that borrows from both managerial accounting and corporate finance.

Some experts refer to financial management as the science of money management. The primary usage of this term is in the world of financing business activities. However, financial management is important at all levels of human existence because every entity needs to look after its finances.

Broadly speaking, the process of financial management takes place at two levels. At the individual level, financial management involves tailoring expenses according to the financial resources of an individual. Individuals with surplus cash or access to funding invest their money to make up for the impact of taxation and inflation. Else, they spend it on discretionary items. They need to be able to take the financial decisions that are intended to benefit them in the long run and help them achieve their financial goals.

The book intends to cover almost most of the aspects pertaining to Finance and Investment Management in a fundamental way. This book is intended to serve as a practical guide to the students, researchers and professionals working in this field.

—*Editor*

1

Overview of Financial Management

FINANCE

Finance is the science of funds management. The general areas of finance are *business finance*, *personal finance*, and *public finance*. Finance includes saving money and often includes lending money. The field of finance deals with the concepts of time, money, risk and how they are interrelated. It also deals with how money is spent and budgeted. One facet of finance is through individuals and business organizations, which deposit money in a bank. The bank then lends the money out to other individuals or corporations for consumption or investment and charges interest on the loans.

Loans have become increasingly packaged for resale, meaning that an investor buys the loan (debt) from a bank or directly from a corporation. Bonds are debt instruments sold to investors for organizations such as companies, governments or charities. The investor can then hold the debt and collect the interest or sell the debt on a secondary market. Banks are the main facilitators of funding through the provision of credit, although private equity, mutual funds, hedge funds, and other organizations have become important as they invest in various forms of debt. Financial assets, known as investments, are financially managed with careful attention to financial risk management to control financial risk. Financial instruments allow many forms of securitized assets to be traded on securities exchanges such as stock exchanges, including debt such as bonds as well as equity in publicly traded corporations.

Central banks, such as the Federal Reserve System banks in the United States and Bank of England in the United Kingdom, are strong players in public finance, acting as lenders of last resort as well as strong influences on monetary and credit conditions in the economy.

OVERVIEW OF TECHNIQUES AND SECTORS OF THE FINANCIAL INDUSTRY

An entity whose income exceeds its expenditure can lend or invest the excess income. On the other hand, an entity whose income is less than its expenditure can raise capital by borrowing or selling equity claims, decreasing its expenses, or increasing its income. The lender can find a borrower, a financial intermediary such as a bank, or buy notes or bonds in the bond market. The lender receives interest, the borrower pays a higher interest than the lender receives, and the financial intermediary earns the difference for arranging the loan. A bank aggregates the activities of many borrowers and lenders. A bank accepts deposits from lenders, on which it pays interest. The bank then lends these deposits to borrowers. Banks allow borrowers and lenders, of different sizes, to coordinate their activity.

Finance is used by individuals (personal finance), by governments (public finance), by businesses (corporate finance) and by a wide variety of other organizations, including schools and non-profit organizations. In general, the goals of each of the above activities are achieved through the use of appropriate financial instruments and methodologies, with consideration to their institutional setting.

Finance is one of the most important aspects of business management and includes decisions related to the use and acquisition of funds for the enterprise.

In corporate finance, a company's capital structure is the total mix of financing methods it uses to raise funds. One method is *debt financing*, which includes bank loans and bond sales. Another method is *equity financing* - the sale of stock by a company to investors. Possession of stock gives the investor ownership in the company in proportion to the number of shares the investor owns. In return for the stock, the company receives cash, which it may use to expand its business or to reduce its debt. Investors, in both bonds and stock, may be *institutional investors* - financial institutions such as investment banks and pension funds - or private individuals, called *private investors* or *retail investors*

Personal Finance

Questions in personal finance revolve around:

- How much money will be needed by an individual (or by a family), and when?
- How can people protect themselves against unforeseen personal events, as well as those in the external economy?
- How can family assets best be transferred across generations (bequests and inheritance)?
- How does tax policy (tax subsidies or penalties) affect personal financial decisions?
- How does credit affect an individual's financial standing?
- How can one plan for a secure financial future in an environment of economic instability?

Personal financial decisions may involve paying for education, financing durable goods such as real estate and cars, buying insurance, e.g. health and property insurance, investing and saving for retirement. Personal financial decisions may also involve paying for a loan, or debt obligations.

Corporate Finance

Managerial or corporate finance is the task of providing the funds for a corporation's activities. For small business, this is referred to as SME finance (Small and Medium Enterprises). It generally involves balancing risk and profitability, while attempting to maximize an entity's wealth and the value of its stock. Long term funds are provided by ownership equity and long-term credit, often in the form of bonds. The balance between these elements forms the company's capital structure. Short-term funding or working capital is mostly provided by banks extending a line of credit. Another business decision concerning finance is investment, or fund management. An investment is an acquisition of an asset in the hope that it will maintain or increase its value. In investment management – in choosing a portfolio – one has to decide *what, how much* and *when* to invest. To do this, a company must:

- Identify relevant objectives and constraints: institution or individual goals, time horizon, risk aversion and tax considerations;
- Identify the appropriate strategy: active *v.* passive – hedging strategy
- Measure the portfolio performance

Financial management is duplicate with the financial function of the Accounting profession. However, financial accounting is more concerned with the reporting of historical financial information, while the financial decision is directed toward the future of the firm.

Capital

Capital, in the financial sense, is the money that gives the business the power to buy goods to be used in the production of other goods or the offering of a service.

The Desirability of Budgeting

Budget is a document which documents the plan of the business. This may include the objective of business, targets set, and results in financial terms, e.g., the target set for sale, resulting cost, growth, required investment to achieve the planned sales, and financing source for the investment. Also budget may be long term or short term. Long term budgets have a time horizon of 5–10 years giving a vision to the company; short term is an annual budget which is drawn to control and operate in that particular year.

Capital Budget

This concerns proposed fixed asset requirements and how these expenditures will be financed. Capital budgets are often adjusted annually and should be part of a longer-term Capital Improvements Plan.

Cash Budget

Working capital requirements of a business should be monitored at all times to ensure that there are sufficient funds available to meet short-term expenses.

The cash budget is basically a detailed plan that shows all expected sources and uses of cash. The cash budget has the following six main sections:

1. Beginning Cash Balance - contains the last period's closing cash balance.
2. Cash collections - includes all expected cash receipts (all sources of cash for the period considered, mainly sales)
3. Cash disbursements - lists all planned cash outflows for the period, excluding interest payments on short-term loans, which appear in the financing section. All expenses that do not affect cash flow are excluded from this list (e.g. depreciation, amortization, etc.)
4. Cash excess or deficiency - a function of the cash needs and cash available. Cash needs are determined by the total cash disbursements plus the minimum cash balance required by company policy. If total cash available is less than cash needs, a deficiency exists.
5. Financing - discloses the planned borrowings and repayments, including interest.
6. Ending Cash balance - simply reveals the planned ending cash balance.

MANAGEMENT OF CURRENT ASSETS

Credit Policy

Credit gives the consumer the opportunity to buy, purchase or acquire goods and services, and pay for them at a later date. This has its advantages and disadvantages as follows:

Advantages of Credit Trade

- Usually results in more customers than cash trade.
- Can charge more for goods to cover the risk of bad debt.
- Gain goodwill and loyalty of customers.
- People can buy goods and pay for them at a later date.

- Farmers can buy seeds and implements, and pay for them only after the harvest.
- Stimulates agricultural and industrial production and commerce.
- Can be used as a promotional tool.
- Increase the sales.
- Modest rates to be filled.
- can be a marketing tool.

Disadvantages of Credit Trade

- Risk of bad debt.
- High administration expenses.
- People can buy more than they can afford.
- More working capital needed.
- Risk of Bankruptcy.

Forms of Credit

- Suppliers credit:
- Credit on ordinary open account
- Installment sales
- Bills of exchange
- Credit cards
- Contractor's credit
- Factoring of debtors
- Cash credit
- Cpf credits
- Exchange of product.

Factors which Influence Credit Conditions

- Nature of the business's activities
- Financial position
- Product durability
- Length of production process
- Competition and competitors' credit conditions
- Country's economic position
- Conditions at financial institutions

First Published 2011

ISBN 978-81-8420-267-0

Published by:

SUMIT ENTERPRISES
4649B/21, Ansari Road, Darya Ganj
New Delhi-110 002
Phone: 011-23279353, 9810217567
E-mail: sumit_enterprises2007@yahoo.co.in

PRINTED IN INDIA

Published by Sri Lokesh Kumar for Sumit Enterprises, New Delhi-110002, Typeset by Abhijeet Typesetters, Printed at Nev Prabhat Printing Press, Tronicacity (UP)

Finance and Investment Management

Dr. Anuradha Monga

SUMIT ENTERPRISES
New Delhi-110 002 (India)

- Discount for early payment
- Debtor's type of business and financial position.

CREDIT COLLECTION

Overdue Accounts

- Attach a notice of overdue account to statement.
- Send a letter asking for settlement of debt.
- Send a second or third letter if first is ineffectual.
- Threaten legal actions.

Effective Credit Control

- Increases sales
- Reduces bad debts
- Increases profits
- Builds customer loyalty
- Builds confidence of financial industry
- Increase company capitalisation
- Increase the customer relationship.

Sources of Information on Creditworthiness

- Business references
- Bank references
- Credit agencies
- Chambers of commerce
- Employers
- Credit application forms.

Duties of the Credit Department

- Legal action
- Taking necessary steps to ensure settlement of account
- Knowing the credit policy and procedures for credit control
- Setting credit limits
- Ensuring that statements of account are sent out
- Ensuring that thorough checks are carried out on credit customers

- Keeping records of all amounts owing
- Ensuring that debts are settled promptly
- Timely reporting to the upper level of management for better management.

Stock

Purpose of stock control:

- Ensures that enough stock is on hand to satisfy demand.
- Protects and monitors theft.
- Safeguards against having to stockpile.
- Allows for control over selling and cost price.

STOCKPILING

This refers to the purchase of stock at the right time, at the right price and in the right quantities. There are several advantages to the stockpiling, the following are some of the examples:

- Losses due to price fluctuations and stock loss kept to a minimum
- Ensures that goods reach customers timeously; better service
- Saves space and storage cost
- Investment of working capital kept to minimum
- No loss in production due to delays.

There are several disadvantages to the stockpiling, the following are some of the examples:

- Obsolescence
- Danger of fire and theft
- Initial working capital investment is very large
- Losses due to price fluctuation.

Rate of Stock Turnover

This refers to the number of times per year that the average level of stock is sold. It may be worked out by dividing the cost price of goods sold by the cost price of the average stock level.

Determining optimum stock levels:

- Maximum stock level refers to the maximum stock level that may be maintained to ensure cost effectiveness.

- Minimum stock level refers to the point below which the stock level may not go.
- Standard order refers to the amount of stock generally ordered.
- Order level refers to the stock level which calls for an order to be made.

CASH

Reasons for Keeping Cash

- Cash is usually referred to as the "king" in finance, as it is the most liquid asset.
- The transaction motive refers to the money kept available to pay expenses.
- The precautionary motive refers to the money kept aside for unforeseen expenses.
- The speculative motive refers to the money kept aside to take advantage of suddenly arising opportunities.

Advantages of Sufficient Cash

- Current liabilities may be catered for meeting the current obligations of the company
- Cash discounts are given for cash payments.
- Production is kept moving
- Surplus cash may be invested on a short-term basis.
- The business is able to pay its accounts in a timely manner, allowing for easily obtained credit.
- Liquidity
- Quick upfront pay.

MANAGEMENT OF FIXED ASSETS

Depreciation

Depreciation is the allocation of the cost of an asset over its useful life as determined at the time of purchase. It is calculated yearly to enforce the matching principle

Insurance

Insurance is the undertaking of one party to indemnify

another, in exchange for a premium, against a certain eventuality.

Uninsured risks:

- Bad debt
- Changes in fashion
- Time lapses between ordering and delivery
- New machinery or technology
- Different prices at different places

Requirements of an insurance contract

- Insurable interest
  * The insured must derive a real financial gain from that which he is insuring, or stand to lose if it is destroyed or lost.
  * The item must belong to the insured.
  * One person may take out insurance on the life of another if the second party owes the first money.
  * Must be some person or item which can, legally, be insured.
  * The insured must have a legal claim to that which he is insuring.
- Good faith
  * *Uberrimae fidei* refers to absolute honesty and must characterise the dealings of both the insurer and the insured.

Shared Services

There is currently a move towards converging and consolidating Finance provisions into shared services within an organization. Rather than an organization having a number of separate Finance departments performing the same tasks from different locations a more centralized version can be created.

Finance of Public Entities

Public finance describes finance as related to sovereign states and sub-national entities (states/provinces, counties, municipalities, etc.) and related public entities (e.g. school districts) or agencies. It is concerned with:

- Identification of required expenditure of a public sector entity
- Source(s) of that entity's revenue
- The budgeting process
- Debt issuance (municipal bonds) for public works projects.

FINANCIAL ECONOMICS

Financial economics is the branch of economics studying the interrelation of financial variables, such as prices, interest rates and shares, as opposed to those concerning the real economy. Financial economics concentrates on influences of real economic variables on financial ones, in contrast to pure finance.

It studies:

- Valuation - Determination of the fair value of an asset
  * How risky is the asset? (identification of the asset-appropriate discount rate)
  * What cash flows will it produce? (discounting of relevant cash flows)
  * How does the market price compare to similar assets? (relative valuation)
  * Are the cash flows dependent on some other asset or event? (derivatives, contingent claim valuation)
- Financial markets and instruments
  * Commodities - topics
  * Stocks - topics
  * Bonds - topics
  * Money market instruments- topics
  * Derivatives - topics
- Financial institutions and regulation

Financial Econometrics is the branch of Financial Economics that uses econometric techniques to parameterise the relationships.

FINANCIAL MATHEMATICS

Financial mathematics is a main branch of applied mathematics concerned with the financial markets. Financial mathematics is the study of financial data with the tools of mathematics, mainly statistics. Such data can be movements of securities—stocks and bonds etc.—and their relations. Another large subfield is insurance mathematics. This is also known as quantitative finance, practitioners as Quantitative analysts.

Experimental Finance

Experimental finance aims to establish different market settings and environments to observe experimentally and provide a lens through which science can analyze agents' behaviour and the resulting characteristics of trading flows, information diffusion and aggregation, price setting mechanisms, and returns processes. Researchers in experimental finance can study to what extent existing financial economics theory makes valid predictions, and attempt to discover new principles on which such theory can be extended. Research may proceed by conducting trading simulations or by establishing and studying the behaviour of people in artificial competitive market-like settings.

Behavioural Finance

Behavioural Finance studies how the psychology of investors or managers affects financial decisions and markets. Behavioural finance has grown over the last few decades to become central to finance.

Behavioural finance includes such topics as:

1. Empirical studies that demonstrate significant deviations from classical theories.
2. Models of how psychology affects trading and prices
3. Forecasting based on these methods.
4. Studies of experimental asset markets and use of models to forecast experiments.

A strand of Behavioural finance has been dubbed Quantitative Behavioural Finance, which uses mathematical and statistical methodology to understand Behavioural biases in conjunction with valuation. Some of this endeavor has been led by Gunduz Caginalp (Professor of Mathematics and Editor of Journal of Behavioural Finance during 2001-2004) and collaborators including Vernon Smith (2002 Nobel Laureate in Economics), David Porter, Don Balenovich, Vladimira Ilieva, Ahmet Duran). Studies by Jeff Madura, Ray Sturm and others have demonstrated significant Behavioural effects in stocks and exchange traded funds. Among other topics, quantitative Behavioural finance studies Behavioural effects together with the non-classical assumption of the finiteness of assets.

FINANCIAL MANAGEMENT

Financial management entails planning for the future of a person or a business enterprise to ensure a positive cash flow. It includes the administration and maintenance of financial assets. Besides, financial management covers the process of identifying and managing risks. The primary concern of financial management is the assessment rather than the techniques of financial quantification. A financial manager looks at the available data to judge the performance of enterprises. Managerial finance is an interdisciplinary approach that borrows from both managerial accounting and corporate finance.

Some experts refer to financial management as the science of money management. The primary usage of this term is in the world of financing business activities. However, financial management is important at all levels of human existence because every entity needs to look after its finances.

FINANCIAL MANAGEMENT: LEVELS

Broadly speaking, the process of financial management takes place at two levels. At the individual level, financial management involves tailoring expenses according to the financial resources of an individual. Individuals with surplus cash or access to funding invest their money to make up for the impact of taxation and inflation. Else, they spend it on discretionary items. They need to be able to take the financial decisions that are intended to benefit them in the long run and help them achieve their financial goals.

From an organizational point of view, the process of financial management is associated with financial planning and financial control. Financial planning seeks to quantify various financial resources available and plan the size and timing of expenditures. Financial control refers to monitoring cash flow. Inflow is the amount of money coming into a particular company, while outflow is a record of the expenditure being made by the company. Managing this movement of funds in relation to the budget is essential for a business. At the corporate level, the main aim of the process of managing finances is to achieve the various goals a company sets at a given point of time. Businesses also seek to generate substantial amounts of profits, following a particular set of financial processes.

Financial managers aim to boost the levels of resources at their disposal. Besides, they control the functioning on money put in by external investors. Providing investors with sufficient amount of returns on their investments is one of the goals that every company tries to achieve. Efficient financial management ensures that this becomes possible.

Strong financial management in the business arena requires managers to be able to:

1. Interpret financial reports including income statements, Profits and Loss or P&L, cash flow statements and balance sheet statements
2. Improve the allocation of working capital within business operations
3. Review and fine tune financial budgeting, and revenue and cost forecasting
4. Look at the funding options for business expansion, including both long and short term financing
5. Review the financial health of the company or business unit using ratio analyses, such as the gearing ratio, profit per employee and weighted cost of capital
6. Understand the various techniques using in project and asset valuations
7. Apply critical financial decision making techniques to assess whether to proceed with an investment

8. Understand valuations frameworks for businesses, portfolios and intangible assets

TAKING CONTROL

Financial management involves taking a historic view of your group's finances. By looking at your past records of income and expenditure, you can form an accurate idea of what you are likely to receive and spend in the future - otherwise known as budgeting and forecasting.

Budgeting and Forecasting

Budgets are much more than an arithmetical exercise - they are a fundamental element of planning and management. Management is about decision taking and this means making assumptions about the future. The best way to get an accurate forecast is to study the past performance of the organisation and identify trends. Looking at monthly figures rather than annual performance figures will naturally give earlier warning of any change in trend. Clearly if income can be predicted with a high degree of certainty, a finance manager can agree to future expenditure. In a less certain income climate, management will need to find ways of protecting the organisation from risk by reducing commitments and increasing reserves.

Costs

Its very important to accurately measure the cost of your activities. List your various activities then systematically look at the costs of running each of them. It is helpful to categorise them as either fixed or variable costs. Fixed costs are those which stay the same whatever the volume of output and variable costs increase or decrease directly in proportion to volume.

Think of the cost of using a car over a year - the fixed costs will include tax and insurance, whereas the costs of petrol and repairs, which will change according to how much the car is used, are variable. For more information about fixed and variable costs and calculating your break-even point - see the costs activity and break-even activity. Services provided by the voluntary sector might not always be the most cost-effective, and any financial manager will have a difficult juggling act trying to provide high quality services that users can afford, while keeping a close eye on the financial health of the organisation.

Comparisons Between the Commercial and non-profit Sectors

Charity Financial Managers	*Business Financial Managers*
Less complex workload, but important to understand commercial operations.	More complex, structural questions about how to use shareholders funds-pay dividends or plough back?
Ability to deal with numerous different grants and stakeholders-requiring different types of accounting.	More straightforward 'textbook' business accounting.
No bottom line profit means problems of motivation, performance measurement and control.	Measurement of success or failure should be easier.

Monitoring and Reporting

Measuring performance in non-profit organisations is much more problematic than in a commercial enterprise, where the return on an investor's capital is the key performance indicator.

There is a legal obligation for all organisations to account for their income and expenditure. Management reporting requirements are less prescriptive as they tend to deal with matters of judgement and details peculiar to an individual organisation. Good practice requires that financial management information should be available on a regular basis, as often as necessary for decision taking and at frequent regular intervals for monitoring purposes. For the smaller charity quarterly reports may be sufficient but for larger charities should aim for monthly management accounts. Being on top of your cash-flow is crucial. Be certain about how much money is in the bank and what you can afford. If a large number of receipts are coming in, it's advisable to report on a daily basis. Financial reports are rarely sufficient in themselves and should be accompanied by quantitative information wherever possible. This is especially important in the case of services to beneficiaries.

A Financial Procedures Manual

It is well worth keeping a financial procedures manual. This will allow the relevant staff - and your management committee - to consult and operate within its specifications. You will need to decide which of your members or employees is allowed to authorise spending, and how much each person is able to spend before they must check with their manager. An office assistant, for example, might have a spending limit of £100 for items of petty cash, while a department manager might have a limit of £5,000. All these details need to be recorded in the procedures manual and included in training programs.

Tax Matters

In general, non-profit organisations are exempt from income tax under the Taxes Act 1988 and from capital gains under the Chargeable Gains Act 1992. Where a charity has trading subsidiaries it is common to transfer any profit away from the subsidiary into the charity by way of a profit-shedding covenant, thereby reducing or eliminating any liability for tax on profits.

In general financial managers should make sure they properly classify receipts on which tax may be recoverable. There are specific reliefs, which include:

- Covenanted donations.
- Gift aid relief for single gifts.
- Gifts free of capital gains tax.
- Gifts free of inheritance tax.
- Gifts from charitable trusts.
- Covenanted salaries.

Needless to say these aspects of financial management are affected by complex statutory regulations which are liable to change from year to year. You may need professional advice to keep abreast of opportunities and threats in this area.

SCOPE OF FINANCIAL MANAGEMENT

To obtain finances, it is important to make an evaluation of the real conditions of finances and to explore sources from where these finances can be increased. Two important functions of financial management are to obtain finances for businesses and to make the effective use of it. Moreover, the decision about the policy of dividend also concerns the range of financial management. This can be named as a planning for the supply of finances.

The decision concerning the way of calculating the benefit (not distributed surpluses included, the deduction for depreciation etc) and the way of distributing it among the shareholders are inseparable from financial management. Thus, the functions managers there important of finances are decision of investment, decision of financing and decision of dividend. He must also decide for which the activities will finance are necessary and, which those are advantageous activities or not. For example, the investment of capital probably plots to require the substantial investment as the will as arrangement to obtain the working capital of exploitation for existing businesses are included in this function of finances.

There are two approaches identified with the range of financial management the traditional and modern approach. Under the traditional approach, the role of the finance manager is confined to only increase funds. It does not regard the effective use of the funds as part of function of financial management. On the one hand the modern approach underlines the two functions of financial management, namely, to increase funds and manufacture of the effective use of the funds. Thus the traditional approach represents a narrow sight of the range of financial management, whereas the modern approach is an overall sight of the same thing. The explanation of the name finance function, that is, the opinion about the function of a financial management had undergone the constant from time to time.

Functions of Financial Management

The finance department of an enterprise performs several functions in order to achieve the above objectives. The scope of finance function is very wide. It consists of the following activities:

Estimating the Requirement of Funds

The finance department must estimate the capital requirements of the firm accurately for long term and short term needs. In estimating the capital requirements of the business, the finance department must take help of the budgets of various activities of the business e.g. sales budget, production budget, expenses budget etc. prepared by the concerned departments. In the initial stage, the estimate is done by promoters but in a growing concern, it is done by the finance department. Unless the financial forecast is correct, business is likely to run into difficulties due to excess or shortage of funds. Correct estimates ensure the availability of funds as and when they are needed. In estimating the requirement of funds, nature and size of the business, modernization and expansion plan should be given due consideration.

Determining the Capital Structure

By capital structure we mean the kind and proportion of different securities for raising the required funds. Once the total requirement of funds is determined, a decision regarding the type of securities to be issued and the relative proportion between them is to be taken. The finance department must determine the proper mix of debt and equity. It should also decide the ratio between long term and short term debts. In determining these ratios, cost of raising finance from different sources, period for which funds are required and several other factors should be considered. A proper balance between risk and returns should be maintained.

Choice of Sources of Finance

A company can raise funds from different sources e.g. shareholders, debenture holders, banks, financial institutions, public deposits etc. Before raising the funds, it has to decide the source from which the funds are to be raised. The choice of the source of finance should be made very carefully by taking a number of factors into account such as cost of raising funds, conditions attached, charge on assets, burden of fixed charges, dilution of ownership and control etc. For example, if the company does not want to dilute the ownership, it will depend on any source of finance other than investment in shares.

Investment of Funds

The funds raised from different sources should be prudently invested in various assets -short term as well as long term to optimize the return on investment. In taking decisions for the investment of long term funds, a careful assessment of various alternatives should be made through capital budgeting, opportunity cost analysis and many other techniques used to evaluate the investment proposals.

A part of the long term funds should be invested in working capital of the company. While taking decision for the investment of funds in long term assets, management should be guided by three basic principles, viz. safety, profitability and liquidity. In taking decisions for the investment of funds in working capital, the finance manager must seek cooperation of marketing and production departments in estimating the funds which are to be involved in carrying of inventories in finished product and credit policy of the marketing department and in raw material and factory supplies of the production department.

Management of Cash

It is the prime responsibility of the finance manager to see that an adequate supply of cash is available at proper time for the smooth running of the business. Cash is needed to purchase raw materials, pay off creditors, to pay to workers and to meet the day to day expenses of the business. Availability of cash is necessary to maintain liquidity and credit- worthiness of the business.

Excess cash must be avoided as it costs money. It there is any cash in excess, it should be invested in near cash assets such as investments etc. which may be converted into cash within no time. A cash flow statement should be prepared by the department to know the correct need of cash is essential to achieve the goal of profitability and liquidity. The finance manager should decide in advance how much cash he should retain to meet current obligations of the company.

Disposal of Surplus

One of the prime function of the finance department is to allocate the surplus. After paying all taxes, the available surplus of the business can be allocated for three purposes -(a) for paying dividend to the shareholders as a return on their investment, (b) for distributing bonus to workmen and company's contribution to other profit sharing plans, and (c) for ploughing back of profits for the expansion of business. As far as the second alternative is concerned, the amount to be paid to workers is generally fixed either by statute or by agreement and therefore, there is no problem in allocating surplus for this purpose. But a considerable, attention is to be paid in so far as first and third alternatives are concerned i.e., how much to be paid to shareholders as dividend and how much to be retained in the business. For this purpose factors like the trend of the earning of the company, trend of the market price of its shares; the requirement of funds for the purpose of expansion and future prospects should be considered.

Financial Controls

The financial manager is under an obligation to check the financial performance of the funds invested in the business. There are a number of techniques to evaluate the performance viz. Return on Investment (ROI), budgetary control, cost control, internal audit, ratio analysis and break-even point analysis. The financial manager must lay emphasis on financial planning as well.

GOAL OF FINANCIAL MANAGEMENT

The goals of financial management At first thought, we might simply say that the goal of financial management is to aid in the maximisation of owner wealth, or more simply, maximisation of the firm's profits. Profits are, after all the bottom line. That's true, but as all managers know, the corporate environment has many other goals.

Maximisation of sales.

Maximisation of market share.

Maximisation of the growth rate of sales.

Maximisation of the market price of the firm's share value.

From the perspective of financial management there are two overriding goals.

1. Profitability.
2. Viability.

The firm wants to be profitable, and it wants to continue in business. It is possible to be profitable and yet fail to continue in business because of a lack of funds to operate (solvency).

Profitability

In maximising profits there is always a tradeoff with risk. The greater the risk we must incur, the greater the anticipated profit we demand. Certainly, given two equally risky projects we would always choose to undertake the one with a greater anticipated return. More often than not, however, our situation revolves around whether the return on a specific investment is great enough to justify the risk involved.

Viability

Firms have no desire to go bankrupt, so it is no surprise that one of the crucial goals of financial management is ensuring financial viability. This goal is often measured in terms of liquidity and solvency. Liquidity is simply a measure of the amount of resources a firm has that are cash or are convertible to cash in the near-term, to meet the obligations the firm has that are coming due in the near term. Accountants use the phrases "near-term" ,"short-term" and "current" interchangeably. Generally the near-term means one year or less. Thus a firm is liquid if it has enough near-term resources to meet its near-term obligations as they become due for payment.

Solvency is simply the same concept from a long-term perspective. Long-term simply means more than one year. Does the firm have enough cash generation potential over the next three, five, and ten years to meet the major cash needs that will occur over those periods? A firm must plan for adequate solvency well in advance because the potentially large amounts of cash involved may take a long period of planning to generate.

The roots of liquidity crises that put firms out of business are often buried in inadequate long-term solvency planning in earlier years.

So a good strategy is maximisation of your firm's liquidity and solvency, right? No, wrong. The treasurer has a complex problem with respect to liquidity. Every dollar kept in a liquid form (such as cash, treasury bills, or money market funds) is a dollar that could have been invested by the firm in some longer-term, higher yielding project or investment. There is a tradeoff in the area of viability and profitability. The more profitable the treasurer attempts to make the firm by keeping it fully invested, the lower the liquidity and the greater the possibility of a liquidity crisis and even bankruptcy. The more liquid the firm is kept, the lower the profits.

We mentioned that profitability and viability are not synonymous. A firm can be profitable every year of its existence, yet go bankrupt anyway. How can this happen? Frequently it is the result of rapid growth and poor financial planning. Consider a firm whose sales are so good that inventory is constantly being substantially expanded. Such expansion requires cash payments to suppliers well in advance of ultimate cash receipt from sales. Therefore growth implies outlay of substantial amounts of cash for the increased inventory levels needed to handle a growing sales volume. Additionally growth is often accompanied by an expansion of plant and equipment, again well in advance of the ultimate receipt of cash from customers. Do growing companies have to go bankrupt? Obviously not. But they do need to plan their solvency along with their growth. The key is to focus on the long-term plans for cash. It is often said that banks prefer to lend to those who don't need the money. Certainly banks don't like to lend to firms who are desperate for the money.

2

Corporate Finance Management

Corporate finance management entails the decision-making process used in allocating resources to maximize the value of the firm. Resource allocation involves 3 major decision areas:

- Capital budgeting
- Financing
- Dividend policy.

CAPITAL BUDGETING

Capital budgeting decides which investments are to be made with the firm's resources. The goal of capital budgeting is to invest in business projects or activities where the anticipated returns equal or exceed the cost of funds that must be committed to generate the required returns, as well as to divest in those projects or activities when returns fall short of the costs. Whether an investment will generate the required returns is determined by the discounted time-value of money of the investment's expected cash flow, also known as the *internal rate of return* (IRR). When deciding among a number of mutually exclusive investment options, the financial manager will choose the one that both generates the highest rate of return and does not exceed the cost of available funds.

Financing

Financing decides whether to use debt or equity to obtain the resources necessary to invest in a business project. Debt includes loans from banks and bonds purchased by bondholders. Equity includes the insurance of common stock or preferred stock. Whichever source of funds is chosen, the funds should be obtained at the lowest average cost to reduce the required rate of return and increase the net present value of the projects selected.

Dividend Policy

Cash flow that cannot be invested at a profit should be returned to the shareholders. Thus, the financial manager develops a dividend policy that specifies at what level an investment no longer provides the required return and funds should be returned to the equity investors, either through common stock dividends, preferred stock dividends, or stock repurchase by the firm. Typically, the dividend policy maintains dividends at a certain level to convey the proper status of the firm to financial markets and investors. For example, a company may decide to maintain dividends at a low level to demonstrate the future growth potential of the firm. Conversely, a policy that maintains dividends at high levels demonstrates the firm's strong financial structure.

In July 1999, Carleton "Carly" Fiorina assumed the position of CEO of Hewlett-Packard (HP). Investors were pleased with her view of HP's future: She promised 15 percent annual growth in sales and earnings, quite a goal for a company with five consecutive years of declining revenue. Ms. Fiorina also changed the way HP was run.

Rather than continuing to operate as separate product groups, which essentially meant the company operated as dozens of minicompanies, Ms. Fiorina reorganized the company into just two divisions. In 2002, HP announced that it would merge with Compaq Computers. However, in one of the more acrimonious corporate battles in recent history, a group led by Walter Hewlett, son of one of HP's cofounders, fought against the merger. Ms. Fiorina ultimately prevailed, and the merger took place. With Compaq in the fold, the company began a two-pronged strategy. It would compete with Dell in the lower-cost, more commodity-like personal computer segment and with IBM in the more specialized, high-end computing market.

Unfortunately for HP's shareholders, Ms. Fiorina's strategy did not work out as planned, and in February 2005, under pressure from HP's board of directors, Ms. Fiorina resigned her position as CEO. Evidently, investors also felt a change in direction was a good idea; HP's stock price jumped almost seven percent the day the resignation was announced. Understanding Ms. Fiorina's rise from corporate executive to chief executive officer, and finally, ex-employee, takes us into issues involving the corporate form of organization, corporate goals, and corporate control, all of which we discuss in this chapter.

WHAT IS CORPORATE FINANCE?

Suppose you decide to start a firm to make tennis balls. To do this, you hire managers to buy raw materials, and you assemble a workforce that will produce and sell finished tennis balls. In the language of finance, you make an investment in assets such as inventory, machinery, land, and labor. The amount of cash you invest in assets must be matched by an equal amount of cash raised by financing. When you begin to sell tennis balls, your firm will generate cash. This is the basis of value creation. The purpose of the firm is to create value for you, the owner. The value is reflected in the framework of the simple balance sheet model of the firm.

The Balance Sheet Model of the Firm

Suppose we take a financial snapshot of the firm and its activities at a single point in time. The assets of the firm are on the left-hand side of the balance sheet. These assets can be thought of as current and fixed. *Fixed assets* are those that will last a long time, such as buildings. Some fixed assets are tangible, such as machinery and equipment. Other fixed assets are intangible, such as patents and trademarks. The other category of assets, *current assets,* comprises those that have short lives, such as inventory. The tennis balls that your firm has made, but has not yet sold, are part of its inventory. Unless you have overproduced, they will leave the firm shortly.

Before a company can invest in an asset, it must obtain financing, which means that it must raise the money to pay for the investment. The forms of financing are represented on the right-hand side of the balance sheet. A firm will issue (sell) pieces of paper called *debt* (loan agreements) or *equity shares* (stock certificates).

Just as assets are classified as long-lived or short-lived, so too are liabilities. A short-term debt is called a *current liability*. Short-term debt represents loans and other obligations that must be repaid within one year. Long-term debt is debt that does not have to be repaid within one year. Shareholders' equity represents the difference between the value of the assets and the debt of the firm. In this sense, it is a residual claim on the firm's assets. From the balance sheet model of the firm, it is easy to see why finance can be thought of as the study of the following three questions:

1. In what long-lived assets should the firm invest? This question concerns the left-hand side of the balance sheet. Of course, the types and proportions of assets the firm needs tend to be set by the nature of the business. We use the term capital budgeting to describe the process of making and managing expenditures on long-lived assets.
2. How can the firm raise cash for required capital expenditures? This question concerns the right-hand side of the balance sheet. The answer to this involves the firm's capital structure, which represents the proportions of the firm's financing from current and long-term debt and equity.
3. How should short-term operating cash flows be managed? This question concerns the upper portion of the balance sheet. There is often a mismatch between the timing of cash inflows and cash outflows during operating activities. Furthermore, the amount and timing of operating cash flows are not known with certainty. The financial managers must attempt to manage the gaps in cash flow. From a balance sheet perspective, short-term management of cash flow is associated with a firm's net working capital. Net working capital is defined as current assets minus current

liabilities. From a financial perspective, the short-term cash flow problem comes from the mismatching of cash inflows and outflows. It is the subject of short-term finance.

Capital Structure

Financing arrangements determine how the value of the firm is sliced up. The persons or institutions that buy debt from (i.e., loan money to) the firm are called *creditors*. The holders of equity shares are called *shareholders*. Sometimes it is useful to think of the firm as a pie. Initially, the size of the pie will depend on how well the firm has made its investment decisions. After a firm has made its investment decisions, it determines the value of its assets (e.g., its buildings, land, and inventories).

The firm can then determine its capital structure. The firm might initially have raised the cash to invest in its assets by issuing more debt than equity; now it can consider changing that mix by issuing more equity and using the proceeds to buy back (pay off) some of its debt. Financing decisions like this can be made independently of the original investment decisions. The decisions to issue debt and equity affect how the pie is sliced. The pie we are thinking of is depicte. The size of the pie is the value of the firm in the financial markets. We can write the value of the firm, V, as V _ B _ S where B is the value of the debt and S is the value of the equity. The pie diagrams consider two ways of slicing the pie: 50 percent debt and 50 percent equity, and 25 percent debt and 75 percent equity. The way the pie is sliced could affect its value. If so, the goal of the financial manager will be to choose the ratio of debt to equity that makes the value of the pie—that is, the value of the firm, V—as large as it can be Current liabilities.

Shareholders' Equity

The Financial Manager

In large firms, the finance activity is usually associated with a top officer of the firm, such as the vice president and chief financial officer, and some lesser officers. A general organizational structure emphasizing the finance activity within the firm. Reporting to the chief financial officer are the treasurer and the controller. The treasurer is responsible for handling cash flows, managing capital expenditure decisions, and making financial plans. The controller handles the accounting function, which includes taxes, cost and financial accounting, and information systems. We think the most important job of a financial manager is to create value from the firm's capital budgeting, financing, and net working capital activities. How do financial managers create value? The answer is that the firm should:

1. Try to buy assets that generate more cash than they cost.
2. Sell bonds and stocks and other financial instruments that raise more cash than they cost.

Thus, the firm must create more cash flow than it uses. The cash flows paid to bondholders and stockholders of the firm should be greater than the cash flows put into the firm by the bondholders and stockholders. To see how this is done, we can trace the cash flows from the firm to the financial markets and back again. The interplay of the firm's activities with the financial markets is illustrated. The firm to the financial markets and back again. Suppose we begin with the firm's financing activities. To raise money, the firm sells debt and equity shares to investors in the financial markets. This results in cash flows from the financial markets to the firm (*A*). This cash is invested in the investment activities (assets) of the firm (*B*) by the firm's management. The cash generated by the firm (*C*) is paid to shareholders and bondholders (*F*). The shareholders receive cash in the form of dividends; the bondholders who lent funds to the firm receive interest and, when the initial loan is repaid, principal. Not all of the firm's cash is paid out. Some is retained (*E*), and some is paid to the government as taxes (*D*).

Over time, if the cash paid to shareholders and bondholders (*F*) is greater than the cash raised in the financial markets (*A*), value will be created.

IDENTIFICATION OF CASH FLOWS

Unfortunately, it is not all that easy to observe cash flows directly. Much of the information we obtain is in the form of accounting statements, and much of the work of financial analysis is to extract cash flow information from accounting statements. The following example illustrates how this is done.

Timing of Cash Flows

The value of an investment made by a firm depends on the timing of cash flows. One of the most important principles of finance is that individuals prefer to receive cash flows earlier rather than later. One dollar received today is worth more than one dollar received next year. The Midland Company refines and trades gold. At the end of the year, it sold 2,500 ounces of gold for $1 million. The company had acquired the gold for $900,000 at the beginning of the year. The company paid cash for the gold when it was purchased. Unfortunately, it has yet to collect from the customer to whom the gold was sold. The following is a standard accounting of Midland's financial circumstances at year-end:

By generally accepted accounting principles (GAAP), the sale is recorded even though the customer has yet to pay. It is assumed that the customer will pay soon. From the accounting perspective, Midland seems to be profitable. However, the perspective of corporate finance is different. It focuses on cash flows: The perspective of corporate finance is interested in whether cash flows are being created by the gold trading operations of Midland. Value creation depends on cash flows. For Midland, value creation depends on whether and when it actually receives $1 million. The Midland Company is attempting to choose between two proposals for new products. Both proposals will provide additional cash flows over a four-year period and will initially cost $10,000. The cash flows from the proposals are as follows:

Risk of Cash Flows

The firm must consider risk. The amount and timing of cash flows are not usually known with certainty. Most investors have an aversion to risk. At first it appears that new product *A* would be best. However, the cash flows from proposal *B* come earlier than those of *A*. Without more information, we cannot decide which set of cash flows would create the most value to the bondholders and shareholders. It depends on whether the value of getting cash from *B* up front outweighs the extra total cash from *A*. Bond and stock prices reflect this preference for earlier cash, and we will see how to use them to decide between *A* and *B*.

The Midland Company is considering expanding operations overseas. It is evaluating Europe and Japan as possible sites. Europe is considered to be relatively safe, whereas operating in Japan is seen as very risky. In both cases, the company would close down operations after one year. After doing a complete financial analysis, Midland has come up with the following cash flows of the alternative plans for expansion under three equally likely scenarios—pessimistic, most likely, and optimistic: If we ignore the pessimistic scenario, perhaps Japan is the best alternative. When we take the pessimistic scenario into account, the choice is unclear. Japan appears to be riskier, but it also offers a higher expected level of cash flow. What is risk and how can it be defined? We must try to answer this important question. Corporate finance cannot avoid coping with risky alternatives, and much of our book is devoted to developing methods for evaluating risky opportunities.

The Corporate Firm

The firm is a way of organizing the economic activity of many individuals. A basic problem of the firm is how to raise cash. The corporate form of business, that is, organizing the firm as a corporation, is the standard method for solving problems encountered in raising large amounts of cash. However, businesses can take other forms. In this section we consider the three basic legal forms of organizing firms, and we see how firms go about the task of raising large amounts of money under each form.

The Sole Proprietorship

A sole proprietorship is a business owned by one person. Suppose you decide to start a business to produce mousetraps. Going into business is simple: You announce to all who will listen, "Today, I am going to build a better mousetrap." Most large cities require that you obtain a business license. Afterward, you can begin to hire as many people as you need and borrow whatever money you need. At year-end all the profits and the losses will be yours. Here are some factors that are important in considering a sole proprietorship:

1. The sole proprietorship is the cheapest business to form. No formal charter is required, and few government regulations must be satisfied for most industries.
2. A sole proprietorship pays no corporate income taxes. All profits of the business are taxed as individual income.
3. The sole proprietorship has unlimited liability for business debts and obligations. No distinction is made between personal and business assets.
4. The life of the sole proprietorship is limited by the life of the sole proprietor.
5. Because the only money invested in the firm is the proprietor's, the equity money that can be raised by the sole proprietor is limited to the proprietor's personal wealth.

The Partnership

Any two or more persons can get together and form a partnership. Partnerships fall into two categories: (1) general partnerships and (2) limited partnerships. In a *general partnership,* all partners agree to provide some fraction of the work and cash and to share the profits and losses. Each partner is liable for all of the debts of the partnership. A partnership agreement specifies the nature of the arrangement. The partnership agreement may be an oral agreement or a formal document setting forth the understanding.

Limited partnerships permit the liability of some of the partners to be limited to the amount of cash each has contributed to the partnership. Limited partnerships usually require that (1) at least one partner be a general partner and (2) the limited partners do not participate in managing the business. Here are some things that are important when considering a partnership:

1. Partnerships are usually inexpensive and easy to form. Written documents are required in complicated arrangements, including general and limited

partnerships. Business licenses and filing fees may be necessary.

2. General partners have unlimited liability for all debts. The liability of limited partners is usually limited to the contribution each has made to the partnership. If one general partner is unable to meet his or her commitment, the shortfall must be made up by the other general partners.
3. The general partnership is terminated when a general partner dies or withdraws (but this is not so for a limited partner). It is difficult for a partnership to transfer ownership without dissolving. Usually, all general partners must agree. However, limited partners may sell their interest in a business.
4. It is difficult for a partnership to raise large amounts of cash. Equity contributions are usually limited to a partner's ability and desire to contribute to the partnership. Many companies, such as Apple Computer, start life as a proprietorship or partnership, but at some point they choose to convert to corporate form.
5. Income from a partnership is taxed as personal income to the partners.
6. Management control resides with the general partners. Usually a majority vote is required on important matters, such as the amount of profit to be retained in the business.

It is very difficult for large business organizations to exist as sole proprietorships or partnerships. The main advantage to a sole proprietorship or partnership is the cost of getting started. Afterward, the disadvantages, which may become severe, are:

(1) unlimited liability,

(2) limited life of the enterprise, and

(3) difficulty of transferring ownership. These three disadvantages lead to

(4) difficulty raising cash.

The Corporation

Of the many forms of business enterprises, the corporation is by far the most important. It is a distinct legal entity. As such, a corporation can have a name and enjoy many of the legal powers of natural persons. For example, corporations can acquire and exchange property. Corporations can enter into contracts and may sue and be sued. For jurisdictional purposes, the corporation is a citizen of its state of incorporation (it cannot vote, however). Starting a corporation is more complicated than starting a proprietorship or partnership. The incorporators must prepare articles of incorporation and a set of bylaws. The articles of incorporation must include the following:

1. Name of the corporation.
2. Intended life of the corporation (it may be forever).
3. Business purpose.
4. Number of shares of stock that the corporation is authorized to issue, with a statement of limitations and rights of different classes of shares.
5. Nature of the rights granted to shareholders.
6. Number of members of the initial board of directors.

The bylaws are the rules to be used by the corporation to regulate its own existence, and they concern its shareholders, directors, and officers. Bylaws range from the briefest possible statement of rules for the corporation's management to hundreds of pages of text. In its simplest form, the corporation comprises three sets of distinct interests: the shareholders (the owners), the directors, and the corporation officers (the top management).

Traditionally, the shareholders control the corporation's direction, policies, and activities. The shareholders elect a board of directors, who in turn select top management. Members of top management serve as corporate officers and manage the operations of the corporation in the best interest of the shareholders. In closely held corporations with few shareholders, there may be a large overlap among the shareholders, the directors, and the top management. However, in larger corporations, the shareholders, directors, and the top management are likely to be distinct groups. The potential separation of ownership from management gives the corporation several advantages over proprietorships and partnerships:

1. Because ownership in a corporation is represented by shares of stock, ownership can be readily transferred to new owners. Because the corporation exists independently of those who own its shares, there is no limit to the transferability of shares as there is in partnerships.
2. The corporation has unlimited life. Because the corporation is separate from its owners, the death or withdrawal of an owner does not affect its legal existence. The corporation can continue on after the original owners have withdrawn.
3. The shareholders' liability is limited to the amount invested in the ownership shares. For example, if a shareholder purchased $1,000 in shares of a corporation, the potential loss would be $1,000. In a partnership, a general partner with a $1,000 contribution could lose the $1,000 plus any other indebtedness of the partnership.

Limited liability, ease of ownership transfer, and perpetual succession are the major advantages of the corporation form of business organization. These give the corporation an enhanced ability to raise cash. There is, however, one great disadvantage to incorporation. The federal government taxes corporate income (the states do as well). This tax is in addition to the personal income tax that shareholders pay on dividend income they receive. This is double taxation for shareholders when compared to taxation on proprietorships and partnerships.

Today, all 50 states have enacted laws allowing for the creation of a relatively new form of business organization, the limited liability company (LLC). The goal of this entity is to operate and be taxed like a partnership but retain limited liability for owners, so an LLC is essentially a hybrid of partnership and corporation. Although states have differing definitions for LLCs, the more important scorekeeper is the Internal Revenue Service (IRS). The IRS will consider an LLC a corporation, thereby subjecting it to double taxation, unless it meets certain specific criteria. In essence, an LLC cannot be too corporationlike, or it will be treated as one by the IRS. LLCs have become common. For example, Goldman, Sachs and Co., one of Wall Street's last remaining partnerships, decided to convert from a private partnership to an LLC (it later "went public," becoming a publicly held corporation). Large accounting firms and law firms by the score have converted to LLCs.

CORPORATION PARTNERSHIP

Liquidity and Shares can be exchanged without Units are subject to substantial marketability termination of the corporation, restrictions on transferability. There Common stock can be listed on is usually no established trading stock exchange, market for partnership units. Voting rights Usually each share of common stock Some voting rights by limited entitles the holder to one vote per partners. However, general partner share on matters requiring a vote has exclusive control and on the election of the directors, management of operations. Directors determine top management.

Taxation Corporations have double taxation: Partnerships are not taxable. Partners Corporate income is taxable, and pay personal taxes on partnership dividends to shareholders are also profits. Reinvestment and Corporations have broad latitude on Partnerships are generally prohibited dividend payout dividend payout decisions from reinvesting partnership profits.

All profits are distributed to partners. Liability Shareholders are not personally liable Limited partners are not liable for obligations of the corporation obligations of partnerships.

General partners may have unlimited liability. Continuity of existence Corporations may have a perpetual life. Partnerships have limited life.

INTERNATIONAL BUSINESS IN INDIA

The current scenario for 'International Business in India' is more than heartening. With stupendous growth of more than 7% annually, improvement and stabilization of relations with neighboring countries and record setting rise of its stock indexes, India continues to grab international attention. It is destination of opportunity with its high-potential workforce and burgeoning middle class and as an increasingly dynamic competitor. India being a multi-cultural, multilingual and multi-religion state, it is not advisable to formulate a uniform business strategy. The eastern part of the country is known as the 'land of the intellectuals' and is regarded as the cultural hub of the country. The southern part is known for its technology acumen and western part is the commercial-capital of the country. The north is where the political power sits and operates the country. International Business Opportunity in India exists in areas like-

- Information Technology and Electronics Hardware.
- Telecommunication.
- Pharmaceuticals and Biotechnology.
- R&D.
- Banking, Financial Institutions and Insurance & Pensions.
- Capital Market.
- Chemicals and Hydrocarbons.
- Infrastructure.
- Agriculture and Food Processing.
- Retailing.
- Logistics.
- Manufacturing.
- Power and Non-conventional Energy.

Sectors like Health, Education, Housing, Resource Conservation & Management Group, Water Resources, Environment, Rural Development, Small and Medium Enterprises (SME) and Urban Development are untapped and offers huge scope. With highest numbers of technical, medical, business management graduates and highest numbers of Phd.s coupled with an energetic English speaking mass India offers 'services' with 50-70% less cost from their western counterparts. For 'International Business in India' bodies like CII, FICCI and different Chambers of Commerce provides a variety of business facilitation services by-

- Closely working with Government and business promotion organizations in India and the respective partner countries.
- Also hosts high-level Government dignitaries and help build close working relationships between Governments and business organizations.
- It also exchanges business delegations, joint task forces and identify bilateral business co-operation potential and make suitable policy recommendations to Governments.

With opportunities galore for ' International Business in India' the trend is mind boggling. ' India International Business' community along with Indian Domestic Business community is steadily emerging as the Knowledge Capital of the world. The World Bank and different rating organizations have forecast that at 7-8% of Economic growth, she will be worlds second largest economy by 2050.

Indian Businesses

Indian Businesses are slowly shifting their base from agriculture to major industrialization. Numerous types of Businesses in India are coming up. As India is developing the Iron & Steel Businesses in India, IT Businesses in India, Indian Businesses in Travel & Tourism, Indian Businesses in Business Process Outsourcing, Food Business market in India, Soft Drinks Businesses in India and various other types of businesses are coming to the forefront and taking the center stage.

The marketplace for Indian Businesses is quite varied including industries in the field of Agriculture & Forestry, Automobiles, Business Services, Chemicals, Computers, Construction, Education, Electrical, Electronics, Engineering/ Machinery, Entertainment, Import & Export, Fashion & Advertising, Food Processing, Government of India Websites, Immigration, India Neighbourhood, Intelligence, International, IT/ITes, Minerals & Metals, Packaging & Paper, Real Estate in India, Regional Portals, Travel & Tourism and many others. The scope of doing business in India has grown in its magnitude. Some of the major companies in the IT sector are Wipro, Tata

Consultancy Services, Infosys Technologies, HCL Ltd, Satyam Computer Services, Cognizant Technology Solutions, Patni Computers, BFL MphasiS, Polaris, i-flex, IBM, Hewlett-Packard and Accenture. In general the major Indian Businesses are the Tatas, Birlas, Ambanis and many more.

The Government has played a major role in the transformation of the Indian Business scenario in India. The major changes initiated by the Government for the betterment of the Indian Businesses are in the form of macroeconomic reforms, tax reforms, finance reforms and freeing of capital markets, reforms in the regulation of business firms, revitalization of the Indian private sector, removal of exchange controls and convertibility, trade reforms, and foreign direct investment. The Foreign companies are showing massive interest in the Indian Businesses. The number of Businesses in India have increased at an impressive rate. More and more foreign companies are having their branches in India. They are either holding hands with the Indian Businesses by entering into a partnership with them or they are building up their own offices in India. The future of Indian Businesses looks bright and assuring.

TRADING IN CORPORATE SECURITIES

The equity shares of most of the large firms in the United States trade in organized auction markets. The largest such market is the New York Stock Exchange (NYSE), which accounts for more than 85 percent of all the shares traded in auction markets. Other auction exchanges include the American Stock Exchange (AMEX) and regional exchanges such as the Pacific Stock Exchange. In addition to the stock exchanges, there is a large OTC market for stocks. In 1971, the National Association of Securities Dealers (NASD) made available to dealers and brokers an electronic quotation system called NASDAQ (which originally stood for NASD Automated Quotation system and is pronounced "naz-dak").

There are roughly two times as many companies on NASDAQ as there are on NYSE, but they tend to be much smaller in size and trade less actively. There are exceptions, of course. Both Microsoft and Intel trade OTC, for example.

Nonetheless, the total value of NASDAQ stocks is much less than the total value of NYSE stocks.

There are many large and important financial markets outside the United States, of course, and U.S. corporations are increasingly looking to these markets to raise cash. The Tokyo Stock Exchange and the London Stock Exchange (TSE and LSE, respectively) are two well-known examples. The fact that OTC markets have no physical location means that national borders do not present a great barrier, and there is now a huge international OTC debt market. Because of globalization, financial markets have reached the point where trading in many investments never stops; it just travels around the world.

Exchange Trading of Listed Stocks

Auction markets are different from dealer markets in two ways. First, trading in a given auction exchange takes place at a single site on the floor of the exchange. Second, transaction prices of shares traded on auction exchanges are communicated almost immediately to the public by computer and other devices. The NYSE is one of the preeminent securities exchanges in the world. All transactions in stocks listed on the NYSE occur at a particular place on the floor of the exchange called a *post*. At the heart of the market is the specialist. Specialists are members of the NYSE who *make a market* in designated stocks. Specialists have an obligation to offer to buy and sell shares of their assigned NYSE stocks. It is believed that this makes the market liquid because the specialist assumes the role of a buyer for investors if they wish to sell and a seller if they wish to buy.

RELATIONSHIP WITH OTHER AREAS IN FINANCE

Investment Banking

Use of the term "corporate finance" varies considerably across the world. In the United States it is used, as above, to describe activities, decisions and techniques that deal with many aspects of a company's finances and capital. In the United Kingdom and Commonwealth countries, the terms "corporate finance" and "corporate financier" tend to be associated with investment banking - i.e. with transactions in which capital is raised for the corporation. These may include:

- Raising seed, start-up, development or expansion capital
- Mergers, demergers, acquisitions or the sale of private companies
- Mergers, demergers and takeovers of public companies, including public-to-private deals
- Management buy-out, buy-in or similar of companies, divisions or subsidiaries - typically backed by private equity
- Equity issues by companies, including the flotation of companies on a recognised stock exchange in order to raise capital for development and/or to restructure ownership
- Raising capital via the issue of other forms of equity, debt and related securities for the refinancing and restructuring of businesses
- Financing joint ventures, project finance, infrastructure finance, public-private partnerships and privatisations
- Secondary equity issues, whether by means of private placing or further issues on a stock market, especially where linked to one of the transactions listed above.
- Raising debt and restructuring debt, especially when linked to the types of transactions listed above.

Financial Risk Management

Risk management is the process of measuring risk and then developing and implementing strategies to manage that risk. Financial risk management focuses on risks that can be managed ("hedged") using traded financial instruments (typically changes in commodity prices, interest rates, foreign exchange rates and stock prices). Financial risk management will also play an important role in cash management.

This area is related to corporate finance in two ways. Firstly, firm exposure to business and market risk is a direct result of previous Investment and Financing decisions. Secondly, both disciplines share the goal of enhancing, or preserving, firm value. All large corporations have risk management teams, and small firms practice informal, if not formal, risk management. There is a fundamental debate on the value of "Risk Management" and shareholder value that questions a shareholder's desire to optimize risk versus taking exposure to pure risk. The debate links value of risk management in a market to the cost of bankruptcy in that market.

Derivatives are the instruments most commonly used in financial risk management. Because unique derivative contracts tend to be costly to create and monitor, the most cost-effective financial risk management methods usually involve derivatives that trade on well-established financial markets or exchanges. These standard derivative instruments include options, futures contracts, forward contracts, and swaps. More customized and second generation derivatives known as exotics trade over the counter aka OTC.

Personal and Public Finance

Corporate finance utilizes tools from almost all areas of finance. Some of the tools developed by and for corporations have broad application to entities other than corporations, for example, to partnerships, sole proprietorships, not-for-profit organizations, governments, mutual funds, and personal wealth management. But in other cases their application is very limited outside of the corporate finance arena. Because corporations deal in quantities of money much greater than individuals, the analysis has developed into a discipline of its own. It can be differentiated from personal finance and public finance.

3

Banking System of Macroeconomic Developments

Since the 1970s and 1980s, development economics underwent a paradigm shift. The financial system is no longer viewed as a passive mobiliser of funds. Efficiency in financial intermediation i.e., the ability of financial institutions to intermediate between savers and investors, to set economic prices for capital and to allocate resources among competing demands is now emphasised. Developments in endogenous growth theory since the late 1980s indicate that efficiency in financial intermediation is a source of technical progress to be exploited for generating increasing returns and sustaining high growth.

These changes have provided the rationale for many developing countries to undertake wide-ranging reforms of their financial systems so as to prepare them for their true resource allocation function. As important financial in the remediaries, banks have a special role to play in this new dispensation. The sharp downturn in global macroeconomic prospects and the continuing sluggishness in domestic industrial activity have necessitated a revision in the forecast for India's real GDP growth in 2001-02 from 6.0-6.5 per cent expected at the time of the April 2001 Monetary and Credit Policy Statement to 5.0-6.0 per cent in the mid-term review of the policy.

The downward revision is primarily predicated on the outlook for the industrial sector which grew by barely 2.2 per cent in April-October 2001 as against 5.9 per cent in the corresponding period of last year, mainly on account of the slowdown in manufacturing and mining and quarrying. Capital goods production declined by as much as 6.6 per cent and several sectors recorded a slow down in growth rate or an absolute decline. On the other hand, agriculture sector, supported by reasonable monsoon, recorded a rebound in growth.

The kharif output is expected to cross a new peak of 105.6 million tonnes and prospects for the rabi crop are also good. On the external front, merchandise exports increased marginally by 0.5 per cent in the first eight months of 2001-02. While oil imports fell by 13.4 per cent, the non-oil imports showed an increase of 8.4 per cent. Despite a moderate widening of the trade deficit, continuing buoyancy in net invisible receipts has kept the current account deficit very low. According to available data, net capital flows are also likely to be of a higher order than in the preceding year. Foreign exchange reserves rose to US $ 48.0 billion as on December 28, 2001 recording an accretion of the order of the US $ 5.8 billion over the end-March 2001 level. In the context of the recent deceleration in the economy the intermediation role assumes even greater relevance.

Banks and financial institutions should endeavour to play a 'supply-leading' rather than 'demand-following' role in initiating the upturn by energising the financial intermediation process. By virtue of a bird's eye view of the economy and their superior credit assessment of the investment proposals and the efficiency of capital, banks should endeavour to economise on 'search' costs in identifying and nurturing growth impulses in the commodity and service producing sectors of the economy. In the recent period, monetary policy in India has also moved into a counter-cyclical stance signalled by cuts in key interest rates and cash reserve requirements.

At the same time, market operations have ensured adequate liquidity to support the revival of aggregate demand with a clear preference for softening of interest rates within the overall institutional constraints on the interest rate regime. Inflation has been steadily falling and this has had a positive impact on inflation expectations, along with the underlying resilience of the macroeconomic fundamentals of the Indian economy. The

50 basis point reduction in the Bank Rate and the 200 basis point reduction in the CRR, announced recently, are expected to significantly enhance the lendable resources of the banking system. The current situation of comfortable liquidity provides an opportunity for banks to transform idle liquidity into investible resources for growth. The easy interest rate environment would make it possible for banks to 'price in' projects which would have earlier remained unfunded due to inherently lower returns to capital or due to lack of access to prime lending rates.

This will, however, require reassessment of portfolios and internal liquidity constraints, even adjustments in risk profiles and risk management. The deceleration in the industrial growth scenario, of course, opens up the moral hazard of adverse selection and the possibilities of large-scale contamination of portfolios. In a situation of generalised slowdown, unviable projects can look potentially bankable given the scarcity of investment avenues. Nevertheless, the possibilities for financial intermediation in the current situation are too varied and challenging to ignore.

There is no systematic evidence that financial sector reforms by themselves and without supportive policies in other areas, can contribute to a revival of the economy; yet this is a time when the responsibility on the financial system to contribute to the process of economic revival is greater than before. Periods of downturn in economic activity also provide opportunities for banks to undertake consolidation and strengthening. There is a strong complementarity between financial stability and macroeconomic stability. The interests of both are served by a stable and resilient financial system.

In recent years, various measures have been taken to improve the functioning of different segments of the financial markets and thereby, to improve the operational effectiveness of monetary policy. The Liquidity Adjustment Facility (LAF), which was introduced in June 2000 has emerged as an effective and flexible instrument for managing liquidity on a day-to-day basis. In the second stage of the LAF, which commenced from May 2001, variable rate repo auctions replaced the collateralised lending facility and Level I support to primary dealers. Standing facilities were rationalised and a back-stop facility was introduced at variable market-related rates.

Concurrently, LAF operating procedures were recast to improve operational flexibility and complementary measures were undertaken to improve the functioning of money and government securities market segments and to facilitate their orderly integration. In order to enable the call money market to evolve into a pure inter-bank market, lending by non-banks was reduced to 85 per cent of their average daily call lending in 2000-01 from May 2001. The minimum maturity for wholesale term deposits of Rs.15 lakh and above has been reduced to 7 days from the earlier minimum maturity of 15 days. The maintenance of daily minimum cash reserve requirements has been lowered to 50 per cent from 65 per cent for the first seven days of the reporting fortnight. Interest paid on eligible balances under CRR has been raised to the level of the Bank Rate from November 3, 2001. The market has responded positively with an appreciable rise in turnover and a decline in volatility.

Several measures have also been taken to improve the functioning of the government securities market. 14-day and 182-day Treasury Bills were withdrawn and the notified amounts of 91-day Treasury Bills has been simultaneously increased. A Negotiated Dealing System (NDS) is being introduced to facilitate electronic bidding and to disseminate information on trades on a real-time basis. For this purpose, the Reserve Bank has begun the automation of its public debt offices. An important step is the setting up of the Clearing Corporation of India Ltd. (CCIL) to act as counterparty in all trades involving government securities, Treasury Bills, repos and foreign exchange. The entire system will operate in a networked environment and Indian Financial Network (INFINET) will provide the backbone for communication.

PRUDENTIAL NORMS

The calibration of the convergence with international standards is conditioned by the specific realities of our situation; however, the New Capital Accord of the Basel Committee on Banking Supervision which was released in January 2001 adds urgency to the process of convergence. It is against the backdrop of these exigencies that prudential norms are being constantly monitored and refined. In the recent period, banks are being encouraged to build risk-weighted components of their subsidiaries into their own balance sheets and to assign additional capital. Risk weights are being constantly refined to take into recognition additional sources of risk. The concept of 'past due' in the identification of NPAs has been dispensed with. Banks and financial institutions are being urged to prepare to move to the international practice of the '90 day norm' in the classification of assets as non-performing by 2003-04.

The new Basel Accord, as contained in the second Consultative Paper on Capital Adequacy of the Basel Committee on Banking Supervision released in January 2001 is in response to the perceived rigidities in the 1988 Accord's capital requirements, the scope for capital arbitrage and the increased sophistication in the measurement and management of risk. The new Accord rests on three mutually reinforcing pillars i.e., minimum capital requirements, processes of supervisory review and market discipline. Under the first pillar, the current definition of capital and the minimum requirement of 8 per cent of capital to risk weighted assets is retained. Capital requirements would be extended on a consolidated basis to holding companies of banking groups. The primary emphasis of the new Accord is on improving the measurement of risk.

The process of measurement of market risk is maintained. Three alternatives for calculating credit risk capital requirements are proposed to be made available to banks, depending on the complexity of their business and the quality of their risk management operations. The 'standardised approach' which can be employed by less complex banks remains conceptually the same as in the 1988 norms; however, it expands the scale of risk weights and uses external credit ratings to categorise credits. Banks with more advanced risk management capabilities can employ an internal ratings based (IRB) approach - 'foundation' and 'advanced' variants are proposed on a progression scale - in which banks may categorise exposures into multiple credit ratings of their approved internal rating systems. The internally estimated probability of default, the maturity of exposure and the credit type i.e., corporate or retail, will determine risk weights. There is a new explicit capital charge proposed on operational risk. The processes of supervisory review contained in the second pillar emphasise the need for banks to develop sound internal procedures to assess the adequacy of capital based on a thorough evaluation of its risk profile and control environment, and to set commensurate targets for capital.

The internal processes would be subject to supervisory evaluation, review and intervention, when appropriate. The third pillar aims at bolstering market discipline through enhanced disclosure by banks. Disclosure requirements are set out in several areas under the new Accord, including the way in which banks calculate their capital adequacy and their risk assessment methods. The Basel Committee on Banking Supervision has received more than 250 comments on the January 2001 proposals.

The Committee is expected to release a fully specified proposal, based on these comments, in early 2002 and to finalise the Accord during 2002. An implementation date of 2005 is envisaged. The Reserve Bank forwarded its comments to the Basel committee in May 2001. It has supported flexibility, discretion to national supervisors and a phased approach in implementing the Accord. The Accord could initially apply to internationally active - banks with over 15 per cent of their business in cross-border transactions, as proposed by the Reserve Bank - and significant banks whose domestic market share exceeds 1 per cent - with a simplified standardised approach to be evolved for other banks.

Material limits on cross-holdings of capital and eschewing of direct responsibility on external credit rating agencies in the assessment of bank assets have also been proposed by the Reserve Bank. It has also expressed its preference for external credit rating agencies that publicly disclose risk scores, rating processes and methodologies. The new accord, when implemented, is likely to have significant implications for the banking system as a whole. Besides requiring increased capital, it attaches urgency to the development of efficient and comprehensive internal systems for assessment and management of risks, setting up and adhering to adequate internal exposure limits and improving internal control generally. The guidelines for risk management and asset liability management provided by the Reserve Bank serve as a useful foundation for building more sophisticated control systems. The feedback received from few banks indicates the need for substantial upgradation of existing management information systems, risk management practices and technical skills.

Capital allocation is also expected to be more risk sensitive and, therefore, banks and financial institutions will have to plan in advance so that there are no disruptions in the capital structure. Further sophistication in risk management and control mechanisms will have to evolve as experience with preferential risk-weighting and sensitivity to external ratings is accumulated. A key requirement when the new Accord, after further modification, becomes operational is that of high quality human resources to cope with and adapt to the new environment.

Enhancing technical skills and abilities to handle new technologies and new risks, exploiting information flows to price them in, and developing foresight in anticipating changing risk-return relationships will become essential.

Indian Banking System by International Standards

The impetus given to the strengthening of domestic financial systems and the international financial architecture by the Asian crisis has gathered momentum in recent years. An important development in this regard has been the move to set up universally acceptable standards and codes for benchmarking domestic financial systems. Moreover, multilateral assessments of country performance are increasingly focusing on observance of standards. While the process has begun with the predominant involvement of governments and regulators, the search for standards and codes is progressively encompassing the private sector with consideration of issues relating to market discipline, corporate governance, insolvency procedures and credit rights. It is important to recognise that new standards and codes are not being regarded as final goals but as instruments or enabling conditions for enhancing efficiency in financial intermediation while ensuring financial stability.

There are three levels at which action is necessary, viz., legal, policy and procedures, and market practices by participants. In several areas, fundamental changes in the legal and institutional infrastructure are pre-requisites. Since these changes can impinge upon the socio-cultural as well as politico-economic ethos, appropriate adoption and some prioritisation in implementation are unavoidable. We have made some noteworthy progress in generating a constructive debate on the applicability of international standards and codes to the Indian financial system. Participative consultation has been supported by internal self-assessments as well as external assessment. In several areas, the issues are of a technical nature. Accordingly, the Standing Committee on International Standards and Codes, set up in December 1999, constituted ten Advisory Groups comprising eminent experts, generally non-official, to bring objectivity and experience into studying the applicability of relevant international codes and standards to each area of competence.

The Advisory Groups have submitted their reports. They have set out a roadmap for implementation of appropriate standard and codes in the light of existing levels of compliance, the cross-country experience, and the existing legal and institutional infrastructure. The Advisory Group on Banking Supervision has assessed the Indian banking system vis-à-vis the principles of the Basel Committee on Banking Supervision. It has found the level of compliance to be generally of a high order. The Advisory Group on Bankruptcy Laws has, inter alia, recommended a comprehensive bankruptcy code incorporating various aspects including cross-border insolvency and the repeal of the Sick Industrial Companies Act. The Advisory Group on Corporate Governance has made recommendations relating to rules and responsibilities of boards and has advised amendments to the Companies Act. The Advisory Group on Data Dissemination has found that India's data dissemination compares favourably with many other countries and has proposed the compilation of forward-looking indicators.

The Advisory Group on Fiscal Transparency is of the view that current fiscal practices meet the IMF's Code of Good Practices on Fiscal Transparency. It has recommended amplifying the scope of fiscal responsibility legislation in order to include the essential elements of a budget law. The Advisory Group on Insurance regulation has recommended flexible minimum capital requirements depending on the class of business. With regard to actuarial and solvency issues, the Group has found the Indian standards to be at par with international norms.

The Advisory Group on International Accounting and Auditing Standards has set out an agenda for the future for convergence in auditing and accounting practices. It has recommended a single standard setting authority and the need for convergence of corporate and tax laws. The Advisory Group on Transparency in Monetary and Financial Policies has recommended inflation as the single mandated objective for the central bank and necessary autonomy to fulfil the mandate. It has also made recommendations on the operating procedures of monetary policy.

The Advisory Group on Payments and Settlement has recommended legal reforms to empower the Reserve Bank to supervise the payment and settlement system, application of the Lamfalussy standards to deferred net settlement (DNS) and introduction of Real Time Gross Settlement (RTGS). It has also recommended the setting up of the Clearing Corporation and a separate guarantee fund for foreign exchange clearing. The Advisory Group on Securities Market Regulation has compared India against the International Organisation of Securities Commissions (IOSCO) principles and emphasised the need to strengthen inter-regulator cooperation.

Thus, in India, we have made considerable progress in the identification of international standards and codes in relevant areas, expert assessment regarding their applicability, including comparator country evaluation and building up possible course of action for the future. The next step is to sensitise all concerned - policy makers, regulators and market participants - to the issues involved and to seek the widest possible debate on issues as well as expert assessments with a view to generating a broad consensus on implementation of a universally recognised set of codes and standards.

Market Discipline

Processes of transparency and market disclosure of critical information describing the risk profile, capital structure and capital adequacy are assuming increasing importance in the emerging environment. Besides making banks more accountable and responsive to better-informed investors, these processes enable banks to strike the right balance between risks and rewards and to improve the access to markets. Improvements in market discipline also call for greater coordination between banks and regulators. India has been a participant in the international initiatives to ensure improved processes of market discipline that are being worked out in several fora, such as, the multilateral organisations, the BIS, the Financial Stability Forum, and the Core Principles Liaison Group.

Concurrent efforts are underway to refine and upgrade financial information monitoring and flow, data dissemination and data warehousing. Banks are currently required to disclose in their balance sheets information on maturity profiles of assets and liabilities, lending to sensitive sectors, movements in NPAs, besides providing information on capital, provisions, shareholdings of the government, value of investments in India and abroad, and other operating and profitability indicators. Financial institutions are also required to meet these disclosure norms. Banks also have to disclose their total investments made in equity shares, units of mutual funds, bonds and debentures, and aggregate advances against shares in their notes to balance sheets.

From this year onwards, notes to banks' balance sheets will disclose the movement of provisions against NPAs as well as those held towards depreciation on investments. Guidelines relating to non-SLR investments through the private placement route mandate the disclosure of information on issuer composition and non-performing investments in a similar manner. Efforts have been made to identify and monitor early warning indicators of financial crises. The overall approach is to combine the use of micro-prudential indicators with macro-economic indicators in order to develop a set of aggregate macro-prudential indicators.

This brings about a mix between bottom-up and top-down assessment. As the methodology gets refined and the indicators are stress-tested for predictive power, financial stability surveillance will be significantly improved. This process will involve greater transparency and objectivity in the disclosure practices of banks. Efforts have also been made to set up a Credit Information Bureau to collect and share information on borrowers and improve the credit appraisal of banks and financial institutions within the ambit of the existing legislation. The Bureau has been incorporated by the State Bank of India in collaboration with Housing Development Finance Corporation (HDFC) and foreign technology partners. Collection and sharing of some items of information have already been initiated. Efforts are also going into the collection and sharing of information on private placement of debt under the Bureau so that there is greater transparency in such trades. The possibility of collecting and disseminating information on suit-filed accounts by the Bureau (in place of the Reserve Bank) is being explored by a Working Group constituted for this purpose with representation from across the financial system. The Group will also examine the prospects of on-line supply of information and the processing of queries. A draft legislation covering various aspects of information sharing, including issues relating to rights, responsibilities, and privacy has been prepared, which would considerably strengthen the functioning of the Bureau when it is enacted.

4

Working Capital

The number one reason most people look at a balance sheet is to find out a company's working capital (or "current") position. It reveals more about the financial condition of a business than almost any other calculation. It tells you what would be left if a company raised all of its short term resources, and used them to pay off its short term liabilities. The more working capital, the less financial strain a company experiences. By studying a company's position, you can clearly see if it has the resources necessary to expand internally or if it will have to turn to a bank and take on debt.

WHAT IS WORKING CAPITAL?

Every business needs funds for two purposes- for its establishment and to carry out its day to day operations. Long term funds are required to create production facilities through purchase of fixed assets such as plant and machinery, land, building, furniture etc. Investments in these assets represent that part of firm's capital which is blocked on a permanent or fixed basis and is called fixed capital. Funds are also needed for short term purposes for the purchase of raw materials, payment of wages and other day to day expenses, etc. These funds are known as Working Capital. Working Capital may be regarded as lifeblood of a business, while its inefficient management can lead not only to loss of profits but also lead to the ultimate down fall of a concern. Hence, working capital management if carried out effectively, efficiently and consistently, will assure the health of an organization.

CALCULATING WORKING CAPITAL

Working Capital is the easiest of all the balance sheet calculations. Here's the formula.

Current Assets - Current Liabilities = Working Capital

One of the main advantages of looking at the working capital position is being able to foresee any financial difficulties that may arise. Even a business that has billions of dollars in fixed assets will quickly find itself in bankruptcy court if it can't pay its monthly bills. Under the best circumstances, poor working capital leads to financial pressure on a company, increased borrowing, and late payments to creditor - all of which result in a lower credit rating. A lower credit rating means banks charge a higher interest rate, which can cost a corporation a lot of money over time.

Negative Working Capital

Companies that have high inventory turns and do business on a cash basis (such as a grocery store) need very little working capital. These types of businesses raise money every time they open their doors, then turn around and plow that money back into inventory to increase sales. Since cash is generated so quickly, managements can simply stockpile the proceeds from their daily sales for a short period of time if a financial crisis arises. Since cash can be raised so quickly, there is no need to have a large amount of working capital available. A company that makes heavy machinery is a completely different story. Because these types of businesses are selling expensive items on a long-term payment basis, they can't raise cash as quickly. Since the inventory on their balance sheet is normally ordered months in advance, it can rarely be sold fast enough to raise money for short-term financial crises (by the time it is sold, it may be too late). It's easy to see why companies such as this must keep enough working capital on hand to get through any unforeseen difficulties.

Working capital is a measurement of an entity's current assets, after subtracting its liabilities. Sometimes referred to as operating capital, it is a valuation of the amount of liquidity a business or organization has for the running and building of the business. Generally speaking, companies with higher amounts of working capital are better positioned for success. They have the liquid assets needed to expand their business operations as desired. Sometimes, a company will have a large amount of assets, but have very little with which to build the business and improve processes. Even a profitable company may have this problem. This can occur when a company has assets that are not easy to convert into cash.

Working capital can be expressed as a positive or negative number. When a company has more debts than current assets, it has negative working capital. When current assets outweigh debts, a company has positive working capital. Changes in working capital will impact a business' cash flow. When working capital increases, the effect on cash flow is negative. This is often caused by the liquidation of inventory or the drawing of money from accounts that are due to be paid by the business. On the other hand, a decrease in working capital translates into less money to settle short-term debts.

Working capital is among the many important things that contribute to the success of a business. Without it, a business may cease to function properly or at all. Not only does a lack of working capital render a company unable to build and grow, but it may also leave a company with too little cash to pay its short-term obligations. Simply put, a company with a very low amount of working capital may be at risk of running out of money.

When a company has too little working capital, it can face financial difficulties and may even be forced toward bankruptcy. This is true of both very small companies and billion-dollar organizations. A company with this problem may pay creditors late or even skip payments. It may borrow money in an attempt to remain afloat. If late payments have affected the company's credit rating, it may have difficulty obtaining a loan at an affordable interest rate.

In some types of businesses, it isn't as much of a problem to have a lower amount of working capital. Companies that are operated on as cash basis, have fast inventory turnovers, and can generate cash quickly don't necessarily need as much working capital. For example, a grocery store might meet these requirements and do well with less working capital.

NATURE OF WORKING CAPITAL

Working Capital Management is concerned with the problems that arise in attempting to manage the Current Assets, the Current Liabilities and the inter-relationship that exists between them. The term Current Assets refers to those Assets which in the ordinary course of business can be, or will be, converted into Cash within one year without undergoing a diminution in value and without disrupting the operations of the firm. The Major Current Assets are Cash, Marketable Securities, Accounts Receivables and Inventory.

Current Liabilities are those Liabilities, which are intended at their inception, to be paid in the ordinary course of business, within a year out of the current assets or the earnings of the concern .The basic Current Liabilities are Accounts Payable, Bills Payable, Bank Overdraft and outstanding expense. *The goal of Working Capital Management is to manage the firm's Assets and Liabilities in such a way that a satisfactory level of working capital is maintained.* This is so because if the firm cannot maintain a satisfactory level of working capital, it is likely to become insolvent and may even be forced into bankruptcy.

The Current Assets should be large enough to cover its current liabilities in order to ensure a reasonable margin of safety. Each of the current assets must be managed efficiently in order to maintain the liquidity of the firm while not keeping too high a level of any one of them. Each of the short term sources of financing must be continuously managed to ensure that they are obtained and used in the best possible way. *The interaction between current assets and current liabilities is, therefore, the main theme of the theory of management of working capital.*

COMPONENTS OF WORKING CAPITAL

Any enterprise whether industrial, trading or other acquires two types of assets to run its business as has already been emphasised time and again. It requires fixed assets which are necessary for carrying on the production/business such as land and buildings, plant and machinery, furniture and fixtures etc. For a going concern these assets are of permanent nature and are not to be sold. The other types of assets required for day to day working of a unit are known as current assets which are floating in nature and keep changing during the course of business. It is these 'current assets' which are generally referred to as 'working capital'. We are by now already aware of the short term nature of these assets which are classified as current assets. It may be noted here that there may not be any fixed ratio between the fixed assets and floating assets for different projects as their requirement would differ depending upon the nature of project. Big industrial projects may require substantial investment in fixed assets and also large investment for working capital. The trading units may not require heavy investment in fixed assets while they may be carrying huge stocks in trade. The service units may hardly require any working capital and all investment may be blocked in creation of fixed assets.

A set financing pattern is evolved to meet the requirement of a unit for acquisition of fixed assets and current assets. Fixed assets are to be financed by owned funds and long term liabilities raised by a unit while current assets are partly financed by long term liabilities and partly by current liabilities and other short term loans arranged by the unit from the bank. The balance sheet of a unit under such dispensation may be represented as in next page.

The total current assets with the firm may be taken as gross working capital whereas the net working capital with the unit may be calculated as under:

Net Working Capital = Current Assets Current Liabilities
(NWC) (GWC) (including bank borrowings)

This net working capital is also sometimes referred to as 'liquid surplus' with the firm and has been margin available for working capital requirements of the unit. Financing of working capital has been the exclusive domain of commercial banks while they also grant term loans for creation of fixed assets either on their own or in consortium with State level/ All India financial institutions. The financial institutions are also now considering sanction of working capital loans. The current assets in the example given in the earlier paragraph are financed asunder:

Current Assets = Current liabilities + Working capital limits from banks + Margin from long term liabilities

Liabilities	*Assets*
Capital	Fixed Assets
Long-term liabilities	
Margin NWC Liquid Surplus	
Working capitallimits frombanks	Current Assets
Current Liabilities	

(Diagram 1)

This is the normal pattern of financing of current assets. However, a few units may be having a negative net working capital as shown below :

Liabilities	*Assets*
Capital	
Long-termLiabilities	Fixed Assets
Working capital deficit	
CurrentLiabilities	CurrentAssets

(Diagram 2)

It is evident from diagram 2 that current liabilities are more than current assets and a part of short term funds (current liabilities) have been diverted to finance fixed assets. Not only that the unit is not able to provide any margin for working capital from its long term sources, but it is showing a net working capital deficit represented by the bracketed area in the diagram. This situation may not be considered as satisfactory and the unit is experiencing liquidity problems and has a current ratio of less than one. It may also be stated here that a large liquid surplus may also not reveal a very encouraging position, as it would mean idle funds or a lower turnover in working capital. It should, therefore, be the endeavour of every concern to ensure optimum utilisation of all the resources at its command and have just adequate liquid surplus. The assessment of working capital may involve two aspects as under:

- The level of current assets required to be held by any unit which is adequate for its day to day functioning, and
- The mode of financing of these current assets.

The value of inventory as given in the balance sheet is the position as on a particular day on which the balance sheet is drawn and may not be the actual average requirement of the unit. We will have to, therefore, evaluate the actual consumption pattern to arrive at a correct decision.

OPERATING CYCLE CONCEPT

The day to day business operations of a concern of any nature and, size involves many successive steps and final working results would depend on the effective combination of all these steps. The steps in general may include:

- Acquisition and storage of raw material and other stores and spares required for manufacture of any product.
- Actual production process when the raw material is subjected to different processes to bring it to final shape of finished goods.
- Storage of finished goods awaiting sales.
- Sales of finished goods and realisations of sale proceeds.

All these steps put together form an operating cycle which can also be represented diagramatically as under :

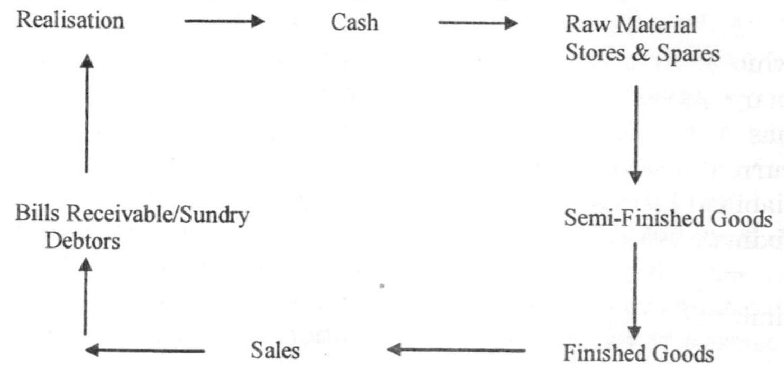

We start from cash to buy raw material etc. and after completing all the steps end up with the cash. The intervening period required for completion of this entire process is the 'Operating Cycle'. The operating cycle may thus be defined as the intervening period from the time the goods or services enter the business till their realisation in cash.

This system of calculation of working capital requirement is not in vogue as it only helps to assess the total requirement of a unit whereas the banks granting working capital limits would be interested in proper classification of its various components. The concept of operating cycle, however, throws light on various components of working capital required for the unit and these components may be classified as under:

- Raw material stores and spares consumed in the production process. The unit must have some stocks of these items for uninterrupted production.
- Manufacturing expenses such as wages, power and fuel etc. to be incurred during the process of manufacture.
- Stocks of work in process/semi finished goods maintained by the unit to complete an operating cycle.
- Stocks of finished goods awaiting sale. All the finished goods may not be immediately sold.
- Administrative and selling expenses during this process.
- Bills receivable/debtors for credit sales.

All or some of these components in varying proportions are required for any business.

Concept of Margin

Margin in relation to working capital has two concepts which need to be clearly understood. The one concept of providing margin by way of liquid surplus i.e. from long term liabilities has already been explained. It must be clear by now that current assets shall partly be financed by capital & long term liabilities for any going concern. This gains importance while fixing overall limits of working capital by the bank.

The other concept of margin as applicable to working capital limits is related to the value of security charged to the bank as cover for these limits. Financial accommodation up to 100% of the value of goods would not be granted by the banks and they would fix a certain margin on the value of security which must be provided by the borrower and the balance amount will be financed by the bank. The percentage of margin fixed on any security is dependent on its nature.

CONCEPT OF WORKING CAPITAL

For the proper understanding of Working Capital, it is necessary to understand the various concepts of Working Capital. The main concepts of Working Capital are as follows:

1. Quantitative or Gross Working Capital Concept;
2. Qualitative or Net Working Capital Concept.

Quantitative or Gross Working Capital Concept

According to this concept Working capital is the total of the entire current asset. This view places more emphasis on the quantitative aspect of working capital rather than its Qualitative aspect. This concept is important due to the following reasons:

a) It enables the enterprise to provide correct amount of Working Capital at the right time;

b) Every management is more interested in the total current assets with which it has to operate than the sources from where it is made available;

c) The gross concept takes into consideration the fact that every increase in the funds of the enterprise would increase its Working Capital;

d) The gross concept of Working Capital is more useful in determination the rate of return on investments in Working Capital.

Qualitative or Net Working Capital Concept

This concept gives more emphasis on the qualitative aspect rather than the quantitative aspect rather than the quantitative aspect of working capital. According to this concept the excess of the current assets over current liabilities is known as working capital. If the current assets and current liabilities are equal; it indicates absents of working capital in the business.

The net working capital concept is important due to the following reasons:

a) It is a qualitative concept which indicates the firm's ability to meet its operating expenses and short term liabilities;

b) It indicates the margin of protection available to the short- term creditors, i.e., the excess of current assets over current liabilities;

c) It is an indicator of the financial soundness of an enterprise;

d) It suggests the need for financing a part of the Working Capital requirements out of permanent sources of funds.

Objective of the Working Capital Management

The basic objectives of the working capital management are as follows:

1. To optimize the investment in current asset and to reduce the level of current liabilities, so that the company can reduce the locking up of funds in working capital and, can improve the return on capital employed in the business;
2. Working capital management is that the company should always be in a position to meet its current obligations which should be properly be supported by the current asset available with the firm. But maintaining excess funds in working capital means locking of funds without return;
3. To manage the firm's current assets in such a way that the marginal return on investment in these assets is not less than the cost of capital employed to finance the current assets.

The Need of Working Capital

The need for working capital cannot be emphasized. Every business needs some amount of working capital. The need for working capital arises due to time gap between production and realization of cash from sales. Thus the working capital is needed for the following purposes:

1. For the purchase of raw materials, components and spares;
2. To pay wages and salaries;
3. To incur day to day expenses and overhead costs such as fuel, power and office expenses, etc;
4. To meet the selling costs facilities to the customers;
5. To provide credit facilities to the customers;
6. To maintain the inventories of raw material, work-in – progress, stores and spares and finished stock.

Variable Working Capital;

Working capital can be divided into following categories on the basis of Concepts:

- Gross Working Capital: Gross Working Capital is the amount of funds invested in the various components of current assets.
- Net working Capital: The net working capital is the difference between the current assets and current liabilities.
- On the Basis of Necessities: Working capital can be divided into following categories on the basis of necessities:
- Fixed (Permanent or Core) working Capital: This refers to that minimum amount of investment in all current assets which is required at all times to carry out minimum level of business activities. In other words, it represents the current assets required on a continuing basis over the entire year.
- Variable (Temporary or seasonal) Working Capital: The amount of such working capital keeps on fluctuating from time to time on the basis of business activities.

COMPONENT OF WORKING CAPITAL

There are two of the major following components of the Working Capital:

Current Assets

Current assets are those assets which can be converted

into cash in the normal course of business within a short period- say a maximum of one year. They are also called floating or circulating assets because they cannot be put to constant use. They are meant for resale or produced for the purpose of sale i.e., converting them into cash. In brief , the list of current assets comprises of :

I. Cash in hand and bank balances;
II. Bills receivables;
III. Sundry debtors (less provision for bad debts);
IV. Short-term loans and advances;
V. Inventories of stocks as:
- Raw- material,
- Work-in-progress,
- Stores and spares,
- Finished goods.

VI. Temporary Investments of surplus funds;
VII. Prepaid Expense;
VIII. Accrued Incomes.

Current Liabilities

Current liabilities are those liabilities which are intended to be paid in the ordinary course of business within a short period of normally one accounting year out of the current assets or the income of the business. Such as:

I. Bills Payable;
II. Sundry creditors or accounts payable;
III. Accrued or outstanding Expenses;
IV. Short-term loan, advances and deposits;
V. Dividends Payable;
VI. Bank overdrafts;
VII. Provision for taxation.

SOURCES OF WORKING CAPITAL

A firm can arrange working capital from the following two sources:

1) Long-term sources
2) Short-term Sources.

Long-term sources

The sources of long term financing can be broadly classified into the following two categories:

- Owned sources:

I. Issue of share: Arrangement of working capital through issue of shares dose not create a fixed obligation on incomes of the business. Thus it is preferable to arrange the permanent working capital through issue of shares.

II. Retained Earnings: A firm can meet its working capital requirement by reinvesting the profits earned by it. Reinvestment the profits earned profit is a regular and cost less sources of funds.

III. Reserves: Like retained earnings, the use of reserves for financing the working capital requirement is also a costless sources of finance.

Borrowed Sources

It mainly includes the issue of debentures or long-term loans.

Short-term Sources

Internal Sources

It mainly includes depreciation provision, outstanding liabilities and provision for taxation.

External sources

Short-term external sources of financing working capital include the following:

I. Trade credit: Usually the manufacturing concerns, wholesalers and retailers avail this type f credit. Such credit is extended by suppliers of goods or raw-materials. This facility is given for a short period which may extend for a few weeks or a few months, based on prevailing market usage. No interest is charged by the suppliers if payment is made by the customer before the expiry of the credit period.

II. Bank credit: Normally companies obtain short-term working capital from banks in the form of short-term loans, cash credit, and overdraft and through discounting the bill of exchange.

III. Short-Term Loans From Financial Institutions: The requirement of working capital can also be stratified by arranging short-term loans from financial institution.

IV. Public Deposits: Business firms sometimes succeed in mobilizing enough funds by way of short-term deposits from publics. By and large attraction of higher rate of interest prompts the public to put their savings as short-term deposits with business firms.

V. Advance from Customers: Advance form customers are also considered as a principle source of short-term working capital finance.

COMPONENTS OF WORKING CAPITAL

A company starting with cash purchase raw-materials, components etc., on cash credit basis. These materials will be converted into finished goods after undergoing the stage of work-in-progress. For this purpose in the company has to make payments towards wages, salaries and other manufacturing costs. Payments to suppliers have to be made on purchase in the case of credit purchase. Further, the company has to meet other operating costs such as selling and distribution costs (interest on borrowed capital). In case the company sells its finished goods on a credit basis, it will pass through one more stage, viz, accounts receivable and gets back cash along with profit on the expiry of credit period. Once again the cash will be used for the purchase of materials and or payment to suppliers and the whole cycle termed as working capital or operating cycle itself. This process indicates the dependence of each stage or component of working capital on its previous stage or component.

Working Capital on the Balance Sheet

A balance sheet contains funding and operating items. Funding items includes equity and debt. Operating components include working capital and non-current assets

Working capital consists of Current Assets and Current Liabilities. These are defined below.

Current Assets

Accounts Receivable

This is money owed to the organization by customers. It appears on the balance sheet under current assets.

Accounts Receivable Linked to the Income Statement

The balance sheet amount for Accounts receivable *is related to the sales amount* in the income statement / profit and loss. It is the amount of sales that have not yet been paid for. It relates to credit sales only. (Cash sales would appear on the balance sheet under Cash at bank).

Accounts Receivable Days

The money owed to the organization by customers is expressed in days.

Inventory

This is the stock of goods available for resale, valued at the lower of cost or net realizable value. How is Inventory linked to the income statement: The balance sheet amount for inventory *is related to the cost of sales amount* in the income statement / profit and loss.

Inventory Days

The stock of goods available for resale is expressed in days.

Other Inventory

This is inventory of consumables.

Inventory WIP

The stock of work in process valued at the lower of cost or net realizable value is shown here.

WIP Days

This is the work in process amount expressed in days. The balance sheet amount is valued at the lower of cost or net realizable value and is related to the *cost of sales amount* on the profit and loss.

Other Current Assets

Current assets that are not included above are entered here.

Current Liabilities

Accounts Payable

This is money owed by the organization to suppliers of inventory and other variable cost of sales. Accounts payable appears on the balance sheet under current liabilities.

How is Accounts payable linked to the income statement:

The balance sheet amount for Accounts payable *is related to the cost of sales amount* and *expenses amount* in the income statement / profit and loss. It is the amount of goods and services that have not yet been paid for.

Accounts Payable Days

This is the Accounts Payable amount expressed in days.

Income Tax Liability

Provision for tax is a liability. It is tax payable arising from the current years operations but not yet paid. Provision for tax is not a funding provision because it is closely linked to the trading cycle. It is entered as part of working capital on the operations side of the balance sheet as "income tax liability".

Accruals and Accruals as % of Fixed exp

Accruals are current liabilities and relate to fixed expenses which were incurred but not paid for in the period shown. They can be expressed as a percentage of fixed expenses.

Other Current Liabilities

This is used for current liabilities that are not included above.

Bank and Cash at Bank

Traditionally working capital includes cash at bank and bank overdraft. Financial analysis demands a change in the format so that the funding components of the organization are separated out.

Working Capital Management

Working capital management is managing the use of current assets and current liabilities to make the most of the business's short-term liquidity. There is a direct correlation between business performance and working capital management.

DETRIMANTS OF WORKING CAPITAL

Working capital management is an indispensable functional area of management. However the total working capital requirements of the firm are influenced by the large number of factors. It may however be added that these factors affect differently to the different units and these keep varying from time to time. In general, the determinants of working capital which are common to all organizations can be summarized as under:

a. Nature and Size of Business
b. Production Cycle
c. Business Cycle
d. Production Policy
e. Credit Policy
f. Growth & Expansion
g. Proper availability of raw materials
h. Profit level
i. Inflation
j. Operating Efficiency.

OPERATING CYCLE AND CASH CYCLE

Operating cycle and cash cycle are two important components of working capital management. Together they determine the efficiency of a firm regarding working capital management.

Operating cycle refers to the delay between the buying of raw materials and the receipt of cash from sales proceeds. In other words, operating cycle refers to the number of days taken for the conversion of cash to inventory through the conversion of accounts receivable to cash. It indicates towards the time period for which cash is engaged in inventory and accounts receivable. If an operating cycle is long, then there is lower accessibility to cash for satisfying liabilities for the short term.

Operating cycle takes into consideration the following elements: accounts payable, cash, accounts receivable, and inventory replacement.

The following formula is used for calculating operating cycle:

Operating cycle = age of inventory + collection period

Cash cycle is also termed as net operating cycle, asset conversion cycle, working capital cycle or cash conversion cycle.

Cash cycle is implemented in the financial assessment of a commercial enterprise. The more the figure is increased, the higher is the period for which the cash of a commercial entity is engaged in commercial activities and is inaccessible for other functions, for instance investments. The cash cycle is interpreted as the number of days between the payment for inputs and getting cash by sales of commodities manufactured from that input.

The fundamental formula that is applied for the calculation of cash conversion cycle is as follows:

Cash cycle = (Average Stockholding Period) + (Average Receivables Processing Period) - (Average Payables Processing Period)

Here

Average Receivables Processing Period (in days) = Accounts Receivable/Average Daily Credit Sales Average Stockholding Period (in days) = Closing Stock/Average Daily Purchases Average Payable Processing Period (in days) = Accounts Payable/ Average Daily Credit Purchases

A short cash cycle reflects sound management of working capital. On the other hand, a long cash cycle denotes that capital is occupied when the commercial entity is expecting its clients to make payments.

There is always a probability that a commercial enterprise can face negative cash conversion cycle, in which case they are getting payments from the clients before any payment is made to the suppliers. Instances of such business entities are commonly those companies, which apply JIT or Just in Time techniques, for example Dell, as well as commercial enterprises, which purchase on terms and conditions of longer duration credits and perform sales against cash, for instance Tesco.

The more the manufacturing procedure is extended, the higher the amount of cash should be kept engaged in inventories by the company. Likewise, the more time is taken for the clients for the purpose of bill payment, the more is the accounts receivable amount. From another viewpoint, if a company is able to detain the payment for its internal inputs, it can decrease the amount of money required. Put differently, the net working capital is diminished by accounts payable.

THE IMPORTANCE OF THE OPERATING CYCLE

Let's take the example of a greengrocer, who is "cashing up" one evening. What does he find? First, he sees how much he spent in cash at the wholesale market in the morning and then the cash proceeds from fruit and vegetable sales during the day. If we assume that the greengrocer sold all the produce he bought in the morning at a mark-up, the balance of receipts and payments for the day will deliver a cash surplus.

Unfortunately, things are usually more complicated in practice. Rarely is all the produce bought in the morning sold by the evening, especially in the case of a manufacturing business. A company processes raw materials as part of an operating cycle, the length of which varies tremendously, from a day in the newspaper sector to 7 years in the cognac sector. There is thus a time lag between purchases of raw materials and the sale of the corresponding finished goods.

And this time lag is not the only complicating factor. It is unusual for companies to buy and sell in cash. Usually, their suppliers grant them extended payment periods, and they in turn grant their customers extended payment periods. The money received during the day does not necessarily come from sales made on the same day. As a result of customer credit, supplier credit and the time it takes to manufacture and sell products or services, the operating cycle of each and every company spans a certain period, leading to timing differences between operating outflows and the corresponding operating inflows.

Each business has its own operating cycle of a certain length that, from a cash flow standpoint, may lead to positive or negative cash flows at different times. Operating outflows and inflows from different cycles are analysed by period, e.g., by month or by year. The balance of these flows is called operating cash flow. Operating cash flow reflects the cash flows generated by operations during a given period. In concrete terms, operating cash flow represents the cash flow generated by the company's day-to-day operations. Returning to our initial example of an individual looking at his bank statement, it represents the difference between the receipts and normal outgoings, such as on food, electricity and car maintenance costs.

Naturally, unless there is a major timing difference caused by some unusual circumstances (start-up period of a business, very strong growth, very strong seasonal fluctuations), the balance of operating receipts and payments should be positive.

THE IMPACT OF THE OPERATING CYCLE ON CASH FLOW

Many small business owners consult with the Small Business Development Center, CPAs, private business consultants, and lenders in an effort to address their working capital needs. Most owners believe the solution to their problems is a line of credit or a lump sum of cash to sustain the growth. The real solution, however, lies in understanding the operating cycle, also known as the cash conversion cycle, and its impact on cash flow.

The operating cycle is simply the sum of days of sales outstanding (DSO) and days of sales in inventory (DSI) minus days of payables outstanding (DPO):

Operating Cycle: DSO + DSI – DPO

To illustrate the use of the operating cycle, consider the following: company A has average daily sales of $1,000, 100% of sales are on credit with 30-days term, inventory is turned weekly, and payables are due in fifteen days.

The operating cycle for company A is: 30 days + 7 days – 15 days = 22 days.

Company A needs $22,000 in cash to sustain its operations at the current level ($1,000 X 22 days). As a company grows, so does the need for cash to sustain the growth. This cycle would force the company to constantly seek financing. To avoid such a problem, the company should make policy changes that would reduce its operating cycle and hence the need for capital. Three possible solutions exist: reduce days of sales outstanding, reduce days of sales in inventory, or increase days of payables outstanding.

Days of sales outstanding can be reduced by offering incentives to re-pay sooner than later or even prepay. Typical incentives can be 2/10 net 30 or 50% down payment. Factoring can also be used to reduce days of sales outstanding since a factor is going to pay immediately upon purchase of accounts receivable.

Days of sales in inventory can be reduced by locating nearer suppliers to reduce the delivery time and hence the required safety inventory level. Just in Time inventory is another method that can be used to reduce inventory. Days of Payables Outstanding can be increased by negotiating better credit terms.

Visit your nearest SBDC office to meet with a counsellor who can provide for further assistance in understanding your operating cycle and your cash needs.

5

Ethical Issues in Financial Management

FINANCIAL MANAGEMENT

Financial management in the small firm is characterized, in many different cases, by the need to confront a somewhat different set of problems and opportunities than those confronted by a large corporation. One immediate and obvious difference is that a majority of smaller firms do not normally have the opportunity to publicly sell issues of stocks or bonds in order to raise funds. The owner-manager of a smaller firm must rely primarily on trade credit, bank financing, lease financing, and personal equity to finance the business. One, therefore faces a much more severely restricted set of financing alternatives than those faced by the financial vice president or treasurer of a large corporation.

On the other hand, many financial problems facing the small firm are very similar to those of larger corporations. For example, the analysis required for a long-term investment decision such as the purchase of heavy machinery or the evaluation of lease-buy alternatives, is essentially the same regardless of the size of the firm. Once the decision is made, the financing alternatives available to the firm may be radically different, but the decision process will be generally similar.

One area of particular concern for the smaller business owner lies in the effective management of working capital. Net working capital is defined as the difference between current assets and current liabilities and is often thought of as the "circulating capital" of the business. Lack of control in this crucial area is a primary cause of business failure in both small and large firms. The business manager must continually be alert to changes in working capital accounts, the cause of these changes and the implications of these changes for the financial health of the company. One convenient and effective method to highlight the key managerial requirements in this area is to view working capital in terms of its major components:

CASH AND EQUIVALENTS

This most liquid form of current assets, cash and cash equivalents (usually marketable securities or short-term certificate of deposit) requires constant supervision. A well planned and maintained cash budgeting system is essential to answer key questions such as: Is the cash level adequate to meet current expenses as they come due? What are the timing relationships between cash inflows and outflows? When will peak cash needs occur? What will be the magnitude of bank borrowing required to meet any cash shortfalls? When will this borrowing be necessary and when may repayment be expected?

ACCOUNTS RECEIVABLE

Almost all businesses are required to extend credit to their customers. Key issues in this area include: Is the amount of accounts receivable reasonable in relation to sales? On the average, how rapidly are accounts receivable being collected? Which customers are "slow payers?" What action should be taken to speed collections where needed?

INVENTORIES

Inventories often make up 50 percent or more of a firm's current assets and therefore, are deserving of close scrutiny. Key questions which must be considered in this area include: Is the level of inventory reasonable in relation to sales and the operating characteristics of the business? How rapidly is inventory turned over in relation to other companies in the same industry? Is any capital invested in dead or slow moving stock? Are sales being lost due to inadequate inventory levels?

If appropriate, what action should be taken to increase or decrease inventory?

ACCOUNTS PAYABLE AND TRADE NOTES PAYABLE

In a business, trade credit often provides a major source of financing for the firm. Key issues to investigate in this category include: Is the amount of money owed to suppliers reasonable in relation to purchases? Is the firm's payment policy such that it will enhance or detract from the firm's credit rating? If available, are discounts being taken? What are the timing relationships between payments on accounts payable and collection on accounts receivable?

Notes Payable

Notes payable to banks or other lenders are a second major source of financing for the business. Important questions in this class include: What is the amount of bank borrowing employed? Is this debt amount reasonable in relation to the equity financing of the firm? When will principal and interest payments fall due? Will funds be available to meet these payments on time?

Accrued Expenses and Taxes Payable

Accrued expenses and taxes payable represent obligations of the firm as of the date of balance sheet preparation. Accrued expenses represent such items as salaries payable, interest payable on bank notes, insurance premiums payable, and similar items. Of primary concern in this area, particularly with regard to taxes payable, is the magnitude, timing, and availability of funds for payment. Careful planning is required to insure that these obligations are met on time.

As a final note, it is important to recognize that although the working capital accounts above are listed separately, they must also be viewed in total and from the point of view of their relationship to one another: What is the overall trend in net working capital? Is this a healthy trend? Which individual accounts are responsible for the trend? How does the firm's working capital position relate to similar sized firms in the industry? What can be done to correct the trend, if necessary?

Webster's Collegiate Dictionary defines "ethics" as the "discipline dealing with what is good and bad and with moral duty and obligation," "a set of moral principles or value" or "a theory or system of moral values." Ethics assists individuals in deciding when an act is moral or immoral, right or wrong. Ethics can be grounded in natural law, religious tenets, parental and family influence, educational experiences, life experiences, and cultural and societal expectations.

Ethics in business, or business ethics as it is often called, is the application of the discipline, principles, and theories of ethics to the organizational context. Business ethics have been defined as "principles and standards that guide behaviour in the world of business." Business ethics is also a descriptive term for the field of academic study in which many scholars conduct research and in which undergraduate and graduate students are exposed to ethics theory and practice, usually through the case method of analysis.

Ethical behaviour in business is critical. When business firms are charged with infractions, and when employees of those firms come under legal investigation, there is a concern raised about moral behaviour in business. Hence, the level of mutual trust, which is the foundation of our free-market economy, is threatened.

Although ethics in business has been an issue for academics, practitioners, and governmental regulators for decades, some believe that unethical, immoral, and/or illegal behaviour is widespread in the business world. Numerous scandals in the late 1990s and early 2000s seemed to add credence to the criticism of business ethics. Corporate executives of WorldCom, a giant in the telecommunications field, admitted fraud and misrepresentation in financial statements. WorldCom's former CEO went on trial for alleged crimes related to this accounting ethics scandal.

A similar scandal engulfed Enron in the late 1990s and its former CEO, Ken Lay, also faced trial. Other notable ethical lapses were publicized involving ImClone, a biotechnological firm; Arthur Andersen, one of the largest and oldest public accounting firms; and Healthsouth, a large healthcare firm located in the southeast United States. These companies eventually suffered public humiliation, huge financial losses, and in some cases, bankruptcy or dissolution. The ethical and legal problems resulted in some corporate officials going to prison, many employees losing their jobs, and thousands of stockholders losing some or all of their savings invested in the firms' stock.

Although the examples mentioned involved top management, huge sums of money, and thousands of stakeholders, business ethics is also concerned with the day-to-day ethical dilemmas faced by millions of workers at all levels of business enterprise.

It is the awareness of and judgments made in ethical dilemmas by all that determines the overall level of ethics in business. Thus, the field of business ethics is concerned not only with financial and accounting irregularities involving billions of dollars, but all kinds of moral and ethical questions, large and small, faced by those who work in business organizations.

The discussion that follows is organized into three parts: (1) the major theories or "moral philosophies" that are applied to business ethics; (2) a well-established model of ethical decision-making in business; and (3) the factors that affect individual ethical decision-making in the business context.

APPROACHES TO ETHICAL DECISION-MAKING

Philosophers have studied and written about ethics for thousands of years. The moral philosophies or ethical "theories" that have been developed form the foundation for ethics in business. Table 1 shows some of the major ethical philosophies that are applied to business ethics. Each of the ethical philosophies is briefly considered in this section.

Teleology

Teleological theories of ethics focus on the consequences caused by an action and are often referred to as "consequentialist" theories. By far the most common teleological theories are egoism and utilitarianism.

Egoism

Egoism defines right and wrong in terms of the consequences to one's self. Egoism is defined by self-interest. An egoist would weigh an ethical dilemma or issue in terms of how different courses of action would affect his or her physical, mental, or emotional well being. Thus, an egoist, when faced with a business decision, would tend to choose the course of action that he or she believes would best serve self-interest.

Although it seems likely that egoism would potentially lead to unethical and/or illegal behaviour, this philosophy of ethics is, to some degree, at the heart of a free-market economy. Since the time of political economist Adam Smith, advocates of a free market unencumbered by governmental regulation have argued that individuals, each pursuing their own self-interest, would actually benefit society at large.

Teleological	Actions are judged as ethical or unethical based on their results.
Egoism	Actions are judged as ethical or unethical based on the consequences to one's self. Actions that maximize self-interest are preferred.
Utilitarianism	Actions are judged as ethical or unethical based on the consequences to "others." Actions that maximize the "good" (create the greatest good for the greatest number) are preferred.
Deontological	Actions are judged as ethical or unethical based on the inherent rights of individual and the intentions of the actor. Individuals are to be treated as means and not ends. It is the action itself that must be judged and not its consequences.
Justice	Actions are judged as ethical or unethical based on the fairness shown to those affected. Fairness may be determined by distributive, procedural, and/or interactional means.
Relativism	Actions are judged as ethical or unethical based on subjective factors that may vary from individual to individual, group to group, and culture to culture.

This point of view is notably espoused by the famous economist Milton Friedman, who suggested that the only moral obligation of business is to make a profit and obey the law. However, it should be noted that Smith, Friedman, and most others who advocate unregulated commerce, acknowledge that some restraints on individuals' selfish impulses are required.

Utilitarianism

In the utilitarian approach to ethical reasoning, one emphasizes the utility, or the overall amount of good, that might be produced by an action or a decision. For example, companies decide to move their production facilities from one country to another. How much good is expected from the move? How much harm? If the good appears to outweigh the harm, the decision to move may be deemed an ethical one, by the utilitarian yardstick.

This approach also encompasses what has been referred to as cost-benefit analysis. In this, the costs and benefits of a decision, a policy, or an action are compared. Sometimes these can be measured in economic, social, human, or even emotional terms. When all the costs are added and compared with the results, if the benefits outweigh the costs, then the action may be considered ethical.

One fair criticism of this approach is that it is difficult to accurately measure costs and benefits. Another criticism is that the rights of those in the minority may be overlooked.

Utilitarianism is like egoism in that it advocates judging actions by their consequences, but unlike egoism utilitarianism focuses on determining the course of action that will produce the greatest good for the greatest number of people. Thus, it is the ends that determine the morality of an action and not the action itself (or the intent of the actor).

Utilitarianism is probably the dominant moral philosophy in business ethics. Utilitarianism is attractive to many business people, since the philosophy acknowledges that many actions result in good consequences for some, but bad consequences for others. This is certainly true of many decisions in business.

Deontology

Deontological theories of ethics focus on (1) the rights of all individuals and (2) the intentions of the person(s) performing an action. Deontological theories differ substantially from utilitarian views on ethics and would not allow, for example, the harming of some individuals in order to help others. To the deontologist, each person must be treated with the same level of respect and no one should be treated as a means to an end. Deontology proposes that the principles of ethics are permanent and unchanging—and that adherence to these principles is at the heart of ethical behaviour. Many deontologists believe that the rights of individuals are grounded in "natural law." Deontology is most closely associated with the German philosopher Immanuel Kant.

Justice

Justice-based theories of ethics concern the perceived fairness of actions. A just (ethical) action is one that treats all fairly and consistently in accord with ethical or legal standards. Justice theories of ethics are closely associated with the philosopher John Rawls. To determine the fairness of an action, one often appeals to distributive, procedural, and/or interactional rules. Distributive fairness is based on the outcomes received by individuals and their perceptions of these outcomes. Procedural fairness is based on the processes (policies, procedures, rules) employed to reach decisions. Individuals evaluate the fairness of these processes in addition to (or instead of) the outcomes received.

Finally, interactional fairness relates to the personal treatment one receives in the administration of a decision-making process. Interpersonal fairness has to do with the respect and consideration shown in the administration of decisions. Informational fairness has to do with the explanations and accounts provided for the decisions made. The study of organizational justice has become a major field within organizational behaviour. To date, however, there has not been a complete integration between justice perceptions and ethical theory.

Relativism

Teleological, utilitarian, and justice theories of ethics are all "universal" theories, in that they purport to advance principles of morality that are permanent and relatively enduring. Relativism states that there are no universal principles of ethics and that right and wrong must be determined by each individual or group. The relativist believes that standards of right and wrong change over time and are different across cultures—and does not accept that some ethical standards or values are superior to others. The concept of relativism can probably be summarized as "What's right for one may not be right for another," or "When in Rome, do as the Romans do."

INDIVIDUAL ETHICAL DECISION-MAKING

There are many approaches to the individual ethical decision-making process in business. However, one of the more common was developed by James Rest and has been called the four-step or four-stage model of individual ethical decision-making. Numerous scholars have applied this theory in the business context. The four steps include: ethical issue recognition, ethical (moral) judgment, ethical (moral) intent, and ethical (moral) behaviour.

Ethical Issue Recognition

Before a person can apply any standards of ethical philosophy to an issue, he or she must first comprehend that the issue has an ethical component. This means that the ethical decision-making process must be "triggered" or set in motion by the awareness of an ethical dilemma. Some individuals are likely to be more sensitive to potential ethical problems than others.

Ethical (Moral) Judgment

If an individual is confronted with a situation or issue that he or she recognizes as having an ethical component or posing an ethical dilemma, the individual will probably form some overall impression or judgment about the rightness or wrongness of the issue. The individual may reach this judgment in a variety of ways, as noted in the earlier section on ethical philosophy.

Ethical (Moral) Intent

Once an individual reaches an ethical judgment about a situation or issue, the next stage in the decision-making process is to form a Behavioural intent. That is, the individual decides what he or she will do (or not do) in regard to the perceived ethical dilemma. According to research, ethical judgments are a strong predictor of Behavioural intent. However, individuals do not always form intentions to behave that are in accord with their judgments, as various situational factors may act to influence the individual otherwise.

Ethical (Moral) Behaviour

The final stage in the four-step model of ethical decision-making is to engage in some behaviour in regard to the ethical dilemma. Research shows that Behavioural intentions are the strongest predictor of actual behaviour in general, and ethical behaviour in particular. However, individuals do now always behave consistent with either their judgments or intentions in regard to ethical issues. This is particularly a problem in the business context, as peer group members, supervisors, and organizational culture may influence individuals to act in ways that are inconsistent with their own moral judgments and Behavioural intentions. Some specific factors that influence the individual ethical decision-making process, as outlined above, are presented in the final section of this essay.

FACTORS AFFECTING ETHICAL DECISION-MAKING

In general, there are three types of influences on ethical decision-making in business: (1) individual difference factors, (2) situational (organizational) factors, and (3) issue-related factors.

Individual Difference Factors

Individual difference factors are personal factors about an individual that may influence their sensitivity to ethical issues, their judgment about such issues, and their related behaviour. Research has identified many personal characteristics that impact ethical decision-making. The individual difference factor that has received the most research support is "cognitive moral development." This framework, developed by Lawrence Kohlberg in the 1960s and extended by Kohlberg and other researchers in the subsequent years, helps to explain why different people make different evaluations when confronted with the same ethical issue. It posits that an individual's level of "moral development" affects their ethical issue recognition, judgment, Behavioural intentions, and behaviour.

According to the theory, individuals' level of moral development passes through stages as they mature. Theoretically, there are three major levels of development. The lowest level of moral development is termed the "pre-conventional" level. At the two stages of this level, the individual typically will evaluate ethical issues in light of a desire to avoid punishment and/or seek personal reward. The pre-conventional level of moral development is usually associated with small children or adolescents.

The middle level of development is called the "conventional" level. At the stages of the conventional level, the individual assesses ethical issues on the basis of the fairness to others and a desire to conform to societal rules and expectations. Thus, the individual looks outside him or herself to determine right and wrong. According to Kohlberg, most adults operate at the conventional level of moral reasoning.

The highest stage of moral development is the "principled" level. The principled level, the individual is likely to apply principles (which may be utilitarian, deontological, or justice) to ethical issues in an attempt to resolve them. According to Kohlberg, a principled person looks inside him or herself and is less likely to be influenced by situational (organizational) expectations. The cognitive moral development framework is relevant to business ethics because it offers a powerful explanation of individual differences in ethical reasoning. Individuals at different levels of moral development are likely to think differently about ethical issues and resolve them differently.

Situational (Organizational) Factors

Individuals' ethical issue recognition, judgment, and

behaviour are affected by contextual factors. In the business ethics context, the organizational factors that affect ethical decision-making include the work group, the supervisor, organizational policies and procedures, organizational codes of conduct, and the overall organizational culture. Each of these factors, individually and collectively, can cause individuals to reach different conclusions about ethical issues than they would have on their own. This section looks at one of these organizational factors, codes of conduct, in more detail.

Codes of conduct are formal policies, procedures, and enforcement mechanisms that spell out the moral and ethical expectations of the organization. A key part of organizational codes of conduct are written ethics codes. Ethics codes are statements of the norms and beliefs of an organization. These norms and beliefs are generally proposed, discussed, and defined by the senior executives in the firm. Whatever process is used for their determination, the norms and beliefs are then disseminated throughout the firm.

An example of a code item would be, "Employees of this company will not accept personal gifts with a monetary value over $25 in total from any business friend or associate, and they are expected to pay their full share of the costs for meals or other entertainment (concerts, the theatre, sporting events, etc.) that have a value above $25 per person." Hosmer points out that the norms in an ethical code are generally expressed as a series of negative statements, for it is easier to list the things a person should not do than to be precise about the things a person should. Almost all large companies and many small companies have ethics codes. However, in and of themselves ethics codes are unlikely to influence individuals to be more ethical in the conduct of business. To be effective, ethics codes must be part of a value system that permeates the culture of the organization. Executives must display genuine commitment to the ideals expressed in the written code—if their behaviour is inconsistent with the formal code, the code's effectiveness will be reduced considerably.

At a minimum, the code of conduct must be specific to the ethical issues confronted in the particular industry or company.

It should be the subject of ethics training that focuses on actual dilemmas likely to be faced by employees in the organization. The conduct code must contain communication mechanisms for the dissemination of the organizational ethical standards and for the reporting of perceived wrongdoing within the organization by employees. Organizations must also ensure that perceived ethical violations are adequately investigated and that wrongdoing is punished. Research suggests that unless ethical behaviour is rewarded and unethical behaviour punished, that written codes of conduct are unlikely to be effective.

Issue-Related Factors

Conceptual research by Thomas Jones in the 1990s and subsequent empirical studies suggest that ethical issues in business must have a certain level of "moral intensity" before they will trigger ethical decision-making processes. Thus, individual and situational factors are unlikely to influence decision-making for issues considered by the individual to be minor.

Certain characteristics of issues determine their moral intensity. In general, the research suggests that issues with more serious consequences are more likely to reach the threshold level of intensity. Likewise, issues that are deemed by a societal consensus to be ethical or unethical are more likely to trigger ethical decision-making processes.

In summary, business ethics is an exceedingly complicated area, one that has contemporary significance for all business practitioners. There are, however, guidelines in place for effective ethical decision making. These all have their positive and negative sides, but taken together, they may assist the businessperson to steer toward the most ethical decision possible under a particular set of circumstances.

THE GOAL OF FINANCIAL MANAGEMENT

The financial manager in a corporation makes decisions for the stockholders of the firm. Given this, instead of listing possible goals for the financial manager, we really need to answer a more fundamental question: From the stockholders' point of view, what is a good financial management decision?

If we assume that stockholders buy stock because they seek to gain financially, then the answer is obvious: Good decisions increase the value of the stock, and poor decisions decrease the value of the stock. Given our observations, it follows that the financial manager acts in the shareholders' best interests by making decisions that increase the value of the stock. The appropriate goal for the financial manager can thus be stated quite easily: The goal of financial management is to maximize the current value per share of the existing stock. The goal of maximizing the value of the stock avoids the problems associated with the different goals we listed earlier.

There is no ambiguity in the criterion, and there is no short-run versus long-run issue. We explicitly mean that our goal is to maximize the *current* stock value. If this goal seems a little strong or one-dimensional to you, keep in mind that the stockholders in a firm are residual owners.

By this we mean that they are only entitled to what is left after employees, suppliers, and creditors (and everyone else with a legitimate claims) are paid their due. If any of these groups go unpaid, the stockholders get nothing. So, if the stockholders are winning in the sense that the leftover, residual portion is growing, it must be true that everyone else is winning also. Because the goal of financial management is to maximize the value of the stock, we need to learn how to identify those investments and financing arrangements that favorably impact the value of the stock. This is precisely what we will be studying. In fact, we could have defined corporate finance as the study of the relationship between business decisions and the value of the stock in the business.

Possible Goals

If we were to consider possible financial goals, we might come up with some ideas like the following:

- Survive.
- Avoid financial distress and bankruptcy.
- Beat the competition.
- Maximize sales or market share.
- Minimize costs.

- Maximize profits.
- Maintain steady earnings growth.

These are only a few of the goals we could list. Furthermore, each of these possibilities presents problems as a goal for the financial manager. For example, it's easy to increase market share or unit sales; all we have to do is lower our prices or relax our credit terms.

Similarly, we can always cut costs simply by doing away with things such as research and development. We can avoid bankruptcy by never borrowing any money or never taking any risks, and so on. It's not clear that any of these actions are in the stockholders' best interests. Profit maximization would probably be the most commonly cited goal, but even this is not a very precise objective. Do we mean profits this year? If so, then we should note that actions such as deferring maintenance, letting inventories run down, and taking other short-run cost-cutting measures will tend to increase profits now, but these activities aren't necessarily desirable. The goal of maximizing profits may refer to some sort of "long-run" or "average" profits, but it's still unclear exactly what this means.

First, do we mean something like accounting net income or earnings per share? Second, what do we mean by the long run? As a famous economist once remarked, in the long run, we're all dead! More to the point, this goal doesn't tell us what the appropriate trade-off is between current and future profits. The goals we've listed here are all different, but they do tend to fall into two classes.

The first of these relates to profitability. The goals involving sales, market share, and cost control all relate, at least potentially, to different ways of earning or increasing profits. The goals in the second group, involving bankruptcy avoidance, stability, and safety, relate in some way to controlling risk. Unfortunately, these two types of goals are somewhat contradictory. The pursuit of profit normally involves some element of risk, so it isn't really possible to maximize both safety and profit. What we need, therefore, is a goal that encompasses both factors.

A More General Goal

Given our goal as stated in the preceding section (to maximize the value of the stock), an obvious question comes up: What is the appropriate goal when the firm has no traded stock? Corporations are certainly not the only type of business; and the stock in many corporations rarely changes hands, so it's difficult to say what the value per share is at any given time. As long as we are dealing with for-profit businesses, only a slight modification is needed. The total value of the stock in a corporation is simply equal to the value of the owners' equity. Therefore, a more general way of stating our goal is as follows: Maximize the market value of the existing owners' equity. With this in mind, it doesn't matter whether the business is a proprietorship, a partnership, or a corporation. For each of these, good financial decisions increase the market value of the owners' equity and poor financial decisions decrease it. In fact, although we choose to focus on corporations in the chapters ahead, the principles we develop apply to all forms of business. Many of them even apply to the not-for-profit sector.

Finally, our goal does not imply that the financial manager should take illegal or unethical actions in the hope of increasing the value of the equity in the firm. What we mean is that the financial manager best serves the owners of the business by identifying goods and services that add value to the firm because they are desired and valued in the free marketplace.

Agency Problem and Control of the Corporation

We've seen that the financial manager acts in the best interests of the stockholders by taking actions that increase the value of the stock. However, in large corporations ownership can be spread over a huge number of stockholders.

This dispersion of ownership arguably means that management effectively controls the firm. In this case, will management necessarily act in the best interests of the stockholders? Put another way, might not management pursue its own goals at the stockholders' expense? In the following pages, we briefly consider some of the arguments relating to this question.

Agency Relationships

The relationship between stockholders and management is called an *agency relationship*. Such a relationship exists whenever someone (the principal) hires another (the agent) to represent his/her interests. For example, you might hire someone (an agent) to sell a car that you own while you are away at school. In all such relationships, there is a possibility of a conflict of interest between the principal and the agent. Such a conflict is called an agency problem. Suppose you hire someone to sell your car and you agree to pay that person a flat fee when he/she sells the car. The agent's incentive in this case is to make the sale, not necessarily to get you the best price. If you offer a commission of, say, 10 percent of the sales price instead of a flat fee, then this problem might not exist. This example illustrates that the way in which an agent is compensated is one factor that affects agency problems.

Management Goals

To see how management and stockholder interests might differ, imagine that the firm is considering a new investment. The new investment is expected to favourably impact the share value, but it is also a relatively risky venture. The owners of the firm will wish to take the investment (because the stock value will rise), but management may not because there is the possibility that things will turn out badly and management jobs will be lost. If management does not take the investment, then the stockholders may lose a valuable opportunity. This is one example of an *agency cost*. More generally, the term agency costs refers to the costs of the conflict of interest between stockholders and management. These costs can be indirect or direct. An indirect agency cost is a lost opportunity, such as the one we have just described. Direct agency costs come in two forms. The first type is a corporate expenditure that benefits management but costs the stockholders. Perhaps the purchase of a luxurious and unneeded corporate jet would fall under this heading.

The second type of direct agency cost is an expense that arises from the need to monitor management actions. Paying outside auditors to assess the accuracy of financial statement information could be one example. It is sometimes argued that, left to themselves, managers would tend to maximize the amount of resources over which they have control or, more generally, corporate power or wealth. This goal could lead to an overemphasis on corporate size or growth.

For example, cases in which management is accused of overpaying to buy up another company just to increase the size of the business or to demonstrate corporate power are not uncommon. Obviously, if overpayment does take place, such a purchase does not benefit the stockholders of the purchasing company. Our discussion indicates that management may tend to overemphasize organizational survival to protect job security. Also, management may dislike outside interference, so independence and corporate self-sufficiency may be important goals.

Do Managers Act in the Stockholders' Interests?

Whether managers will, in fact, act in the best interests of stockholders depends on two factors. First, how closely are management goals aligned with stockholder goals? This question relates, at least in part, to the way managers are compensated. Second, can management be replaced if they do not pursue stockholder goals? This issue relates to control of the firm. As we will discuss, there are a number of reasons to think that, even in the largest firms, management has a significant incentive to act in the interests of stockholders.

Managerial Compensation

Management will frequently have a significant economic incentive to increase share value for two reasons.

First, managerial compensation, particularly at the top, is usually tied to financial performance in general and oftentimes to share value in particular.

For example, managers are frequently given the option to buy stock at a bargain price. The more the stock is worth, the more valuable is this option. In fact, options are often used to motivate employees of all types, not just top management. The second incentive managers have relates to job prospects. Better performers within the firm will tend to get promoted. More generally, those managers who are successful in pursuing stockholder goals will be in greater demand in the labor market and thus command higher salaries. In fact, managers who are successful in pursuing stockholder goals can reap enormous rewards. For example, one of America's best paid executives in 2004 was Rueben Mark, the CEO of Colgate-Palmolive for the past 20 years; according to Forbes magazine, he made $148 million in that year. By way of comparison, Mark made less than Mel Gibson and Oprah Winfrey ($210 million each) but more than Tiger Woods ($80 million). Over the period 2000–2004, Oracle CEO Larry Ellison was the highest paid executive, earning about $836 million. Dell CEO Michael Dell earned slightly less over the same period, only $526 million.

Control of the Firm

Control of the firm ultimately rests with stockholders. They elect the board of directors, who, in turn, hire and fire management. The fact that-stockholders control the corporation was made abundantly clear by Carly Fiorina's experience at HP, which we described to open the chapter. Even though she had reorganized the corporation, there came a time when shareholders, through their elected directors, decided that HP would be better off without her, so out she went.

An important mechanism by which unhappy stockholders can act to replace existing management is called a *proxy fight*. A proxy is the authority to vote someone else's stock. A proxy fight develops when a group solicits proxies in order to replace the existing board, and thereby replace existing management. For example, the proposed merger between HP and Compaq, which we mentioned in our chapter opener, triggered one of the most widely followed, bitterly contested, and expensive proxy fights in history, with an estimated price tag of well over $100 million.

Another way that management can be replaced is by takeover. Those firms that are poorly managed are more attractive as acquisitions than well-managed firms because a greater profit potential exists. Thus, avoiding a takeover by another firm gives management another incentive to act in the stockholders' interests. For example, in 2004, Comcast, the cable television giant, announced a surprise bid to buy Disney at a time when Disney's management was under close scrutiny for its performance. Not too surprisingly, Disney's management strongly opposed being acquired, and Comcast ultimately decided to withdraw, in part because of improvements in Disney's financial performance.

The available theory and evidence are consistent with the view that stockholders control the firm and that stockholder wealth maximization is the relevant goal of the corporation. Even so, there will undoubtedly be times when management goals are pursued at the expense of the stockholders, at least temporarily.

Stakeholders

Our discussion thus far implies that management and stockholders are the only parties with an interest in the firm's decisions. This is an oversimplification, of course. Employees, customers, suppliers, and even the government all have a financial interest in the firm. Taken together, these various groups are called stakeholders in the firm. In general, a stakeholder is someone other than a stockholder or creditor who potentially has a claim on the cash flows of the firm. Such groups will also attempt to exert control over the firm, perhaps to the detriment of the owners.

Dealer Versus Auction Markets

There are two kinds of secondary markets: *dealer* markets and *auction* markets. Generally speaking, dealers buy and sell for themselves, at their own risk. A car dealer, for example, buys and sells automobiles. In contrast, brokers and agents match buyers and sellers, but they do not actually own the commodity that is bought or sold. A real estate agent, for example, does not normally buy and sell houses. Dealer markets in stocks and long-term debt are called *over-the-counter* (OTC) markets.

Most trading in debt securities takes place over the counter. The expression *over the counter* refers to days of old when securities were literally bought and sold at counters in offices around the country. Today, a significant fraction of the market for stocks and almost all of the market for long-term debt have no central location; the many dealers are connected electronically.

Auction markets differ from dealer markets in two ways. First, an auction market or exchange has a physical location (like Wall Street). Second, in a dealer market, most of the buying and selling is done by the dealer. The primary purpose of an auction market, on the other hand, is to match those who wish to sell with those who wish to buy. Dealers play a limited role.

6

Budget: The Fiscal Policy

Fiscal Policy Overview

The Union Budget 2008-09 was presented in the backdrop of impressive growth in the Indian economy which clocked about 9 per cent of average growth in the last four years. This striking performance coupled with significant improvement in fiscal indicators, during the Fiscal Responsibility and Budget Management (FRBM) Act, 2003 regime definitely put the country on a higher growth trajectory inspiring confidence in the medium to long term prospects of the economy. The process of fiscal consolidation during these years has resulted in improvement in fiscal deficit from 5.9 per cent of GDP in 2002-03 to 2.7 per cent of GDP in 2007-08. During the same period, revenue deficit has declined from 4.4 per cent to 1.1 per cent of GDP.

In tune with the philosophy of equitable growth, the process of fiscal consolidation was taken forward without constricting the much-required social sector and infrastructure related expenditure. This improvement in the state of public finances was achieved through higher revenue buoyancy, driven by efficient tax administration and improved compliance which is evident from increase in the tax to GDP ratio from 8.8 per cent in 2002-03 to 12.5 per cent in 2007-08.

Riding on the path of fiscal consolidation, the Union Budget 2008-09 was presented with fiscal deficit estimated at 2.5 per cent of GDP and revenue deficit at 1 per cent of GDP. However after the presentation of the Union Budget in February 2008, the world economy was hit by three unprecedented crises — first, the petroleum price rise; second, rise in prices of other commodities; and third, the breakdown of the financial system.

The combined effect of these crises of these orders are bound to affect emerging market economies and India was no exception. The first two crises resulted in serious inflationary pressure in the first half of 2008-09. The focus of the monetary as well as fiscal policy shifted from fuelling growth to containing inflation, which had reached 12.9 per cent in August, 2008.

Series of fiscal measures both on tax revenue and expenditure side were undertaken with the objective of easing supply side constraints. These measures were supplemented by monetary initiatives through policy rate changes by the Reserve Bank of India, and contributed to the softening of domestic prices.

Headline inflation fell to 4.39 per cent in January, 2009. However, the fiscal measures undertaken through tax concessions and increased expenditure on food, fertiliser and petroleum subsidies along with increased wage bill for implementing the Sixth Central Pay Commission recommendations significantly altered the deficit position of the Government.

The global financial crisis in the second half of the financial year which heralded recessionary trends the world over, also impacted the Indian economy causing the focus of fiscal policy to be shifted to providing growth stimulus. The moderation in growth of the economy and the impact of the fiscal measures taken to stimulate growth can be seen reflected in the estimates for gross tax revenue which stand reduced from Rs 6,87,715 crore in B.E.2008-09 to Rs 6,27,949 crore in R.E.2008-09.

Additional budgetary resources of Rs.1,50,320 crore provided as part of stimulus package and various committed liabilities of Government including rising subsidy requirement, provision under NREGS, implementation of Central Sixth Pay Commission recommendations and Agriculture Debt Waiver and Debt Relief Scheme for Farmers contributed to the higher fiscal deficit of 6 per cent of GDP in RE 2008-09 as compared to 2.5 per cent of GDP in B.E.2008-09.

The Country is facing difficult economic situation, the cause of which is not emanating from within its boundaries. However, left unattended, the impact of this crisis is going to affect us in medium to long term.

The Government had two policy options before it. In view of falling buoyancy in tax receipts, the Government could have taken a decision to cut expenditure and thereby live within the estimated deficit for the year. The second option was to increase public expenditure, even with reduced receipts, to stimulate economy by creating demand and maintain the growth trajectory which the country was witnessing in the recent past. The Government took the second option of adopting fiscal measures to increase public expenditure to boost demand and increase investment in infrastructure sector. Ensuring revival of the higher growth of the economy will restore revenue buoyancy in medium term and afford the required fiscal space to revert to the path of fiscal consolidation.

Fiscal Policy for the ensuing financial year

The Interim Budget 2009-2010 is being presented in the backdrop of uncertainties prevailing in the world economy. The impact of this is seen in the moderation of the recent trend in growth of the Indian economy in 2008-09 which at 7.1 per cent still however makes India the second fastest growing economy in the World. The measures taken by Government to counter the effects of the global meltdown on the Indian economy, have resulted in a short fall in revenues and substantial increases in government expenditures, leading to a temporary deviation from the fiscal consolidation path mandated under the FRBM Act during 2008-09 and 2009-2010.

The revenue deficit and fiscal deficit for R.E.2008-09 and B.E.2009-2010 are, as a result, higher than the targets set under the FRBM Act and Rules. The grounds due to which this temporary deviation has taken place, are detailed in the Fiscal Policy Overview above and also in the Macro-economic Framework Statement being presented in the Parliament. The fiscal policy for the year 2009-2010 will continue to be guided by the objectives of keeping the economy on the higher growth trajectory amidst global slowdown by creating demand through increased public expenditure in identified sectors. However, the medium term objective will be to revert to the path of fiscal consolidation at the earliest, with improvement in the economic situation.

TAX POLICY

Indirect Taxes

During the first half of the fiscal year, the global spurt in commodity prices (crude petroleum, food items and metals) led to increases in domestic prices of essential items and industrial inputs, putting a severe inflationary pressure on the economy. Hence, the Government took several measures after the presentation of the Union Budget 2008-09, particularly on the Customs side, to contain the rising inflation, as detailed below:-

Customs

On 21.3.2008, to curb the inflationary trends in the economy arising out of a rise in prices of food items, a sharp reduction was effected in the import duty rates on various food items such as semi-milled or wholly milled rice (70% to nil) and crude and refined edible oils (from 40%-75% to 20%-27.5%). On 01.04.2008, a further reduction was effected in the import duty rate- on all crude edible oils duty was reduced to nil, and on refined edible oils duty was reduced to 7.5%.

Export duty of Rs 8,000 PMT was imposed on exports of Basmati rice with effect from 10.5.2008. With effect from 10.5.2008, import duties on crude petroleum was reduced to nil and on petrol and diesel to 2.5% (earlier 7.5%). Customs duty on other petroleum products was reduced from 10% to 5% on 04.06.2008.

Import duties were reduced to nil on many iron and steel items as well as on specified inputs for this sector (zinc, ferro-alloys, metcoke) on 29.4.2008. Further, in order to increase the domestic availability and bring about moderation in prices, export duties were imposed on many items in the iron and steel sector @ 15% ad valorem on pig iron, sponge iron, iron and steel scrap, iron or steel pencil ingots, semi finished products and HR coils/sheets, etc. On 08.07.2008, raw cotton was also fully exempted from customs duties so as to contain the prices of raw cotton and augment the domestic supply.

Excise

With effect from 04.06.2008, excise duty on unbranded motor spirit (MS) was reduced from Rs 6.35 per litre to Rs 5.35 per litre and on unbranded high speed diesel (HSD), excise duty was reduced from Rs 2.6 per litre to Rs 1.6 per litre. In the post-October stage, while the inflationary pressures on the economy were subdued, the global meltdown and resultant slowdown of the Indian economy required review of the existing policy in favour of maintaining the growth momentum and retaining export markets. As such, the following policy changes were effected which would be reviewed in the ensuing financial year in the light of the macroeconomic situation particularly the growth of the manufacturing sector:

Service Tax

The refund of service tax paid by exporters on various taxable services attributable to export of goods has been further extended to include clearing and forwarding agents services. The upper limit of refund of service tax paid by exporters on foreign commission agent services has been enhanced from 2% of FOB value to 10% of FOB value of export goods. Drawback benefit can now be availed of simultaneously with refund of service tax paid in respect of exports. In order to mitigate the genuine hardships of goods transport agencies, eight specified services which are provided to goods transport agency have also been fully exempted from service tax.

Excise

With effect from 07.12.2008, a fiscal stimulus package was implemented. As part of this package, Government implemented an across-the board reduction of 4 percentage points in the ad valorem rates of excise duty on non-petroleum items, with a few exceptions. Thus the three major ad valorem rates of Central Excise duty viz. 14%, 12% and 8% have been reduced to 10%, 8% and 4%, respectively. The specific rates of duty applicable to cement and cement clinker were also reduced proportionately.

Customs

Export duties on iron and steel items were withdrawn w.e.f. 31.10.2008. Aviation turbine fuel was fully exempted from basic customs duty for the benefit of the aviation industry w.e.f. 31.10.2008. In addition, to provide a level playing field to the domestic industry, some customs duty exemptions provided earlier to combat inflation, on iron and steel items, zinc and ferro-alloys, were withdrawn w.e.f. 18.11.2008. As an incentive to the infrastructure sector, the CVD and Special CVD exemption granted to imports of cement has been withdrawn w.e.f. 2nd January, 2009 to provide a cushion to domestic cement industry and boost demand.

In the power sector, customs duty on naphtha used for generation of electricity by electrical generating stations has been fully exempted w.e.f. 2nd January, 2009 till the end of this financial year.

Direct Taxes

Over the last five years, widespread reforms have been ushered in the area of direct taxes. The reform strategy comprises the following elements: - Minimizing distortions within the tax structure by expanding the tax base and rationalizing the tax rates. Enabling the tax administration to provide quality taxpayer services and also enhance deterrence levels. Both these objectives reinforce each other and have promoted voluntary compliance.

Re-engineering business processes in the Income-tax Department through extensive use of information technology, viz., e-filing of returns; issue of refunds through ECS and refund bankers; selection of returns for scrutiny through computers; e-payment of taxes; establishing a Centralized Processing Centre and an effective taxpayer information system. These measures have substantially enhanced the direct tax revenue productivity from 3.81 per cent of GDP in 2003-04 to an estimated 6.35 per cent of GDP in 2008-09. Further, the share of direct taxes in the Central tax revenues is now significantly higher than the share of indirect taxes resulting in a substantial improvement in the equity of the tax system.

Therefore, the reform strategy in the medium term is to consolidate the achievements of the past.

Since there is no change in the tax base and rates, the prospects of growth in direct tax collection in the ensuing financial year will remain unchanged vis-a-vis the revised estimate for the financial year 2008-09.

Contingent and other Liabilities

The FRBM Act mandates the Central Government to specify the annual target for assuming contingent liabilities in the form of guarantees. Accordingly the FRBM Rules prescribe a cap of 0.5 per cent of GDP in any financial year on the quantum of guarantees that the Central Government can assume in the particular financial year. The Central Government extends guarantees primarily on loans from multilateral/bilateral agencies, bond issues and other loans raised by various Public Sector Undertakings/Public Sector Financial Institutions.

The stock of contingent liabilities in the form of guarantees given by the government has reduced from Rs 1,07,957 crore at the beginning of the FRBM Act regime i.e. 2004-05 to Rs 1,04,872 crore at the end of 2007-08. As a percentage of GDP, it has reduced from 3.4 per cent in 2004-05 to 2.3 per cent in year 2006-07 and further to 2.2 per cent for the year 2007-08.

The disclosure statement on outstanding Guarantees as prescribed in the FRBM Rules, 2004 is appended in the Receipts Budget as Annex 3 (iii). Assumption of contingent liability in the form of guarantee by the sovereign helps to leverage private sector participation in areas of national priorities. In the current situation, wherein a large number of infrastructure projects are being cleared for implementation under the Public Private Partnership (PPP) mode, difficulties are being faced in reaching financial closure due to the current uncertainties in the global financial market. Within the given fiscal constraints and with a view to supporting financing of above mentioned PPP projects, the India Infrastructure Financing Company Limited (IIFCL) has been authorized to raise Rs 10,000 crore through Government guaranteed tax free bonds, by the end of 2008-09 and additional Rs 30,000 crore on the same basis as per requirement in the next financial year. The capital so raised will be used by IIFCL to refinance bank lending of longer maturity to eligible infrastructure projects. This initiative of the government is expected to result in leveraging of bank financing to PPP programmes of about Rs one lakh crore. The likely assumption of contingent liability in the form of guarantee for 2008-09, including the above mentioned Rs 10,000 crore for IIFCL, will amount to Rs 36,606 crore which will be 0.67 percentage of GDP during 2008-09, higher than the target of 0.5 per cent of GDP set under the FRBM Rules.

This deviation has been necessiated in the larger interest of re-invigorating the economy in the background of the current economic scenario, to stimulate demand and increase investment in infrastructure sector projects. In the medium term while this may not have a potential budgetary impact, the additional demand thus created will help restore the economy to its higher growth path and contribute to higher revenue buoyancy which has shown a slump in the current financial year due to moderation in the growth in economy.

Government Borrowings, Lending and Investments

The Government policy towards borrowings to finance its deficit continues to remain anchored on the following principles namely (i) greater reliance on domestic borrowings over external debt, (ii) preference for market borrowings over instruments carrying administered interest rates, (iii) elongation of the maturity profile and consolidation of the debt portfolio and (iv) development of a deep and wide market for Government securities to improve liquidity in secondary market.

In the first half of the current financial year, the government borrowing was in line with the indicated auction calendar decided upon in consultation with the Reserve Bank of India. However, due to the need to provide the fiscal stimulus to counter the situation created by the effects of the global financial crisis, the borrowing calendar of the government had to be revised in the second half of the current financial year. The gross and net market borrowings (dated securities and 364-day Treasury Bills) of the Central Government during 2008-09 (up to February 9, 2009) amounted to Rs 2,40,167 crore and

Rs 1,68,710 crore, respectively. As part of policy to elongate maturity profile, Central Government has been issuing securities with maximum 30—year maturity. The weighted average maturity of dated securities issued during 2008-09 (up to February 9, 2009) was 14.45 years which was marginally lower than 14.90 years during the corresponding period of the previous year. The weighted average yield of dated securities issued during 2008-09 (up to February 9, 2009) was 7.91 per cent and was lower than 8.12 per cent during the corresponding period of last year.

Consequent to the transition to the FRBM Act mandated environment, recourse to borrowing from RBI under normal circumstances is prohibited. During the year 2008-09 (up to February 7, 2009) the Central Government resorted to ways and means advance to meet the temporary mismatch in receipts and expenditure for 77 days as compared with 91 days a year ago. The daily average utilization of ways and means advance by the Central Government was Rs 7,383 crore as compared with Rs 14,498 crore a year ago. The Central Government also availed of Overdraft (OD) for 24 days up to February 7, 2009. The daily average of OD was Rs.11,233 crore as compared with Rs 6,381 crore a year ago.

The outstanding balance under Market Stabilization Scheme (MSS) on 1st April, 2008 was Rs 1,70,554 crore. Notwithstanding fresh issuance of Rs 43,500 crore during 2008-09, the outstanding balance under the MSS declined to Rs 1,05,773 crore mainly reflecting the change in policy and unwinding MSS through buyback of Rs 47,544 crores. This was done in order to ease liquidity in the system in the backgrounds of the additional borrowing plan during the second half of 2008-09 to finance the increased deficit.

In order to have prudent management of debt and greater focus on carrying cost as well as meeting secondary market liquidity, the government has set up a Middle Office which in due course will merge with the proposed Debt Management Office.

Central Government has stopped playing the role of financial intermediary for State Government for domestic market borrowings and the trends in the current year shows that this transition has been very smooth resulting in reduction in cost for the State Governments while at the same time bringing in a sense of market discipline.

Government has set up National Investment Fund (NIF) to which the disinvestment proceeds from Central PSUs are being transferred. This fund is being managed by professional fund managers. The receipts in the Fund are not reckoned as resources for the purpose of financing the fiscal deficit. The income from investments under NIF is used to finance social infrastructure and provide capital to viable public sector enterprises without depleting the corpus of NIF.

Initiatives in Public Expenditure Management

The focus has shifted from financial outlays to outcomes for ensuring that the budgetary provisions are not merely spent within the financial year but have resulted in intended outcomes. Initiatives have been taken to evenly pace plan expenditure during the year and also to avoid rush of expenditure at the year end which results in poor quality of expenditure. The practice of restricting the expenditure in the month of March to 15 per cent of budget allocation within the fourth quarter ceiling of 33 per cent is being enforced religiously. The quarterly exchequer control based cash and expenditure management system which inter alia involves preparing a Monthly Expenditure Plan (MEP) continues to be followed in select Demands for Grants. The emphasis is on right pacing plan expenditure by ensuring adequate resources for execution of budgeted schemes. At the same time, steps have also been taken in the form of austerity instructions to reduce expenditure in non-priority areas without compromising on operational efficiency. This has resulted in availability of adequate resources from realised receipts for priority schemes.

Delays in receipts of utilization certificate are broadly indicative of poor implementation strategy, diversion of funds or delay in utilization of funds for intended purposes. Monitoring of utilization certificates and unspent balances with the implementing authorities is reviewed at the highest level in the Ministry of Finance. Necessary control mechanisms have been put in place with the help of the office of the Controller General of Accounts (CGA) to avoid parking of funds and to track expenditure.

A central monitoring, evaluation and accounting system for the 1258 centrally sponsored schemes and central sector schemes of the Government has been instituted under the Central Plan Schemes Monitoring System. All sanctions issued by the Central Ministries under these schemes are now identified with a unique sanction ID that enables the tracking of release as per their accounting and budget heads across the different implementing agencies. This central system is hosted on the e-lekha portal of the CGA.

In addition pilots are currently underway in the States of Punjab , Karnataka and Uttarakhand for testing a system for expenditure filing and direct payment to beneficiaries under the schemes. The results of the pilot would form the basis of designing comprehensive IT based Decision Support System and Management Information System for all the centrally sponsored schemes and central sector schemes. This initiative assumes special significance in the light of the significant increase in the social sector spending by the Government.

The application software COMPACT has been extended to all civil ministries of the Government and expenditure data is being uploaded on a daily basis by the Pay and Accounts Offices on e-lekha. This is a significant step towards faster and accurate compilation of the accounts for the Government of India and will lead to the development of a core accounting solution.

Policy Evaluation

The process of fiscal consolidation during the FRBM Act regime has created necessary fiscal space to undertake much needed social sector expenditure and provide for higher infrastructure outlays. The performance up to 2007-08 was heartening. Fiscal deficit was brought down from 4.5 per cent of GDP in 2003-04 to 2.7 per cent in 2007-08. Similarly, revenue deficit was reduced from 3.6 per cent of GDP in 2003-04 to 1.1 per cent in 2007-08. The government was steadfast in following the fiscal consolidation path which is reflected in the deficit estimates of B.E.2008-09. However, subsequent to the global meltdown, there was a compelling need to adjust the fiscal policy to take care of exceptional circumstances through which the economy has been passing. The result of the fiscal measures taken by the Government for containing inflation has been positive as is evident from headline inflation dropping from high of 12.9 per cent in August 2008 to 4.39 per cent in January 2009. Similarly the intervention of the Government has ensured that the economy grows at a healthy rate of 7.1 per cent in a difficult year when most of the developed economies are facing recession. The fiscal consolidation process has to be put on hold temporarily. The process of fiscal consolidation will be back on track once there is an improvement in economic conditions.

THE LIMITATIONS OF FISCAL POLICY

Fiscal policy has been a great success in developed countries but only partially so in developing countries. The tax structure in the developing countries is rigid and narrow. Thus, conditions conducive to the growth of well-knit and integrated tax policies are absent and sorely missed. Following are some of the reasons that are hindrances for its implementation in developing countries:

1. A sizeable portion of most developing economies is non-monetized, rendering fiscal measures of the government ineffective and self-defeating.
2. Lack of statistical information as regards the income, expenditure, savings, investment, employment etc. makes it difficult for the public authorities to formulate a rational and effective fiscal policy.
3. Fiscal policy cannot succeed unless people understand its implications and cooperate with the government in its implication. This is due to the fact that, in developing countries, a majority of the people are illiterate.
4. Large-scale tax evasion, by people who are not conscious of their roles in development, has an impact on fiscal policy.
5. Fiscal policy requires efficient administrative machinery to be successful. Most developing economies have corrupt

and inefficient administrations that fail to implement the requisite measures vis-a-vis the implementation of fiscal policy.

Among the various tools of fiscal policy, the following are the most important:

Reflationary Fiscal Policy

It may be used to boost the level of economic activity during periods of recession or deceleration in economic activity. This is done by lowering taxes or increasing government expenditure.

Deflationary Fiscal Policy

During a boom, i.e., when the economy is growing beyond its capacity, inflation and balance of payment problems might result. This can be achieved by increasing taxes or by reducing government expenditure. It would perhaps be too simplistic to conclude that fiscal policy is the most important tool of financial correction and consolidation, especially that undertaken by the government. However, there is no reason to neglect this very powerful tool that is in the hands of governments and central banks the world over. Used properly, fiscal policy can determine the broad direction the economy of a given country is going to take.

FISCAL POLICY: WHEN THEORY COLLIDES WITH REALITY

The term fiscal comes from the Latin word fiscalis which in turn comes from fiscus, i.e. a basket used for collecting money. In Italian "il fisco" refers to the agency that collects taxes. Thus "fiscal policy" means policy related to taxes. The same is the case in Spanish, French, and Portuguese. In English the expression "fiscal policy" was apparently first used by Edwin R.A. Seligman, a prominent professor of public finance at Columbia University in the early part of the 20th century. He used the expression to criticize Adolf Wagner, a German economist, who had suggested that governments should engage in some redistribution of income through their budgetary activities. This seems to be the genesis of the "redistribution branch" of the trilogy m. de popular by Richard Musgrave

(1959). The Keynesian revolution changed the meaning of fiscal policy moving it away from the tax or revenue side of the budget to include both revenue and spending. For the Keynesians, fiscal policy refers to the manipulation of taxes and public spending to influence aggregate demand. Thus we had the genesis of the "stabilization branch" in Musgrave's trilogy.

The Theory of Fiscal Policy

The theory of fiscal policy owes much to North European economists such as Jan Tinbergen, Bent Hansen, Leif Johansen, and others who five decades ago developed it. In spirit, if not in geography, Richard Musgrave could be placed among this group. There were obviously also contributors from North America such as: Alvin Hansen, Lawrence Klein, Abba Lerner, Robert Solow, Paul Samuelson, and others, but, in their writing, they focused mostly on the stabilization role of fiscal policy. The Keynesian stabilization policy is only a part, though an important part, of the modern theory of fiscal policy. In the conception of this theory, especially well developed in Musgrave's (1959) and in Johansen's (1965) treatises, the goals of fiscal policy extend beyond stabilization because fiscal tools can be used also for redistributing income and for reallocating resources I will sketch the "Theory of Fiscal Policy" in its most essential elements and will outline the assumptions implicit in it. I will then argue that the reality can be far removed from this theory, at least in some countries.

In contrasting the theory with the reality, I will use Italian examples. The reason is that, having been part of the Italian government, I know the Italian situation best and not necessarily because that situation is farthest from the theory. In fact my knowledge of other countries and discussions with foreign colleagues with inside knowledge of particular countries have convinced me the conclusions of this paper are also valid, to varying degrees, for many other countries. However, this discussion may be less representative of the countries in the North of Europe for which the theory was originally developed. Let me start with the main elements of this theory. Policymakers are assumed to have no other objectives but the promotion of the social welfare or the public interest of the citizens. The social welfare does not depend on any single variable or indicator, but on several indicators, some of an economic nature and some of a social nature.

The way in which the policymakers rank these indicators change with time or with the government in power. In representative democracies this ranking is assumed to reflect the preferences of the citizens and changes in those preferences. Examples of economic indicators are: economic growth, growth of employment, growth of productivity, the rate of inflation, income distribution, unemployment among particular groups, and so on. Examples of social indicators are: life expectancy, incidence of crime, literacy rates, the quality of the physical environment, the incidence of illnesses, and so on.

The policymakers responsible for economic policy will naturally focus on

economic indicators. They have some perception of the weight that each of these indicators, yi, has on the welfare function, W1. Thus we can write the equation, (1) W = f (y1,y2.......yn)

The policymakers are aware that the indicators, yi can be influenced by changes in particular policy instruments, xj. These instruments are the "handles" available to the policymakers to modify the social welfare and to steer it toward an optimum. Therefore, each indicator is a function of the policy instruments. Thus, we can write the equation,

(2) yi = f (x1, x2, x3....xj)

Often a particular instrument xi is especially efficient in influencing a specific indicator yi. Efficiency in this context means the change in an instrument, "x, necessary to change an indicator by a given amount, "y. If a small or realistic change in an instrument can produce a significant change in an indicator, then the instrument is considered efficient with respect to that indicator When efficient instruments are available to promote desirable objectives economic, policy becomes easier. Examples of policy instruments are: various taxes; particular features of taxes such as deductions and rates;

various categories of expenditures; particular features of expenditures; and so on. Fiscal deficits can also be seen as indirect instruments to pursue stabilization policies. They are influenced by changing taxes and spending. Non-fiscal economic instruments are the exchange rate, the interest rate, regulations and so on.

They also influence the socio-economic indicators but they will be ignored in this discussion, which is focused on fiscal policy. If some technical conditions are satisfied then the implicit system of equation formed by the relationships mentioned above can be solved for the values of the instruments that would maximize the social welfare, W.[3] This mathematical solution may require too large changes in the instruments. However, if the instruments are efficient, the solution of the equation will require changes in their value that are technically or politically feasible.

Stripped to the bare bones, this is the Theory of Fiscal Policy. It provided the essential theoretical framework or guidance for much of the fiscal work in the past half century. Jan Tinbergen got the first Nobel Prize in Economics largely for his contribution to the development of this theory.

Assumptions of the Theory

Most theories contain assumptions. Sometimes the assumptions are explicit; often they are not. Sometimes they are realistic; often they are not. What are the important assumptions implicit in the Theory of Fiscal Policy? And how realistic are they? I will discuss the main ones.

First Assumption: The existence of a Nerve Centre, that is of an office or a place where that rather abstract concept that we call the "government" decides which policy instruments to use to influence the economic objectives that it considers important to promote and to maximize the social welfare. The existence of a Nerve Centre implies to a large extent: (a) a unitary form of government; (b) a unified budget; and (c) a prime minister, president or finance minister with the political power to set the desired objectives and to change the policy instruments in the desired direction and by the needed magnitude. This first assumption implies the existence of an all-inclusive budgetary process. No public finance decision is made outside the budget; or, at least, all decisions, whether in or out of the formal budget are directly or indirectly controlled by the Nerve Centre. There cannot be any fragmentation of decision making either because of different levels of government, each with independent power, or because of policy differences among ministries or between agencies. This also implies that the budget for sub-national governments, or for extra-budgetary institutions, must not be a soft one. When differences in objectives or in the use of instruments exist among policymakers, they must be ironed out within the Nerve Centre. This assumption deals essentially with political power and administrative controls and with how fragmented the political power is and how it can be used. Obviously, the political power is partly the result of the support that the government receives from the electorate and partly the result of institutional arrangements determined by a country's constitution. It is also partly the result of the real control that the government has over the bureaucracy and the legislature.

Second Assumption: Those who represent the government have only the public interest of the citizens in mind when they make the policy decisions. They are not influenced by their personal interests, or by the special interests of particular groups or geographical areas. There are no effective lobbies operating outside the electoral process and there is no scope for corruption, rent seeking or "state capture."

Policymakers avoid "populist" policies, that go against the public interest, even when these policies have short run appeal that could help those in power win the next election. Thus the electoral cycle plays no role in budgetary decisions.

Third Assumption: When it makes the budgetary decisions, the government has available to it the best economic analyses that money can buy. These analyses must be based on reliable data, on unbiased forecasts, and on accepted economic principles that establish links between changes in policy instruments and changes in policy objectives. From these analyses, the policymakers must be able to determine, with a reasonable degree of accuracy, that a given change in policy instrument is expected to cause a given change in a particular objective. These analyses rule out policy decisions based on "gut feelings," impressions, ideology, wrong data, biased forecasts, electoral promises, or simply antagonism toward previous governments.

Fourth Assumption: Because the policy instruments are generally imbedded in legislation, they can only be changed by enacting specific new laws or by changing current laws. The bills submitted to parliament and the approved laws are assumed to be clear, specific and to contain as little "noise" as possible. They must not create asymmetric information, or problems of different interpretation, between the government, on one side, and the citizens, on the other; or even between the policymakers and the public servants who write the laws, on one side, and those who must enforce or administer them, on the other. A law must be identifiable, as much as possible, with a specific policy instrument. It must be possible and easy to determine which instrument a specific law wants to change and which policy objective it wants to influence. In other words, the xs in equation (2) above must be identifiable in the laws. To the extent possible, the laws should avoid dealing with, or be directed towards, multiple objectives. It is generally inefficient to try to influence more than one objective with one instrument.

Fifth Assumption: The executive branch must have as much control over the policy instruments (i.e. over the proposed laws) as it is feasible in a democratic society. This assumption has several corollaries some already implicit in the above discussion.

First, parliaments must, of course, have the prerogative to approve or turn down the proposals submitted to them by the executive. They should also have the prerogative to improve the proposals or amend them in some relevant ways. However, they should not have the prerogative to change them in fundamental ways; or to delay unduly action on proposals submitted by the executive. It is the executive branch of government that, within clear constitutional limits, must control the instruments of economic policy, not the parliament.

Second, and related to the first assumption, the various ministries must operate in a harmonious or coordinated way and must not push for conflicting legislation. What we have called the Nerve Centre must solve any internal conflicts.

Third, most spending or taxing decisions must be exercised during the budget period, which is normally one year but can be longer. The authorization to spend money authorized in a budget must not stretch out over several budget periods, except for spending connected with large capital projects that by necessity take several years to complete. Unspent resources or unpaid liabilities should not characterize the end of the budget period. When this happens, the impact of fiscal policy on the economy and the budgetary outcome become more difficult to determine. Fourth, decisions made upstream, by the executive, and approved by parliament, must not be distorted downstream by the existence of principal-agents problems. Principal-agents problems can occur at the level of ministries, institutions, departments, or even at the level of local offices. When principal-agents problems are significant, the signals sent from the top can change in various ways in their application.

THE REALITY OF FISCAL POLICY

What I described above is the framework that many economists have in mind (even though they might not be aware of it) when they write theoretical papers dealing with fiscal policy. For sure that framework is still reflected in textbooks. As I described it, that theory of fiscal policy originated in the writings of mostly North European economists in the 1950s and 1960s. It was a "normative" theory, that is, a theory that tells us how the world should behave, not how it does. Or, perhaps it was a "naive positive theory" based on a view of the world as seen by the citizens of particular countries. Unfortunately, it was far from the reality that exists in other countries, both industrial and especially developing countries. Thus, while the theory is still useful in telling us what the world should be like, it is less useful in telling us how much of the world actually behaves.

There have been two main challenges over the years to this theory. An earlier one coming from the "Public choice School" and a more recent one coming from "The Positive Theory of Fiscal Policy." Both have been influenced by present or past works of Italian economists. The "School of Public choice", largely developed by James Buchanan, Gordon Tullock and others, and inspired by the "Scienze delle Finanze," the literature that prevailed in Italy about a century ago, would not accept the "Theory of Fiscal Policy" because of its deep suspicion of governments and its skepticism that policymakers and bureaucrats can be separated from their personal interests and incentives in the pursuit of the "public interest".

The "positive theory of fiscal policy" developed by economists such Alberto Alesina, Guido Tabellini, Alan Drazen, Torsten Persson, J. Von Hagen and others seems less suspicious about the notices of policymakers and bureaucrats and more attentive to the institutions and institutional set up that determine policy outcomes. This school seems to conclude that with better institutions and better institutional arrangements good policies could be pursued and better objectives could be achieved. In other words, the "Positive Theory of Fiscal Policy" does not necessarily invalidate the "Theory of Fiscal Policy" but it argues that the latter can be valid only if given institutions are in place. In the rest of this paper I shall take the assumptions outlined above and assess them for their degree of realism. The conclusion will be one of skepticism that, in realistic circumstances, the premises of the Theory of Fiscal Policy can be realized. First Assumption: The existence of a Nerve Centre where all the economic decisions are made and intragovernmental differences are ironed out. What impressed me most in my two years as an Undersecretary in the Ministry of Economy and Finance was the absence of such a centre. The prime minister's office did not play such a role. The ministry of economy and finance, in spite of, or perhaps because of, its enormous power, was in frequent conflict with other ministries, which pushed for a different allocation of budgetary resources.

These conflicts originated from different objectives which, in turn, reflected different party affiliations or even geographical areas represented. This made it difficult for the ministry of economy and finance to guide economic policy. The various parties in the government coalition were often in sharp disagreements with one another on specific policies and these disagreements were not ironed out within the government. Rather they often went public, giving the impression that the government did not have a clear sense of direction. Each group saw the public interest in a different way. Some parties were continually threatening to leave the coalition and some ministers were threatening to resign unless policies of interest to their supporters were enacted. Out of this situation it would have been difficult to come out with a coordinated set of policies that would put in motion changes in policy instruments that would in turn lead to changes in objectives consistent with the "public interest." Putting it bluntly, there was no clear compass to guide the government in a specific direction. Therefore, in spite of the absolute parliamentary majority of the government, which made it possible for it to pass any law on which the parties that formed the governing coalition could agree, the political power necessary to make coherent economic policy was either missing or could not be exercised. The result was inaction on several fronts so that essential reforms were not made or when made were watered down.

Second Assumption: The government has the public interest in mind and only promotes the social welfare of the citizens. I must confess that I always had difficulty with the concept of public interest and social welfare. In a real sense I could never see precisely what it meant. The public interest or the social welfare, should be the outcome of many objectives. Different citizens, or regions, or ethnic groups, or demographic cohorts, or different political parties inevitably give different weights to each of these objective. Thus, to determine what the public interest is and to promote it, it must be possible to give values to and to weigh, the various objectives that contribute it. But how is this possible? Who decides on the trade offs among the objectives? When can one say that the government is not following the public interest? There is often no place within the political structure of most countries where the basic question of interest to economists is asked: what is the public interest and what can we do to promote it?

It can be argued that the more even is the income distribution of a country, and the more homogeneous is the population, the easier it should be to determine "the public interest." In these circumstances, as a first approximation, it could be assumed that the citizens would rank and value the objectives in similar ways. The countries where the theory of fiscal policy originated, the Northern European countries, especially in the 1950s and 1960s had in fact, fairly homogeneous populations and low Gini coefficients. However, today many countries are characterized by great heterogeneity of the populations, uneven income distributions, cultural, ethnic, and income differences among regions of the same country and other characteristics that would make it difficult, even in theory, to determine the public interest. The increase in income inequality, the growing cross-country movement of people, and the aging of the population may have increased the heterogeneity of the populations making economic policy more difficult. Third Assumption: The government bases its policy decisions on the best economic analysis possible. The naked truth is that often there is no economic analysis behind a policy decision. The decisions often appear out of nowhere, or, sometimes, are justified because they reflect some electoral promise.

Ideology becomes a substitute for analysis. Or the analysis may be the one provided mainly by lobbies interested in promoting a specific policy. Often there has not been a serious assessment of what effects a policy decisions will produce, or how much it will cost, or will generate in revenue. This is especially the case with proposals promulgated in the last few days before the budget is sent to parliament for discussion and approval. In Italy the submission of bills to the two commissions in each "camera" in Parliament that deal with budget or finance issues must be accompanied by some numbers on their costs, or their revenue generations and their probable effects. The Italian Constitution specifically requires the provision of these estimates. These estimates are prepared by the Ragioneria Generale dello Stato, if they involve spending, or by the Dipartimento per le Politiche Fiscali, if they involve revenue. The staff of these offices is made up for the most part by lawyers whose expertise is in drafting laws or in checking whether existing laws are being observed. They have little specific training in analyzing the economic or fiscal consequences of policy proposals. Perhaps more importantly, they are given little time to prepare these estimates. In spite of their best efforts, it is no surprise that their estimates are often widely off.

Take as an example a law that, by providing specific incentives, was intended to make individuals working in so-called underground economic activities emerge and become officially registered workers. The estimate that was prepared and was sent to parliament predicted that a total of 900,000 workers would emerge. The actual number that emerged was about 450 (sic) workers. Errors in estimates are normal, but errors of this magnitude point to deeper problems. On the other hand a law that encouraged the "repatriation" of capital illegally held abroad (a kind of amnesty) had been estimated to encourage the "repatriation" of about 50 billion euro. By sheer coincidence the actual figure came close to it.

But it was just a coincidence. The 50 billion euro had been largely picked out of thin air. Major tax reforms are at times made after a lot of preparatory work. This was, for example, the case with the Carter Commission in Canada, the Meade Commission in the United Kingdom, and the 1986 Reagan reform in the United States. At times, however, little work goes into them. The Legge Delega (Loi Cadre) which set the stage for the 2002-2003 Italian tax reform, was prepared with no quantitative analysis even though it aimed at drastically changing the Italian tax system. In a country with a very high public debt and fragile public accounts one would have expected that, before sending a proposal for a major tax reform to Parliament, its potential revenue implications, as well as the redistributional impact of the reform and its impact on economic variables, should have been assessed carefully and in detail. It was not the case. The reform was sent to Parliament before any serious empirical evaluation of it was made. The impression that one got was that such an evaluation was not necessary because the tax reform responded to an electoral promise and electoral promises do not require empirical analyses or evaluations. If the reform did not fit the macroeconomic situation, so be it. In any case, it was promised that "fiscal space" would be created in future budgets to accommodate it. There was no explanation of where this space would come from in a situation of deteriorating fiscal accounts. I could provide other examples but the above should convey the essence of the problem.

Fourth Assumption: Matching of proposed laws with specific policy instruments and economic objectives. And clarity of the laws. The theoretical view of fiscal policy in a democratic setting must assume that a country's laws are the (fiscal) instruments through which policymakers aim at changing the policy objectives in the desired direction. It also requires, for efficiency reasons, that an instrument should not aim at promoting more than one objective. Each law should, thus, preferably aim at promoting a single objective. Unfortunately the real world is more complicated than that. Parliaments tend to be law factories. They produce too many laws. Furthermore, most laws are very complex, deal with multiple objectives, and are written in a language too arcane for the common citizen to understand. According to different estimates, there are now somewhere between thousand and 150 thousand laws in existence in Italy. Many of these laws do not deal with economic objectives. But many do. Some of these laws may be a hundred years old but are still valid. One curious feature is that laws are almost never abrogated. They are just amended. These laws are the instruments through which the government aims, or better was aiming at the time the laws were enacted, at influencing particular social or economic objectives. Thus, they are, in effect, the xs in equation (2) above. Since the desired objectives cannot be that many, there is obviously an over abundance of instruments. It would be difficult to claim that many of these laws are efficient policy instruments.

Many laws contain hidden tax incentives or tax expenditures even when they do not deal explicitly with taxation or spending. Many of them attempt to promote indirectly some redistributional objectives. In Italy there is almost an obsession to use most instruments for some broadly defined and vague equity objective. This makes many laws inefficient vis-a-vis their original, intended purposes. When a bill is presented to Parliament for approval into law and begins to make the round through the various parliamentary commissions, amendments begin to be attached to what may already be a complex bill. Many of these amendments are proposed by the government itself. More will be proposed in the discussion in the full Parliament, often encouraged, behind the scene, by some interested minister. At times these amendments are in the thousands. This Christmas tree approach, in which every member of Parliament can, in theory, hang something on the initial proposal, often produces a final product (the law that is approved) that is quite different from the initial or the intended one. This also means that it becomes progressively more difficult to estimate the impact of the law on the fiscal accounts or on the intended objective, even though the relevant offices try hard to produce estimates of that impact. These offices must, at times, prepare these estimates for major revisions literally within hours of the time the revisions are proposed. This is especially the case when the proposals for changing the budget document are discussed in Parliament just before Christmas.

In Italy there is a legal requirement to limit the content of bills, presented to Parliament for approval into laws, to single issues. This requirement is consistently violated. In 2002, this problem became so acute that the President of Italy. for this reason, took the extraordinary step of refusing to sign into law some bills already approved by Parliament, that had been sent to his office for his final official imprimatur, before they became laws. This is not an exclusively Italian problem. It exists, for example, in the United States where, occasionally, totally unrelated spending requests are attached to a bill that deals with some other issue.

The clarity of the laws also deserves a comment. Laws are directed at citizens and thus the citizens should be able to read and understand them so that they can follow their directives. This was the case with the laws were written on stones in old times. Often in the modern world this is not the case. More than once I found myself in situations in which a particular bill presented to Parliament dealt with topics in which I was considered, and considered myself, an expert. In spite of this, I had great difficulty in understanding what the bill said. This was in part a consequence of the "legalese" or archaic language used by those who draft these laws. In part it was due to the fact that most bills make reference to, and are linked on, existing laws that may have been on the books for decades and that themselves may have been amended several times before. Without consulting these past laws, and without spending a lot of time doing it, it would be impossible for a normal person, even one with some relevant training, to understand the content of specific bills. When there are tens of thousands of laws, it is easy to see the difficulty for the normal citizens. The Romans used to say that ignorance of the law is no excuse. often wondered whether non-understanding can become an excuse.

The result is the creation of de facto asymmetric information between the bureaucrats who write the laws, and the citizens, who must observe them, or even the parliamentarians who approve the laws. This asymmetry gives a lot of power to a few, well-placed bureaucrats and leads to the creation of an extensive industry of advisors, consultants, and facilitators on whom the citizens must depend for interpreting the laws and for abiding by some of their requirements. There are important consequences that follow from this situation. First, the industry of advisors, consultants, and facilitators is a largely unproductive activity; it is a dead weight. However, it is an industry that attracts a lot of very able people because of the high incomes that it makes possible. By absorbing much valuable human capital, which could have been put to more directly productive uses, it must slow down the rate of growth of the country. Second, estimates of costs and revenues (for the public accounts) made for these bills are often wrong leading to potential fiscal difficulties. Third, the specific role of the state that the government tries to promote through these laws is difficult to identify. As a consequence, it is difficult to identify the public interest that is being pursued and the causal relation between a law (as a policy statement) and a particular objective. Fourth, as it almost surely happens with the many tax incentives buried in hundreds of laws that are strictly not tax laws, some of the objectives pursued by the laws are likely to neutralize one another. Fifth, many citizens often live with the uncertainty as to whether they have complied with the requirements of the tax laws. Uncertainty is not good for economic development, as Kydland and Prescott, the 2004 winners of the Nobel Prize in Economics have shown. This is certainly the case with tax laws.

Finally, I often asked myself whether what was not clear to me, as a public finance expert with a lot of training and experience, could possibly be clear to the members of the Italian Parliament most of whom had far less training and experience than I had. The only reasonable answer to this question is that most of them probably pay attention only to those features of bills that interest them personally, or interest directly their supporters or their region. For the rest of the budget, they largely follow party instructions, which in turn follow the advice of the civil servants politically close to their party. But again, it should be stressed that this problem is far from being confined to Italy.

Fifth Assumption: Government control over the policy instruments. This assumption has various components. However, the key question is whether the group of policymakers that make up "the government" truly controls the policy instruments, coordinates their use, determines the objectives to be pursued, and has full and timely information on what is going on. On the issue of control of policy instruments and determination of the objectives to be pursued, I argued earlier that (a) the absence of a powerful Nerve Centre; (b) frequent disagreements on the use of instruments and on the goals to be pursued among ministries and coalition parties; (c) the power of each member of parliament to propose amendments to legislative proposals; and (d) the existence of asymmetric information between policymakers, on one side, and, on the other side, the civil servants who draft the legislative proposals and, as importantly, the regulations that give specific content to these proposals (the "regolamenti attuativi"), imply that the government's control over the instruments is often tenuous.

Some of these issues would require a lot of time and space to discuss in detail. Rather than discuss them, I will address briefly a topic of particular interest to macroeconomists, namely the pursuit of fiscal policy for stabilization, the issue of concern for the Stability and Growth Pact and for the use of fiscal rules in general. This topic is closely related to the question of control over policy instruments. Thus, it provides a good example of some of the issues discussed above. How much real control do the policy makers have on the fiscal instruments necessary for countercyclical policy?.

7

Investment Management

Investment management is the professional management of various securities (shares, bonds and other securities) and assets (e.g., real estate) in order to meet specified investment goals for the benefit of the investors. Investors may be institutions (insurance companies, pension funds, corporations etc.) or private investors (both directly via investment contracts and more commonly via collective investment schemes e.g. mutual funds or exchange-traded funds). The term asset management is often used to refer to the investment management of collective investments, (not necessarily) while the more generic fund management may refer to all forms of institutional investment as well as investment management for private investors. Investment managers who specialize in *advisory* or *discretionary* management on behalf of (normally wealthy) private investors may often refer to their services as wealth management or portfolio management often within the context of so-called "private banking".

The provision of 'investment management services' includes elements of financial statement analysis, asset selection, stock selection, plan implementation and ongoing monitoring of investments. Investment management is a large and important global industry in its own right responsible for caretaking of trillions of yuan, dollars, euro, pounds and yen. Coming under the remit of financial services many of the world's largest companies are at least in part investment managers and employ millions of staff and create billions in revenue. Fund manager (or investment adviser in the United States) refers to both a firm that provides investment management services and an individual who directs fund management decisions.

INDUSTRY SCOPE

The business of investment management has several facets, including the employment of professional fund managers, research (of individual assets and asset classes), dealing, settlement, marketing, internal auditing, and the preparation of reports for clients. The largest financial fund managers are firms that exhibit all the complexity their size demands. Apart from the people who bring in the money (marketers) and the people who direct investment (the fund managers), there are compliance staff (to ensure accord with legislative and regulatory constraints), internal auditors of various kinds (to examine internal systems and controls), financial controllers (to account for the institutions' own money and costs), computer experts, and "back office" employees (to track and record transactions and fund valuations for up to thousands of clients per institution).

Key Problems of Running such Businesses

Key problems include:

- revenue is directly linked to market valuations, so a major fall in asset prices causes a precipitous decline in revenues relative to costs;
- above-average fund performance is difficult to sustain, and clients may not be patient during times of poor performance;
- successful fund managers are expensive and may be headhunted by competitors;
- above-average fund performance appears to be dependent on the unique skills of the fund manager; however, clients are loath to stake their investments on the ability of a few individuals- they would rather see firm-wide success, attributable to a single philosophy and internal discipline;
- analysts who generate above-average returns often

become sufficiently wealthy that they avoid corporate employment in favour of managing their personal portfolios.

Representing the Owners of Shares

Institutions often control huge shareholdings. In most cases they are acting as fiduciary agents rather than principals (direct owners). The owners of shares theoretically have great power to alter the companies they own via the voting rights the shares carry and the consequent ability to pressure managements, and if necessary out-vote them at annual and other meetings.

In practice, the ultimate owners of shares often do not exercise the power they collectively hold (because the owners are many, each with small holdings); financial institutions (as agents) sometimes do. There is a general belief that shareholders - in this case, the institutions acting as agents—could and should exercise more active influence over the companies in which they hold shares (e.g., to hold managers to account, to ensure Boards effective functioning). Such action would add a pressure group to those (the regulators and the Board) overseeing management.

However there is the problem of how the institution should exercise this power. One way is for the institution to decide, the other is for the institution to poll its beneficiaries. Assuming that the institution polls, should it then: (i) Vote the entire holding as directed by the majority of votes cast? (ii) Split the vote (where this is allowed) according to the proportions of the vote? (iii) Or respect the abstainers and only vote the respondents' holdings?

The price signals generated by large active managers holding or not holding the stock may contribute to management change. For example, this is the case when a large active manager sells his position in a company, leading to (possibly) a decline in the stock price, but more importantly a loss of confidence by the markets in the management of the company, thus precipitating changes in the management team.

Some institutions have been more vocal and active in pursuing such matters; for instance, some firms believe that there are investment advantages to accumulating substantial minority shareholdings (i.e. 10% or more) and putting pressure on management to implement significant changes in the business. In some cases, institutions with minority holdings work together to force management change. Perhaps more frequent is the sustained pressure that large institutions bring to bear on management teams through persuasive discourse and PR. On the other hand, some of the largest investment managers—such as BlackRock and Vanguard—advocate simply owning every company, reducing the incentive to influence management teams. A reason for this last strategy is that the investment manager prefers a closer, more open and honest relationship with a company's management team than would exist if they exercised control; allowing them to make a better investment decision.

The national context in which shareholder representation considerations are set is variable and important. The USA is a litigious society and shareholders use the law as a lever to pressure management teams. In Japan it is traditional for shareholders to be low in the 'pecking order,' which often allows management and labor to ignore the rights of the ultimate owners. Whereas US firms generally cater to shareholders, Japanese businesses generally exhibit a *stakeholder* mentality, in which they seek consensus amongst all interested parties (against a background of strong unions and labour legislation).

SIZE OF GLOBAL FUND MANAGEMENT INDUSTRY

Conventional assets under management of the global fund management industry increased by 14% in 2009, to $71.3 trillion. Pension assets accounted for $28.0 trillion of the total, with $22.9 trillion invested in mutual funds and $20.4 trillion in insurance funds. Together with alternative assets (sovereign wealth funds, hedge funds, private equity funds and exchange traded funds) and funds of wealthy individuals, assets of the global fund management industry totalled over $105 trillion, an increase of 15% on the previous year. The increase in 2009 followed a 18% decline in the previous year and was largely a result of the recovery in equity markets during the year. Part of the reason for the increase in dollar terms was the depreciation in the value of the US dollar against a number of currencies in 2009.

The US remained by far the biggest source of funds, accounting for around a half of conventional assets under management or some $36 trillion. The UK was the second largest centre in the world and by far the largest in Europe with around 9% of the global total.

Philosophy, Process and People

The 3-P's (Philosophy, Process and People) are often used to describe the reasons why the manager is able to produce above average results.

- Philosophy refers to the over-arching beliefs of the investment organization. For example: (i) Does the manager buy growth or value shares (and why)? (ii) Do they believe in market timing (and on what evidence)? (iii) Do they rely on external research or do they employ a team of researchers? It is helpful if any and all of such fundamental beliefs are supported by proof-statements.
- Process refers to the way in which the overall philosophy is implemented. For example: (i) Which universe of assets is explored before particular assets are chosen as suitable investments? (ii) How does the manager decide what to buy and when? (iii) How does the manager decide what to sell and when? (iv) Who takes the decisions and are they taken by committee? (v) What controls are in place to ensure that a rogue fund (one very different from others and from what is intended) cannot arise?
- People refers to the staff, especially the fund managers. The questions are, Who are they? How are they selected? How old are they? Who reports to whom? How deep is the team (and do all the members understand the philosophy and process they are supposed to be using)? And most important of all, How long has the team been working together? This last question is vital because whatever performance record was presented at the outset of the relationship with the client may or may

not relate to (have been produced by) a team that is still in place. If the team has changed greatly (high staff turnover or changes to the team), then arguably the performance record is completely unrelated to the existing team (of fund managers).

INVESTMENT MANAGERS AND PORTFOLIO STRUCTURES

At the heart of the investment management industry are the managers who invest and divest client investments.

A certified company investment advisor should conduct an assessment of each client's individual needs and risk profile. The advisor then recommends appropriate investments.

Asset Allocation

The different asset class definitions are widely debated, but four common divisions are stocks, bonds, real-estate and commodities. The exercise of allocating funds among these assets (and among individual securities within each asset class) is what investment management firms are paid for. Asset classes exhibit different market dynamics, and different interaction effects; thus, the allocation of money among asset classes will have a significant effect on the performance of the fund. Some research suggests that allocation among asset classes has more predictive power than the choice of individual holdings in determining portfolio return. Arguably, the skill of a successful investment manager resides in constructing the asset allocation, and separately the individual holdings, so as to outperform certain benchmarks (e.g., the peer group of competing funds, bond and stock indices)...

Long-term Returns

It is important to look at the evidence on the long-term returns to different assets, and to holding period returns (the returns that accrue on average over different lengths of investment). For example, over very long holding periods (eg. 10+ years) in most countries, equities have generated higher returns than bonds, and bonds have generated higher returns than cash. According to financial theory, this is because equities are riskier (more volatile) than bonds which are themselves more risky than cash.

Diversification

Against the background of the asset allocation, fund managers consider the degree of diversification that makes sense for a given client (given its risk preferences) and construct a list of planned holdings accordingly. The list will indicate what percentage of the fund should be invested in each particular stock or bond. The theory of portfolio diversification was originated by Markowitz (and many others) and effective diversification requires management of the correlation between the asset returns and the liability returns, issues internal to the portfolio (individual holdings volatility), and cross-correlations between the returns.

Investment Styles

There are a range of different styles of fund management that the institution can implement. For example, growth, value, market neutral, small capitalisation, indexed, etc. Each of these approaches has its distinctive features, adherents and, in any particular financial environment, distinctive risk characteristics. For example, there is evidence that growth styles (buying rapidly growing earnings) are especially effective when the companies able to generate such growth are scarce; conversely, when such growth is plentiful, then there is evidence that value styles tend to outperform the indices particularly successfully.

Performance Measurement

Fund performance is often thought to be the acid test of fund management, and in the institutional context, accurate measurement is a necessity. For that purpose, institutions measure the performance of each fund (and usually for internal purposes components of each fund) under their management, and performance is also measured by external firms that specialize in performance measurement. The leading performance measurement firms compile aggregate industry data, e.g., showing how funds in general performed against given indices and peer groups over various time periods.

In a typical case (let us say an equity fund), then the calculation would be made (as far as the client is concerned) every quarter and would show a percentage change compared with the prior quarter (e.g., +4.6% total return in US dollars). This figure would be compared with other similar funds managed within the institution (for purposes of monitoring internal controls), with performance data for peer group funds, and with relevant indices (where available) or tailor-made performance benchmarks where appropriate. The specialist performance measurement firms calculate quartile and decile data and close attention would be paid to the (percentile) ranking of any fund.

Generally speaking, it is probably appropriate for an investment firm to persuade its clients to assess performance over longer periods (e.g., 3 to 5 years) to smooth out very short term fluctuations in performance and the influence of the business cycle. This can be difficult however and, industry wide, there is a serious preoccupation with short-term numbers and the effect on the relationship with clients (and resultant business risks for the institutions).

An enduring problem is whether to measure before-tax or after-tax performance. After-tax measurement represents the benefit to the investor, but investors' tax positions may vary. Before-tax measurement can be misleading, especially in regimens that tax realised capital gains (and not unrealised). It is thus possible that successful active managers (measured before tax) may produce miserable after-tax results. One possible solution is to report the after-tax position of some standard taxpayer.

Risk-adjusted Performance Measurement

Performance measurement should not be reduced to the evaluation of fund returns alone, but must also integrate other fund elements that would be of interest to investors, such as the measure of risk taken. Several other aspects are also part of performance measurement: evaluating if managers have succeeded in reaching their objective, i.e. if their return was sufficiently high to reward the risks taken; how they compare to their peers; and finally whether the portfolio management results were due to luck or the manager's skill. The need to answer all these questions has led to the development of more sophisticated performance measures, many of which originate in modern portfolio theory. Modern portfolio theory established the quantitative link that exists between portfolio risk and return.

The Capital Asset Pricing Model (CAPM) developed by Sharpe (1964) highlighted the notion of rewarding risk and produced the first performance indicators, be they risk-adjusted ratios (Sharpe ratio, information ratio) or differential returns compared to benchmarks (alphas).

The Sharpe ratio is the simplest and best known performance measure. It measures the return of a portfolio in excess of the risk-free rate, compared to the total risk of the portfolio.

This measure is said to be absolute, as it does not refer to any benchmark, avoiding drawbacks related to a poor choice of benchmark. Meanwhile, it does not allow the separation of the performance of the market in which the portfolio is invested from that of the manager. The information ratio is a more general form of the Sharpe ratio in which the risk-free asset is replaced by a benchmark portfolio. This measure is relative, as it evaluates portfolio performance in reference to a benchmark, making the result strongly dependent on this benchmark choice.

Portfolio alpha is obtained by measuring the difference between the return of the portfolio and that of a benchmark portfolio. This measure appears to be the only reliable performance measure to evaluate active management. In fact, we have to distinguish between normal returns, provided by the fair reward for portfolio exposure to different risks, and obtained through passive management, from abnormal performance (or outperformance) due to the manager's skill (or luck), whether through market timing, stock picking, or good fortune. The first component is related to allocation and style investment choices, which may not be under the sole control of the manager, and depends on the economic context, while the second component is an evaluation of the success of the manager's decisions. Only the latter, measured by alpha, allows the evaluation of the manager's true performance (but then, only if you assume that any outperformance is due to skill and not luck).

Portfolio return may be evaluated using factor models. The first model, proposed by Jensen (1968), relies on the CAPM and explains portfolio returns with the market index as the only factor. It quickly becomes clear, however, that one factor is not enough to explain the returns very well and that other factors have to be considered.

Multi-factor models were developed as an alternative to the CAPM, allowing a better description of portfolio risks and a more accurate evaluation of a portfolio's performance. For example, Fama and French (1993) have highlighted two important factors that characterize a company's risk in addition to market risk.

These factors are the book-to-market ratio and the company's size as measured by its market capitalization. Fama and French therefore proposed three-factor model to describe portfolio normal returns (Fama-French three-factor model). Carhart (1997) proposed to add momentum as a fourth factor to allow the short-term persistence of returns to be taken into account. Also of interest for performance measurement is Sharpe's (1992) style analysis model, in which factors are style indices. This model allows a custom benchmark for each portfolio to be developed, using the linear combination of style indices that best replicate portfolio style allocation, and leads to an accurate evaluation of portfolio alpha

EDUCATION OR CERTIFICATION

Increasingly, international business schools are incorporating the subject into their course outlines and some have formulated the title of 'Investment Management' or 'Asset Management' conferred as specialist bachelors degrees (e.g. Cass Business School, London). Due to global cross-recognition agreements with the 2 major accrediting agencies AACSB and ACBSP which accredit over 560 of the best business school programs, the Certification of MFP Master Financial Planner

Professional from the American Academy of Financial Management is available to AACSB and ACBSP business school graduates with finance or financial services-related concentrations. For people with aspirations to become an investment manager, further education may be needed beyond a bachelors in business, finance, or economics. A graduate degree or an investment qualification such as the Chartered Financial Analyst designation (CFA) or the Certified Financial Markets Practitioner (CFMP) Exam by the Management Laboratory may help in having a career in investment management.

There is no evidence that any particular qualification enhances the most desirable characteristic of an investment manager, that is the ability to select investments that result in an above average (risk weighted) long-term performance . The industry has a tradition of seeking out, employing and generously rewarding such people without reference to any formal qualifications .

LEGISLATION ON TRADE AND INVESTMENT

Legislation concerning foreign trade administration in South Africa includes the International Trade Administration Act, the Import and Export Control Act, and the Customs and Taxation Act. In 2005, South Africa amended its Customs and Taxation Act.

Legislation on Investment Administration

The Export Credit and Foreign Investments Re-insurance Act and the Exchange Control Amnesty and Amendment of Taxation Laws Act are the two major legislation on foreign investment in South Africa.

Other laws pertinent to foreign investment include the Companies Act, the Income Tax Act, the Financial Institution (Investment Funds) Act, and the Labor Act. All the areas of foreign investment come under these laws.

In 2005, South Africa revised, inter alia, its Exchange Control Amnesty and Amendment of Taxation Laws Act and its Income Tax Act.

Another legislation related to foreign investment in South Africa is the Competition Act, which provides strict criteria for approval of mergers and aims to encourage competition between businesses.

In addition to the above-mentioned legislation, investment-related laws in South Africa include the Environment Act as adopted on 31 May 2004.

TRADE ADMINISTRATION

Tariff System

According to its WTO accession commitments, South Africa has significantly reduced its tariff. South Africa's average tariff stands at 5.8 percent at present, with an average tariff of 9.1 percent and 5.3 percent for agricultural and non-agricultural products respectively. In 2005, South Africa cut its import tariff on acetate, acetyl cellulose and related products as well as on some imports subject to specific duties.

According to the Customs Union Agreement signed by South Africa, Botswana, Lesotho, Namibia and Swaziland in 2002, these five countries have established a Southern African Customs Union (SACU) administering a uniform tariff. After the agreement went into effect, member countries divide tariff receipts among themselves according to a pre-arranged formula. The supreme decision-making body for SACU is the Council of Ministers (COM).

Import Administration

Any company registered in South Africa's Department of Trade and Industry can engage in import trade, with no need to apply for special trading rights. The import of most products has been liberalized in South Africa, but certain special products are subject to licensing administration.

In accordance with the Import and Export Control Act, these products include, among others, fish and fishery products, certain vegetables and other agrarian products, certain dairy products, certain red teas, fermented beverages, alcoholic beverages, petroleum and certain petrochemical products, radioactive mineral products, certain footwear, all kinds of waste products, certain medicines and pharmaceutical products, environmentally hazardous products, gambling devices, and arms.

Importers should apply for a license before importing any of these products and no shipment should be made overseas prior to the granting of the import license. Importers should submit import license application to the relevant authorities at least two weeks before shipment to allow sufficient time for the approval. Application materials include the name of the imports and any information demanded by the authorities to be made available about the imports. Once issued by the Import and Export Administration Bureau, the import license is to remain valid for 12 months.

Export Administration

It is required that South African exporters be registered in the Customs House. Export licensing administration is imposed on strategic products, non-regenerable resources, agricultural products, scrap metals and so on. The catalog of products coming under licensing is determined by the South African Minister of Trade and Industry and published on government bulletins.

The exporters of diamond should register in South African Diamond Commission. According to South African regulations, the export of waste metals, which are deemed national resources, is placed under restriction. Before an export license is granted, waste metals should first be made available to South African lower stream enterprises at a discounted rate of their export prices, normally 15 percent discount for non-ferrous metals and 7.5 percent discount for ferrous metals. The government can only issue export licenses if the lower stream enterprises do not respond to the offer or do not need the waste metals. In addition, although no clear regulation in this regard exists, the export of ostrich and its breeding eggs is still prohibited.

Other Related Systems

South Africa has now abolished its foreign exchange control under the current account. However, to guard against financial fraud and money laundering, South African banks have, as required by the Financial Intelligence Center Act, tightened their monitoring over the funds of their clients.

INVESTMENT ADMINISTRATION

South Africa has tried to promote investment, particularly foreign investment, through a number of state-initiated programs. As from 1 January 2001, South Africa has adopted the policy of taxation according to residence. According to the agreements with other countries on the avoidance of double taxation, non-residents in South Africa are still subject to taxation on their earnings in South Africa. The South African taxation categories fall into two broad types – direct taxation and indirect taxation. The former includes income tax, corporate secondary tax, capital earnings tax, and endowment tax, whereas the latter covers value-added tax, real estate inheritance tax, stamp tax, consumption and import tax, circulatory securities tax, district service consulting fees, and skill development fees.

The South African corporate income tax currently stands at 30 percent and value-added tax at 14 percent. The rate of excise duties is 10 percent except that office equipment and motorcycles have a duty at 5 percent; specific excise duties are levied on tobacco and tobacco products, alcoholic and nonalcoholic beverages.

South Africa places no restriction upon stock investment by foreign investors. Foreign investors buying stocks of publicly listed companies in South Africa should confirm that authorized dealers endorse "Non-resident" on stock certificates so that stock returns such as dividends could be remitted home in the future. Generally speaking, no restriction is imposed upon the remittance abroad of investment earnings by non-residents.

COMPETENT AUTHORITIES

The Department of Trade and Industry (DTI) and the International Trade Administration Commission (ITAC) regulate foreign trade in South Africa. The Department of Trade and Industry conducts foreign economic relations and trade negotiations, signs bilateral and multilateral trade agreements, keeps in touch with provincial economic development agencies, and coordinates trade and investment relations between provinces in the country.

On the other hand, the International Trade Administration Commission carries out anti-dumping and countervailing investigations in the SACU region, is responsible for import and export administration, licensing administration, restructuring the tariff regimes, supervision of preferential industrial policies, and has the authority to require local importers and exporters to provide information regarding their business activities.

Other governmental agencies relating to trade and investment administration include the National Economic Development and Labor Council and the Board for Regional Industrial Development.

8

Indian Financial System and Capital Market

OVERVIEW OF INDIAN FINANCIAL SYSTEM

The Indian financial system comprises a set of financial institutions, financial markets and financial infrastructure. The financial institutions mainly consist of commercial and cooperative banks, regional rural banks (RRBs), all-India financial institutions (AIFIs) and non-banking financial companies (NBFCs). The banking sector which forms the bedrock of the Indian financial system, falls under the regulatory ambit of the Reserve Bank of India under the provisions of the Banking Regulation Act, 1949 and the Reserve Bank of India Act, 1934. The Reserve Bank also regulates select AIFIs. Consequent upon amendments to the Reserve Bank of India (Amendment) Act in 1997, a comprehensive regulatory framework in respect of NBFCs was put in place in January 1997.

The financial market in India comprises the money market, the Government securities market, the foreign exchange market and the capital market. A holistic approach has been adopted in India towards designing and development of a modern, robust, efficient, secure and integrated payment and settlement system. The Reserve Bank set up the Institute for Development and Research in Banking Technology (IDRBT) in 1996, which is an autonomous centre for technology capacity building for banks and providing core IT services.

Financial Institutions

Scheduled commercial banks (SCBs) occupy a predominant position in the financial system accounting for around three fourths of the total assets in the financial system. While the public sector banks (PSBs), consisting of eight banks in the State Bank group and 19 nationalised banks, constitute almost three fourths of the total assets of SCBs, the private sector banks, 30 in number, constitute less than one-fifth of the total assets. The 33 foreign banks operating in India account for about 6-7 per cent of the assets of SCBs. The 196 RRBs play a critical role in extending credit to the poorer sections of the rural society. The ownership of RRBs jointly vests with the Central Government, the State Governments and the sponsor banks. The cooperative banking system, with two broad segments of urban and rural cooperatives, forms an integral part of the Indian financial system. While the urban cooperative banking system has a single tier comprising the Primary Cooperative Banks (commonly known as [1]urban cooperative banks – UCBs), the rural cooperative credit system is divided into long-term and short-term cooperative credit institutions which have a multi-tier structure.

The term-lending institutions are mostly Government-owned and have been the traditional providers of long-term project loans. Non-Banking Financial Companies (NBFCs) encompass an extremely heterogeneous group of intermediaries and provide a gamut of financial services. Primary Dealers (PDs) in the Government securities market constitutes a systemically important segment of the NBFCs. At present, there are a total of 17 PDs playing active role in the Government securities market. A majority of them are promoted by banks.

Apart from this, India has a well-established and vibrant insurance sector within the financial system. The Insurance Regulatory and Development Agency (IRDA) has been established to regulate and supervise the insurance sector.

Pre-reforms Phase

Until the early 1990s, the role of the financial system in India was primarily restricted to the function of channelling resources from the surplus to deficit sectors. Whereas the financial system performed this role reasonably well, its operations came to be marked by some serious deficiencies over the years.

The banking sector suffered from lack of competition, low capital base, low productivity and high intermediation cost. After the nationalisation of large banks in 1969 and 1980, the Government-owned banks dominated the banking sector. The role of technology was minimal and the quality of service was not given adequate importance. Banks also did not follow proper risk management systems and the prudential standards were weak. All these resulted in poor asset quality and low profitability. Among non-banking financial intermediaries, development finance institutions (DFIs) operated in an overprotected environment with most of the funding coming from assured sources at concessional terms. In the insurance sector, there was little competition. The mutual fund industry also suffered from lack of competition and was dominated for long by one institution, viz., the Unit Trust of India. Non-banking financial companies (NBFCs) grew rapidly, but there was no regulation of their asset side.

Financial markets were characterised by control over pricing of financial assets, barriers to entry, high transaction costs and restrictions on movement of funds/participants between the market segments. This apart from inhibiting the development of the markets also affected their efficiency.

FINANCIAL SECTOR REFORMS IN INDIA

It was in this backdrop that wide-ranging financial sector reforms in India were introduced as an integral part of the economic reforms initiated in the early 1990s with a view to improving the macroeconomic performance of the economy. The reforms in the financial sector focused on creating efficient and stable financial institutions and markets. The approach to financial sector reforms in India was one of gradual and non-disruptive progress through a consultative process. The Reserve Bank has been consistently working towards setting an enabling regulatory framework with prompt and effective supervision, development of technological and institutional infrastructure, as well as changing the interface with the market participants through a consultative process. Persistent efforts have been made towards adoption of international benchmarks as appropriate to Indian conditions. While certain changes in the legal infrastructure are yet to be effected, the developments so far have brought the Indian financial system closer to global standards.

The reform of the interest regime constitutes an integral part of the financial sector reform. With the onset of financial sector reforms, the interest rate regime has been largely deregulated with a view towards better price discovery and efficient resource allocation. Initially, steps were taken to develop the domestic money market and freeing of the money market rates. The interest rates offered on Government securities were progressively raised so that the Government borrowing could be carried out at market-related rates. In respect of banks, a major effort was undertaken to simplify the administered structure of interest rates. Banks now have sufficient flexibility to decide their deposit and lending rate structures and manage their assets and liabilities accordingly. At present, apart from savings account and NRE deposit on the deposit side and export credit and small loans on the lending side, all other interest rates are deregulated.

Indian banking system operated for a long time with high reserve requirements both in the form of Cash Reserve Ratio (CRR) and Statutory Liquidity Ratio (SLR). This was a consequence of the high fiscal deficit and a high degree of monetisation of fiscal deficit. The efforts in the recent period have been to lower both the CRR and SLR. The statutory minimum of 25 per cent for SLR has already been reached, and while the Reserve Bank continues to pursue its medium-term objective of reducing the CRR to the statutory minimum level of 3.0 per cent, the CRR of SCBs is currently placed at 5.0 per cent of NDTL.

As part of the reforms programme, due attention has been given to diversification of ownership leading to greater market accountability and improved efficiency. Initially, there was infusion of capital by the Government in public sector banks, which was followed by expanding the capital base with equity participation by the private investors.

This was followed by a reduction in the Government shareholding in public sector banks to 51 per cent. Consequently, the share of the public sector banks in the aggregate assets of the banking sector has come down from 90 per cent in 1991 to around 75 per cent in 2004. With a view to enhancing efficiency and productivity through competition, guidelines were laid down for establishment of new banks in the private sector and the foreign banks have been allowed more liberal entry. Since 1993, twelve new private sector banks have been set up. As a major step towards enhancing competition in the banking sector, foreign direct investment in the private sector banks is now allowed up to 74 per cent, subject to conformity with the guidelines issued from time to time.

As a part of the financial sector reforms, the regulatory framework and supervisory practices have almost converged with the best practices elsewhere in the world. The minimum capital to risk assets ratio (CRAR) has been kept at nine per cent which is one percentage point above the international norm; and additionally, banks are required to maintain a separate Investment Fluctuation Reserve (IFR) out of profits, towards interest rate risk. Impressive institutional and legal reforms have been undertaken in relation to the banking sector. There have been a number of measures for enhancing the transparency and disclosures standards. The regulatory framework in India, in addition to prescribing prudential guidelines and encouraging market discipline, is increasingly focusing on ensuring good governance through "fit and proper" owners, directors and senior managers of the banks. Transfer of shareholding of five per cent and above requires acknowledgement from the Reserve Bank and such significant shareholders are put through a 'fit and proper' test. Banks have also been asked to ensure that the nominated and elected directors are screened by a nomination committee to satisfy 'fit and proper' criteria. Directors are also required to sign a covenant indicating their roles and responsibilities. The Reserve Bank has recently issued detailed guidelines on ownership and governance in private sector banks emphasizing diversified ownership.

In 1994, a Board for Financial Supervision (BFS) was constituted comprising select members of the Reserve Bank Board with a variety of professional expertise to exercise 'undivided attention to supervision' and ensure an integrated approach to supervision of commercial banks, development finance institutions, non-banking finance companies, urban cooperatives banks and primary dealers. Certain amendments are being considered by the Parliament to enhance Reserve Bank's regulatory and supervisory powers.

Over the last few years, the several policy initiatives undertaken in the form of recapitalisation of the weak RRBs, deregulation of deposits and lending rates and relaxation to lend to nontarget groups, have improved their operational efficiency, governance and regulation and brought them almost at par with the rural branches of commercial banks.

The cooperative banks besides suffering from the problem of multiple supervisory authorities, also face the challenge of reconciling the democratic character with financial discipline and modernising systems and procedures. The Task Force on Cooperatives constituted by the Government (December 2004) has made several suggestions for the revival of the sector to be implemented in consultation with the State Governments. The Reserve Bank has adopted a cautious approach regarding granting licenses for new banks and branches of urban cooperative banks (UCBs), while focusing on consolidation within the sector through mergers and amalgamations. In addition, initiatives have been undertaken to gradually tighten the prudential norms for regulation and supervision of UCBs. As a prelude to revamping the sector, a vision document for UCBs has been released by the Reserve Bank, highlighting the importance of a differentiated regulatory regime for the sector.

The ongoing restructuring of AIFIs is evident in the recent conversion of Industrial Credit and Investment Corporation of India (ICICI) and Industrial Development Bank of India (IDBI) into banks. The Board of Directors of Industrial Finance Corporation of India (IFCI) Ltd. have approved, in principle, the merger with a bank. In view of the deteriorating financial position of Industrial Investment Bank of India (IIBI) Ltd., the Government has undertaken a programme of restructuring its liabilities. Apart from Infrastructure Development Finance Company Ltd. (IDFC), there are three refinancing institutions *viz.*, National Bank of Agriculture and Rural Development (NABARD), Small Industries Development Bank of India (SIDBI) and National Housing Bank (NHB), and EXIM Bank. At the State level, the State Financial Corporations registered under the State Financial Corporations Act, 1951 and the State Industrial Development Corporations (SIDCs)-purvey credit to industries/sectors in different States. On balance, the development financial institution (DFI) model has become increasingly unsustainable and AIFIs are fast adopting the business model of a bank for long-term commercial viability.

Non-Banking Financial Companies (NBFCs) encompass an extremely heterogeneous group of intermediaries. The main area of concern has been the substantial growth in deposits of the Residuary Non-Banking Companies (RNBCs), with just two companies accounting for more than 80 per cent of the total deposits held by NBFCs. The Indian banking sector is gradually heading towards consolidation of core competencies of different financial intermediaries, which would engender greater economic efficiency in the form of lower transaction cost, and greater product sophistication.

FINANCIAL SYSTEM: CURRENT STATUS

There has been a notable reduction in the ratio of non-performing assets (NPAs) to advances in response to various initiatives, such as, improved risk management practices and greater recovery efforts driven, *inter alia,* by the recently enacted Securitisation and Reconstruction of Financial Assets and Enforcement of Security Interest (SARFAESI) Act, 2002. The financial performance of most of the PSBs has improved in recent times as reflected in their comfortable capital adequacy ratios and declining NPL ratios. The CRAR in respect of all categories of banks has improved. New private sector banks have displayed impressive performance particularly in terms of efficiency and customer service

Financial Markets

A major objective of reforms in the financial sector was to develop various segments of the financial market as also eliminate segmentation across various markets in order to smoothen the process of transmission of impulses across markets, easing the liquidity management process and making resource allocation process more efficient across the economy. The strategy adopted for meeting these objectives involved removal of restrictions on pricing of assets, building the institutional structure and technological infrastructure, introduction of new instruments, and fine-tuning of the market microstructure.

The 1990s saw the significant development of various segments of the financial market. At the short end of the spectrum, the money market saw the emergence of a number of new instruments such as CP and CDs and derivative products including FRAs and IRS. Repo operations, which were introduced in the early 1990s and later refined into a Liquidity Adjustment Facility, allow the Reserve Bank to modulate liquidity and transmit interest rate signals to the market on a daily basis. The process of financial market development was buttressed by the evolution of an active government securities market after the Government borrowing programme was put through the auction process in 1992-93.

The development of a market for Government paper enabled the Reserve Bank to modulate the monetisation of the fiscal deficit. The foreign exchange market deepened with the opening up of the economy and the institution of a market-based exchange rate regime in the early 1990s.

Although there were occasional episodes of volatility in the foreign exchange market, these were swiftly controlled by appropriate policy measures. The capital market also underwent some metamorphic changes during the 1990s. The development of the financial markets was well supported by deregulation of balance sheet restrictions in respect of financial institutions, allowing them to operate across markets. This resulted in increased integration among the various segments of the financial markets.

OVERVIEW OF INDIAN CAPITAL MARKET

The Indian capital market is more than a century old. Its history goes back to 1875, when 22 brokers formed the Bombay Stock Exchange (BSE). Over the period, the Indian securities market has evolved continuously to become one of the most dynamic, modern, and efficient securities markets in Asia. Today, Indian market confirms to best international practices and standards both in terms of structure and in terms of operating efficiency.

Indian securities markets are mainly governed by

a) The Company's Act 1956,

b) the Securities Contracts (Regulation) Act 1956 (SCRA Act), and

c) the Securities and Exchange Board of India (SEBI) Act, 1992.

A brief background of these above regulations are given below:

a) The Companies Act 1956 deals with issue, allotment and transfer of securities and various aspects relating to company management. It provides norms for disclosures in the public issues, regulations for underwriting, and the issues pertaining to use of premium and discount on various issues.

b) SCRA provides regulations for direct and indirect control of stock exchanges with an aim to prevent undesirable transactions in securities. It provides regulatory jurisdiction to Central Government over stock exchanges, contracts in securities and listing of securities on stock exchanges.

c) The SEBI Act empowers SEBI to protect the interest of investors in the securities market, to promote the development of securities market and to regulate the security market.

The Indian securities market consists of primary (new issues) as well as secondary (stock) market in both equity and debt. The primary market provides the channel for sale of new securities, while the secondary market deals in trading of securities previously issued. The issuers of securities issue (create and sell) new securities in the primary market to raise funds for investment. They do so either through public issues or private placement. There are two major types of issuers who issue securities. The corporate entities issue mainly debt and equity instruments (shares, debentures, etc.), while the governments (central and state governments) issue debt securities (dated securities, treasury bills). The secondary market enables participants who hold securities to adjust their holdings in response to changes in their assessment of risk and return. A variant of secondary market is the forward market, where securities are traded for future delivery and payment in the form of futures and options. The futures and options can be on individual stocks or basket of stocks like index. Two exchanges, namely National Stock Exchange (NSE) and the Stock Exchange, Mumbai (BSE) provide trading of derivatives in single stock futures, index futures, single stock options and index options. Derivatives trading commenced in India in June 2000.

Major Reforms in the Indian Capital Market

The major reforms in the Indian capital market since the 1990s are presented below:

- As a first step to reform the capital market, the Securities and Exchange Board of India (SEBI), which was earlier set up in April 1988 as a nonstatutory body under an administrative arrangement, was given statutory powers in January 1992 through an enactment of the SEBI Act, 1992 for regulating the securities markets. Twin objectives mandated in the SEBI Act are investor protection and orderly development of the capital market.
- The most significant development in the primary capital market has been the introduction of free pricing. The issuers of securities are now allowed to raise the capital from the market without requiring any consent from any authority either for making the issue or for pricing it. However, the issue of capital has been brought under SEBI's purview in that issuers are required to meet the SEBI guidelines for Disclosure and Investor Protection,

which, in general, cover the eligibility norms for making issues of capital (both public and rights) at par and at a premium by various types of companies, reservation in issues, *etc*.

- The abolition of capital issues control and the freeing of the pricing of issues led to unprecedented upsurge of activity in the primary capital market as the corporates mobilised huge resources. It, *inter alia*, exposed certain inadequacies of the regulations. Therefore, without seeking to control the freedom of the issuers to enter the market and freely price their issues, the SEBI further strengthened the norms for public issues in April 1996. Alongside, SEBI raised the standards of disclosure in public issues to enhance their transparency for improving the levels of investor protection. Issuers of capital are now required to disclose information on various aspects, such as, track record of profitability, risk factors, *etc*. Issuers now also have the option of raising resources through fixed price floatations or the book building process.
- Trading infrastructure in the stock exchanges has been modernised by replacing the open outcry system with on-line screen based electronic trading, unlike several of the developed countries where the two systems still continue to exist on the same exchange. In all, 23 stock exchanges in India have approximately 8,000 trading terminals spread all over the country. This improved the liquidity of the Indian capital market and a better price discovery.
- The trading and settlement cycles were initially shortened from 14 days to 7 days. Subsequently, to further enhance the efficiency of the secondary market, rolling settlement was introduced on a T+5 basis. With effect from April 1, 2002, the settlement cycle was further shortened to T+3 for all listed securities. The settlement cycle is now T+2.
- All stock exchanges in the country have established clearing houses. Consequently, all transactions are

settled through the clearing house only and not directly between members, as was practiced earlier.

- Several measures have been undertaken/strengthened to ensure the safety and integrity of the market. These are: margining system, intra-day trading limit, exposure limit and setting up of trade/settlement guarantee fund.
- Securities, which were earlier held in physical form, have been demateralised and their transfer is done through electronic book entry, which has eliminated some of the disadvantages of securities held in physical form. There are two depositories operating in the country.
- In India, all listed companies are now required to furnish to the stock exchanges and also publish unaudited financial results on a quarterly basis. To enhance the level of continuous disclosure by the listed companies, the SEBI decided to amend the Listing Agreement to incorporate the Segment Reporting, Accounting for Taxes on Income, Consolidated Financial Results, Consolidated Financial Statements, Related Party Disclosures and Compliance with Accounting Standards.
- The Indian capital market is also increasingly integrating with the international capital markets. One of the significant steps towards integrating Indian capital market with the international capital markets was the permission given to Foreign Institutional Investors (FIIs) such as, mutual funds, pension funds and country funds to operate in the Indian markets. Indian firms have also been allowed to operate in the Indian markets. Indian firms have also been allowed to raise capital from international capital markets through issues of Global Depository Receipts (GDRs), American Depository Receipts (ADRs), Euro Convertible Bonds (ECBs), *etc.*
- Boards of various stock exchanges, which in the past included mainly brokers, have been broad-based in order to make them more widely representative so that they represent different interests and not just the interests of their members. Reconstituted Governing Boards have

now broker and non-broker representation in the ratio of 50-50 apart from the Executive Director who has a seat on the Board and is required to be a non-broker professional. To remove the influence of brokers in the functioning of stock exchanges, the SEBI decided that no broker member of the stock exchange shall be an office bearer of an exchange or hold the position of President, Vice President, Treasurer, *etc*. Efforts are afoot to demutualise and corporatise the stock exchanges.

- Apart from stock exchanges, various intermediaries, such as mutual funds, stock brokers and sub-brokers merchant bankers, portfolio managers, registrars to an issue and share transfer agents, underwriters, debenture trustees, bankers to an issue, custodian of securities, venture capital funds and issuers have been brought under the SEBI's regulatory purview.
- There are now regulations in place governing substantial acquisition of shares and takeovers of companies. The Regulations are aimed at making the takeover process more transparent and to protect the interests of minority shareholders.
- Trading in derivative products, such as stock index future, stock index options and futures and options in individual stocks have also been introduced.

BASIC CONSIDERATIONS IN MANAGING CAPITAL

Now that we understand the importance of capital, let's focus on how we manage capital within an organization. The overall objective is to find an "optimal" capital structure - the right mix of capital sources (debt and equity) that minimizes the overall cost of capital and maximizes values to the shareholders (owners of the business). When we raise capital, we have two choices - issue debt or issue stock. Debt is represented by bonds which are long-term instruments sold to investors. Stock is the ownership interest of the business and depending upon the rules of incorporation, stockholders will have certain rights. Therefore, we start our understanding of capital management by looking at the advantages and disadvantages of the two sources of capital:

Some advantages to using stock are:

- No fixed payments are required to investors; dividends are paid only as earnings are available.
- No maturity date on the security, the invested capital does not have to be repaid.
- Improves the credit worthiness of the company.

Some disadvantages to using stock are:

- Dilutes the earnings per share to shareholders.
- Issuance costs are higher than debt.
- Issuing more stock can increase the overall cost of capital.
- Dividend payments to shareholders are not tax deductible.

Some advantages to using debt are:

- Interest payments are tax deductible.
- Does not dilute earnings per share or control within the company.
- Cost is fixed; interest and principal do not change.
- Expected returns to investors are usually lower than stock.

Some disadvantages to using debt are:

- Fixed charges must be paid regardless of available earnings or cash flow.
- Adds more risk to the business.
- Has a maturity date and the capital invested must be repaid to investors.

In addition to understanding the pros and cons of financial securities, we also need to recognize that several conditions will impact how we raise capital. These conditions include:

Economic Conditions: The demand and supply of capital in the marketplace can impact how capital is raised. For example, expectations of inflation will influence the cost that is paid for capital. Higher rates of inflation erode the values of investments and thus, investors will demand higher rates of return.

Market Conditions: The demand for higher rates of return will increase the cost of capital. For example, if we raise capital with a security that is not highly marketable, investors will require higher rates of return for the increased risk.

Operating Conditions: The level of fixed costs used to operate the business needs to be considered. For example, higher fixed costs can result in wider variations to operating income from numerous factors - increased competition, slower economic growth, etc. This is referred to as business risk.

Financial Conditions: The existing levels of outstanding debt will impact how capital will be raised. Higher levels of debt (including preferred stock) can result in wider variations to earnings due to higher fixed obligations that must be paid (interest to debt holders and fixed dividends to preferred stock holders). This is referred to as financial risk.

Not only do we need to look at various conditions, but we need to consider how financing will impact capital structure. Capital structure appears on the right side of the Balance Sheet as liabilities and equity; i.e. the long-term sources of funds to finance assets. Assets appear on the left side of the Balance Sheet. Capital structure is the permanent financing of the business through the use debt and stock. The total of all liabilities and equity is referred to as Financial Structure. Therefore, Capital Structure = Financial Structure - Current Liabilities.

Finding the right capital structure encompasses numerous considerations - growth rates in sales, risk attitudes of management, liquidity of assets, control position of the company, etc. Finding the right capital structure also involves finding the right amount of financial leverage. Financial leverage is the financing of assets with fixed obligations - debt and preferred stock. The use of financial leverage increases return on equity up to a certain level of operating income. As you use more financial leverage (debt and preferred stock), higher levels of operating income are needed to cover the additional fixed obligations (interest on debt and fixed dividends on preferred stock).

Generally, the use of financial leverage will improve financial performance whenever returns are higher than the costs of obtaining funds. In a perfect world, management would favour more leverage whenever return on capital exceeds the after tax costs of debt.

However, higher returns also result in higher risk to the business (risk return tradeoff). Therefore, the use of financial leverage is a balancing act between higher returns for shareholders vs. higher risk to shareholders.

Financial leverage can be measured with ratios such as debt to total assets. Financial leverage is also expressed as the Degree of Financial Leverage or DFL. DFL is the percentage change in earnings given a change in operating income (Earnings Before Interest & Taxes or EBIT). The higher the DFL, the riskier the business. We can use the following formula to calculate DFL:

DFL = EBIT / EBIT - I - (P / (1-TR)) where I is Interest and P is Preferred Dividends and TR is the tax rate.

Example 1 - Calculate Degree of Financial Leverage (DFL)

Mason Corporation has sales of $ 400,000 with total operating costs consisting of $ 330,000 in variable costs and $ 30,000 in fixed costs. Annual interest is $ 6,000 and preferred dividends are $ 2,000 per year. The tax rate is 20%.

Sales	$ 400,000
Less Variable Costs	(330,000)
Less Fixed Costs	(30,000)
EBIT	$ 40,000

DFL = $ 40,000 / $ 40,000 - $ 6,000 - ($ 2,000 / .80) = 1.27

In addition to financial leverage, there is operating leverage. Operating leverage is the use of fixed costs in production over variable costs. For example, replacing production workers (variable cost) with robots (fixed cost) would be an example of increased operating leverage.

As operating leverage increases, more sales are needed to cover the increased fixed costs. Since variable costs have been reduced, profits will increase more given an increase in sales after the breakeven point has been reached. High levels of fixed costs increase business risk. Like financial leverage, we can measure the Degree of Operating Leverage (DOL) as the percentage change in operating income given a change in sales. The following formula can be used to calculate DOL:

DOL = CM / CM - FC where CM is Contribution Margin and FC is Fixed Cost.

Example 2 - Calculate Degree of Operating Leverage (DOL)

Referring back to Example 1, we can make the following calculations:

Sales	$ 400,000
Less Variable Costs	(330,000)
Contribution Margin	$ 40,000

DOL = $ 40,000 / $ 40,000 - $ 30,000 = 4.0

Usually firms use one form of leverage over the other to finance investments.

For example, manufacturing companies tend to invest heavily in fixed assets and thus operating leverage is used much more than financial leverage. Service type companies have low levels of investment in fixed assets and therefore, financial leverage is widely used to finance the business. Leverage is relative to the type of fixed cost approach that is appropriate for funding the business and leverage by its very definition creates risk. Therefore, the use of leverage will always include a tradeoff between risk and return.

APPROACHES TO MANAGING CAPITAL

One way to understand how to manage capital is to look at the various approaches that can be used for finding the right capital structure. As we previously indicated, the right capital structure is that mix of debt and stock that maximizes the value of the firm while at the same time maintains a relatively low overall cost of capital. Two very different approaches to capital management are the Net Operating Income Approach and the Net Income Approach.

Net Operating Income Approach: This approach to capital management concludes that it does not matter how you mix the capital structure. The value of the business is not determined by how you arrange the right side of the Balance Sheet. Additionally, the overall cost of capital will not change as you change the mix of capital. Therefore, values are determined by the capitalization of operating income or EBIT (Earnings Before Interest Taxes).

Example 3 - Calculate Market Value of Business under Net Operating Income Approach to Capital Management

Norton Company has $ 400,000 in outstanding debt at 7% interest. Norton's cost of capital is 12% and expected operating income or Earnings Before Interest & Taxes (EBIT) is $ 120,000.

Earnings to Shareholders = $ 120,000 - $ 28,000 (7% interest on debt) = $ 92,000.

Total Market Value = $ 120,000 / .12 = $ 1,000,000

Market Value of Stock = $ 1,000,000 - $ 400,000 = $ 600,000

Cost of Equity = $ 92,000 / $ 600,000 = 15.3%

Net Income Approach: In contrast to the Net Operating Income Approach, the Net Income Approach concludes that the capital structure of an organization has a major influence on the value of the organization. Therefore, the use of leverage will change both the cost of capital and the value of the firm. Net Income is capitalized in arriving at the market value of the firm.

Example 4 - Calculate Market Value of Business under Net Income Approach to Capital Management

Referring back to Example 3, we can calculate the following values:

Market Value of Stock = $ 92,000 / 15.3% = $ 601,307

Total Value = $ 601,307 + $ 400,000 = $ 1,001,307

Overall Cost of Capital = $ 120,000 / $ 1,001,307 = 12%

Franco Modigliani and Merton Miller have provided some guidance between the Net Operating Income Approach and the Net Income Approach. Modigliani and Miller concluded that capital structure is not a major factor in the determination of values. Values are determined by the investment and operating decisions that generate cash flows. It is cash flows that give rise to values. This approach to valuation has become a mainstay within financial management. But what about capital structures? Mike Jenson, founder of the Journal of Financial

Economics, may have resolved the answer to this question. Jenson noted that whenever a company makes a change in its capital structure, it sends a signal to investors. This signalling effect does in fact result in changes to valuations. For example, when the Chairman of the Federal Reserve speaks about interest rates, a signal is sent to the marketplace and valuations quickly change. Therefore, shifts in capital structure do impact the value of a business.

Jenson also noticed that managers have a tendency to guard capital and minimize the distribution of dividends to shareholders. This follows with the so-called "pecking order" of financing whereby managers prefer internal sources of capital to external sources of capital. The specific pecking order is as follows:

1. Internal sources of capital - retained earnings / cash
2. External sources of capital - debt
3. External sources of capital - convertible securities
4. External sources of capital - preferred stock
5. External sources of capital - common stock

Consequently, capital structures can impact valuations due to the so-called signalling effect. Additionally, the real source of values will reside in cash flows (more specifically free cash flows). Free cash flows are the excess cash that can be withdrawn from a business after paying everything off. And in order to generate free cash flows, management must generate returns in excess of the cost of capital.

MILER AND MODIGLIANI POSITION

The Modigliani-Miller Theorem is a cornerstone of modern corporate finance. At its heart, the theorem is an irrelevance proposition: The Modigliani-Miller Theorem provides conditions under which a firm's financial decisions do not affect its value. Modigliani (1980, p. xiii) explains the Theorem as follows: ... with well-functioning markets (and neutral taxes) and rational investors, who can 'undo' the corporate financial structure by holding positive or negative amounts of debt, the market value of the firm – debt plus equity – depends *only* on the income stream generated by its assets. It follows, in particular, that the value of the firm should not be affected by the share of debt in its financial structure or by what will be done with the returns – paid out as dividends or reinvested (profitably).

In fact what is currently understood as the Modigliani-Miller Theorem comprises four distinct results from a series of papers (1958, 1961, 1963). The first proposition establishes that under certain conditions, a firm's debt-equity ratio does not affect its market value. The second proposition establishes that a firm's leverage has no effect on its weighted average cost of capital (i.e., the cost of equity capital is a linear function of the debt-equity ratio). The third proposition establishes that firm market value is independent of its dividend policy. The fourth proposition establishes that equity-holders are indifferent about the firm's financial policy.

Miller (1991) explains the intuition for the Theorem with a simple analogy. "Think of the firm as a gigantic tub of whole milk. The farmer can sell the whole milk as it is. Or he can separate out the cream, and sell it at a considerably higher price than the whole milk would bring." He continues, "The Modigliani-Miller proposition says that if there were no costs of separation, (and, of course, no government dairy support program), the cream plus the skim milk would bring the same price as the whole milk." The essence of the argument is that increasing the amount of debt (cream) lowers the value of outstanding equity (skim milk) – selling off safe cash flows to debt-holders leaves the firm with more lower valued equity, keeping the total value of the firm unchanged. Put differently, any gain from using more of what might seem to be cheaper debt is offset by the higher cost of now riskier equity. Hence, given a fixed amount of total capital, the allocation of capital between debt and equity is irrelevant because the weighted average of the two costs of capital to the firm is the same for all possible combinations of the two.

The Theorem makes two fundamental contributions. In the context of the modern theory of finance, it represents one of the first formal uses of a no arbitrage argument (though the "law of one price" is longstanding). More fundamentally, it structured the debate on why irrelevance fails around the

Theorem's assumptions: (i) neutral taxes; (ii) no capital market frictions (i.e., no transaction costs, asset trade restrictions or bankruptcy costs); (iii) symmetric access to credit markets (i.e., firms and investors can borrow or lend at the same rate); and (iv) firm financial policy reveals no information. Modigliani and Miller (1958) also assumed that each firm belonged to a "risk class," a set of firms with common earnings across states of the world, but Stiglitz (1969) showed that this assumption is not essential. The relevant assumptions are important because they set conditions for effective arbitrage: When a financial market is not distorted by taxes, transaction or bankruptcy costs, imperfect information or any other friction which limits access to credit, then investors can costlessly replicate a firm's financial actions. This gives investors the ability to 'undo' firm decisions, if they so desire. Attempts to overturn the Theorem's controversial irrelevance result were a fortiori arguments about which of the assumptions to reject or amend. The systematic analysis of these assumptions led to an expansion of the frontiers of economics and finance.

The importance of taxes for the irrelevance of debt versus equity in the firm's capital structure was considered in Modigliani and Miller's original paper (1958). Miller and Modigliani (1963) and Miller (1977) addressed the issue more specifically, showing that under some conditions, the optimal capital structure can be complete debt finance due to the preferential treatment of debt relative to equity in a tax code. For example, in the U.S. interest payments on debt are excluded from corporate taxes. As a consequence, substituting debt for equity generates a surplus by reducing firm tax payments to the government. Firms can then pass this surplus on to investors in the form of higher returns. This raised the further provocative question – were firms that issued equity leaving stockholder money on the table in the form of unnecessary corporate income tax payments? Miller (1977) resolved this problem by showing that a firm could generate higher after-tax income by increasing the debt-equity ratio, and this additional income would result in a higher payout to stockholders and bondholders, but the value of the firm need not increase. The crux of the argument is that as debt is substituted for equity, the proportion of firm payouts in the form of interest on debt rises relative to payouts in the form of dividends and capital gains on equity. Higher taxes on interest payments than on equity returns reduce or eliminate the advantage of debt finance to the firm.

The remaining Modigliani-Miller assumptions deal with various types of capital market frictions (e.g., transaction costs or imperfect information) that are at the heart of arbitrage. The driving force in a perfect market for a homogeneous good is the "law of one price." If debt and equity are merely different packages of an underlying homogeneous good – capital, and there are no market imperfections, then it follows immediately that the law of one price holds due to arbitrage. Investors simply engage in arbitrage until any deviation in the price of the two forms of capital is eliminated. Thus, the remaining discussion is organized around the three implications of the Theorem for firm capital structure, dividend policy, and the method of capital finance (lease versus buy).

With regard to firm capital structure, the Theorem opened a literature on the fundamental nature of debt versus equity. Are debt and equity distinct forms of capital? Why and in what specific ways? In order to answer these questions about the nature of capital, the optimal contract literature examines debt and equity as financial contracts that arise optimally in response to particular market frictions, when contracting possibilities are complete or incomplete. Complete contracts can be written on all states if this is optimal; incomplete contacts cannot depend on some states of nature.

In one of the earliest contributions, Townsend (1979) combines elements of imperfect information and bankruptcy costs to examine the nature of debt in a complete contracting environment. In his costly state verification model, debt is an optimal response to costly monitoring and differential information: All agents know ex-ante the distribution of firm returns, but only the firm privately and costlessly observes the return ex-post. The lender can acquire this information, but must irrevocably commit to pay a deadweight verification cost. Townsend shows that debt is optimal because it minimizes this cost. When the firm makes the required fixed debt repayment, no cost is incurred. Only when the firm is insolvent, and hence cannot repay its debt fully, does verification occur. Townsend interprets this as costly bankruptcy (liquidation): the firm is shut down; firm assets are seized by a "court," which verifies their magnitude and transfers the residual to the lender, net of the verification cost. Lacker and Weinberg (1989) extend the approach by specifying conditions under which equity is optimal in an analogue of the model, costly state falsification. Neither debt nor equity is ex-post efficient in this class of models because no agent wishes to request costly intervention, and incur the deadweight cost, ex-post. Agents know that bankruptcy occurs only when the firm is truly unable to repay due to a low realization, but they are implicitly assumed to be committed to the decisions they made ex-ante. Otherwise, debt is no longer optimal.

Krasa and Villamil (2000) show that a firm-lender investment problem with multiple stages, costly enforcement, limited commitment and an explicit enforcement decision, can illuminate debt's distinct properties. The analysis also solves the ex-post inefficiency problem in the costly state verification model. Agents write a contract in the initial period, knowing only the distribution of project returns. The contract specifies payments and when enforcement will occur, and can be altered if agents receive new information. In the next period, the borrower privately observes the return and can make the unenforceable payment specified in the original contract or propose an alternative payment (i.e., renegotiate). In the final stage the investor can seek costly enforcement of the contractually specified payment or renegotiate enforcement. The opportunity to renegotiate is important because it introduces a new source of information: Any positive renegotiation payment by the firm would reveal information to the investor about the firm's state. Debt is optimal because it minimizes information revelation. Renegotiation, which imposes a constraint on the contract problem, is only relevant when an agent acquires new information and can use the information to alter the initial contract. Debt weakens agents' incentive to renegotiate by minimizing information revelation (a fixed face value reveals no information about the firm). The contract is ex-post efficient because all decisions are chosen optimally as part of a Perfect Bayesian Nash Equilibrium. This minimal information revelation of debt stands in sharp contrast to the active information revelation in signalling models of equity. For example, in Leland and Pyle (1977) retained equity by a firm signals a profit increase sufficient to offset the owner's foregone diversification. In Myers and Majluf (1984), issuing equity signals bad news – owners with inside information sell shares when markets overvalue them. These signalling models leave open why a firm would use financial decisions to reveal information, a problem that does not arise in Krasa and Villamil.

In incomplete contracting models, control rights are an alternative justification for debt and equity contracts. Aghion and Bolton (1992) view debt as a particular assignment of control rights with important incentive properties. They show that when contracting possibilities are exogenously incomplete and control rights are assigned entirely to the investor or the firm, the first best contract cannot be implemented. If the investor has sole control, the investor may force the firm to expand to a sub-optimal level. Alternatively, if the firm has sole control it may not liquidate optimally. Aghion and Bolton show that, under some conditions, debt is the optimal contract because it assigns control to the firm in good states but to the investor in bad states. This ensures that optimal decisions are made in solvency and default states. Zender (1991) extends the model to include both debt and equity contracts. Grossman and Hart (1988) and Harris and Raviv (1988) examine control in the context of voting rights. They focus on the "one vote per share" property of equity and majority voting, showing circumstances under which equity is optimal and when other "extreme securities" are optimal.

Instead of focusing on the properties of debt and equity per se, Allen and Gale (1988, 1992) examine the properties of optimal securities more broadly – financial innovation. They study the problem of a firm that can issue securities in a market where the transactions cost of issuing securities makes the market incomplete. Market structure is endogenous, in the sense that because firms choose the securities they issue, this determines the transaction costs they incur. Allen and Gale (1988) prohibit short sales and show that neither debt nor equity is optimal. In contrast Allen and Gale (1992) permit unlimited short sales, and show by example that debt and equity can be optimal. They note that the example is a special case; in general their model predicts that optimal securities are much more complex than those typically observed. The debt-equity puzzle unleashed by Modigliani and Miller continues to be an active area of research. The common theme of both the complete and incomplete contracting literatures is that debt, equity, and hybrid securities arise endogenously to overcome frictions in capital markets. Debt and equity have unique properties that resolve these frictions.

The Modigliani and Miller (1961) and Miller (1977) result that firm value is independent of dividend policy has also been examined extensively. Bhattacharya (1979) and others show that firm dividend policy can be a costly device to signal a firm's state, and hence relevant, in a class of models with: (i) asymmetric information about stochastic firm earnings; (ii) shareholder liquidity (a need to sell makes firm valuation relevant); and (iii) deadweight costs (to pay dividends, refinance cash flow shocks or cover under-investment). In a separating equilibrium, only firms with high anticipated earning pay high dividends, thus signalling their prospects to the stock market. As in other costly signalling models, why a firm would use financial decisions to reveal information, rather than direct disclosure, must be addressed. As previously, taxes are another important friction which effect dividend policy.

Finally, Miller and Upton (1976) show that firms are indifferent between leasing and buying capital, except when they face different tax rates. Meyers, Dill and Bautista (1976) develop a formula to evaluate the lease versus buy decision, where different tax rates across firms create different discount rates. They show it is optimal for low tax rate, and hence high discount rate firms, to lease. Alchian and Demsetz (1972) show that leasing involves agency costs due to the separation of ownership and control of capital; a lessee may not have the same incentive as an owner to properly use or maintain the capital. Coase (1972) and Bulow (1986) argue that a durable goods monopolist may lease in order to avoid time inconsistency, and Hendel and Lizzari (1999, 2002) show that it may lease to reduce competition or adverse selection in secondary (used goods) markets. Eisfeldt and Rampini (2005) show that leasing has a repossession advantage relative to buying via secured lending. They trade off the benefit of this enforcement advantage against the cost of the standard ownership versus control agency problem.

In addition to these specific advances in financial structure, an essential part of Modigliani and Miller's innovation was to put agents on equal footing. They, and others, then asked – what types of frictions would cause agents to have different market opportunities, information sets or commitment frictions? This perspective, which was novel at the time, has been used productively to analyze problems in monetary economics, public finance, international economics, and a number of other applications. In summary, the most profound and lasting impacts of the Modigliani-Miller Theorem have been this notion of "even footedness" and the systematic investigation of the Theorem's assumptions. The approach has motivated decades of research in economics and finance in a search for what *is* relevant in a host of economic problems (between borrowers and lenders, governments and citizens, and countries). As Miller (1988) said, "Showing what doesn't matter can also show, by implication, what does."

SIGNALLING THEORY

In this topic, we briefly discuss signalling theory. But, before we begin our discussion of signalling theory, why would a firm be interesting in signalling? In general, a firm's managers use signals to reveal information to the public about firm value. Managers have the incentive to signal if:

1) They have private information about firm value and the public does not (i.e., information asymmetry)
2) The private information is "good" news (therefore, the signal will reveal this good news to the public)
3) Bad firms can't (won't) imitate

4) Managers cannot credibly disclose the positive information without the signal (i.e., they can't simply hold a news conference).

In corporate finance, signalling models have been used (as the textbook describes) to explain the level of investment by an entrepreneur in a firm, debt versus equity choices, the size of dividends, and stock splits. The textbook splits its discussion between "costly" (with exogenous costs) and "costless" signals (with endogenous costs). With either type, the signal is meant to separate good firms from bad firms.

Our discussion centers on one of the foundational papers in "costly" signalling theory: Spence, Michael, "Job market signalling," Quarterly Journal of Economics 87 (1973), 355-374. In the Spence model, hiring an employee is viewed as an investment decision with uncertainty concerning the employee's value. The cost to the firm is the wages paid. The value to the firm is the employee's marginal product (i.e., marginal contribution) to the firm.

Assumptions

1) Employer cannot directly observe the potential employee's (i.e., applicant's) marginal product
2) Employer can observe the attributes of the applicant that are related to his/her marginal product (education, work experience, age, sex, race, height, etc.)
3) Some attributes are fixed (age, sex, race, height), some are not (education, work experience)
4) Fixed attributes are termed "indices," those subject to change by the applicant are termed "signals"
5) Signals are costly and are negatively correlated with the applicant's productive capability. That is, the signal is less costly for applicants with greater productive capabilities.
6) Employer uses indices and signals to determine the wage rate
7) Employers are risk neutral who offer wages equal to the applicant's expected marginal product

8) Employer beliefs about the value implied by the indices and signals can change through time as new data is received

Since the applicant can't alter indices, the only thing they can do to affect the wage rate is to alter their signals. (Spence focuses on the education signal.)

The amount of education acquired by applicant is the amount that maximizes the difference between the offered wages and the cost of education (the signalling cost). Education costs include dollars (tuition), time, mental strain, etc.

Assumption 5 is critical to an effective signal. What would happen if the signal was equally costly to all applicants?

Information feedback loop:

1) Employers have conditional probabilistic beliefs about the relation between indices / signals and applicants' marginal product
2) Employer offers wage schedule (a function of indices and signals)
3) Signalling decisions are made by applicants (taking into account signalling costs)
4) Employer hires applicant, observes relation between indices/signals and marginal product and updates beliefs
5) Go back to #1

Spence (1973) describes a signalling equilibrium in which new incoming data is self-confirming (so no update in beliefs). That is, employers set the wage schedule that induces applicant signalling decisions. Employers then hire and the marginal product of the employees is as expected.

Example one

1) One employer
2) Two types of applicants: Type one have low marginal product (= \$1), the other have high marginal product (= \$2).
3) Proportion of group one: q, proportion of group two: 1-q

4) Signal = education. Signalling costs:
   Group one: cost of education of level $y = y$
   Group two: cost of education of level $y = y/2$
5) Education does not change the applicant's marginal product

To find equilibrium, set initial probabilistic beliefs, then determine if they are confirmed. For example, assume that the employer's probabilistic beliefs are:

6) If $y < y^*$, then productivity = \$1 (with probability 1), if $y\ ^3\ y^*$, then productivity = \$2 (with probability 1). So the employer offers wages of \$1 to applicants with $y < y^*$ and wages of \$2 to applicants with $y\ ^3\ y^*$
7) Applicants will respond by either obtaining education level 0 or y^* (why only these two levels?)
8) For employer beliefs to be confirmed, then all applicants from group one must obtain education level 0 and all applicants from group two must obtain education level y^*
9) Each groups sets y to maximize the difference between wage and signal cost
10) Education selected by applicants is self confirming if:
    For group one: $\$1 > \$2 - y^*$
    For group two: $\$2 - y^* / 2 > \$1$
11) Putting these two conditions together: $\$1 < y^* < \$2$. Note – any y^* in that range is in equilibrium, but not equivalent in terms of welfare. For example, how do members of group one and two think about increasing y^*?
12) Proportion of individuals in each group does not affect the equilibrium.
13) If signalling is not allowed, then wage rate for all applicants is: $\$1q + \$2(1 - q) = \$2 - q$. For example, if $q = 0.4$, then wage rate = \$1.6.
    a. Group one prefers no signalling.
    b. Group two prefers signalling or no signalling depending on the values for y^* and q. Remember, groups two's net return is $\$2 - y^* / 2$. Also remember

that \$1 < y^* < \$2. So, if q £ 0.5, then group two is worse off by signalling.

14) In general, if $y^* < 2q$, then group two is better off in a signalling environment. So, higher q increases benefit to signal for group two, higher y^* decreases the benefit from signalling.

15) Even more in general, if a_1y is the signalling cost for group one and a_2y is the signalling cost for group two, then: group two is better off in a signalling environment if $q > a_2 / a_1$.

Example Two

1) Employer beliefs are:

   If $y < y^*$, then group one (productivity \$1) with probability q and group two (productivity \$2) with probability 1-q.

   If y ³ y^*, then group two (productivity = \$2) with probability 1

2) Levels of y selected are still either 0 or y^*.

3) Wage rate is set at \$2 – q for y = 0 and \$2 for $y = y^*$.

4) Assume y^* set greater than 2q. Then both groups select y = 0.

Group One

y = 0, then net wage = \$2 – q (select this)

$y = y^*$, then net wage = \$2 – y^*

Group Two

y = 0, then net wage = \$2 – q (select this)

$y = y^*$, then net wage = \$2 – $y^*/2$

5) This is "in equilibrium" because employer's beliefs are confirmed (i.e., the wage paid for y = 0 is equal to the marginal product, on average). That is, once this wage schedule is set, no new data will be released to alter the employer beliefs.

6) Yet, no information is provided in this equilibrium.

Example Three

1) There is also a signalling equilibrium in which all

participants pick $y = y^*$. To get this equilibrium, employers believe:

If $y < y^*$, then group one (productivity \$1) with probability 1.

If $y\,^{3}\,y^*$, then group one (productivity \$1) with probability q and group two (productivity \$2) with probability 1-q.

2) Wage rate is set at \$1 for $y = 0$ and \$2 – q for $y = y^*$.
3) These beliefs are self confirming if y^* set less than \$1 – q.
4) In this equilibrium, everyone gets educated to improve their wage rate, but education provides no information about productivity.

Some Closing Observations and Conclusions

1) A negative correlation between signal cost and productivity (or value) is a necessary condition for a signal.
2) However, simply having a negative correlation between signal cost and productivity doesn't imply that people will signal (e.g., if education can only be acquired at levels 1 and 3). Thus, there has to be a sufficient number of possible signals across the cost range.
3) Multiple equilibria are possible, with some inferior to others (e.g., setting y^* greater than a bit over 1 in example 1)
4) Sometimes everyone loses with signalling. Sometimes some people win and others lose.

EPS

Even comparing the earnings of one company to another really doesn't make any sense, if you think about it. Earnings will tell you nothing about how many shares the company has. Because you do not know how many shares a company has, you do not know how many parts that companies earnings have to be divided into. If the company has more shares, the earnings will be divided into more parts.

For example, companies A and B both earn Rs.100, but company A has 10 shares outstanding, so each share holder has in effect earned Rs.10. On the other hand, if company B has 50 shares outstanding and they too have earned Rs.100 then each shareholder has earned Rs.2. So you see it is important to know what is the total number of outstanding shares are as well as the earnings.

Thus it makes more sense to look at earnings per share (EPS), as a comparison tool. You calculate earnings per share by taking the net earnings and divide by the outstanding shares.

EPS = Net Earnings / Outstanding Shares

So looking at the EPS ratio, you should go buy Company A with an EPS of 10, right? EPS is not the only basis of comparing two companies, but it is one of the methods used.

Note that there are three types of EPS numbers:

- Trailing EPS – last year's numbers and the only actual EPS
- Current EPS – this year's numbers, which are still projections
- Forward EPS – future numbers, which are obviously projections

EPS doesn't tell you whether it's a good stock to buy or what the market thinks of it. For that information, we need to look at some other ratios next....

EBIT

Just like Net profit after tax (NPAT), there are not too many more important numbers than the Earnings Before net Interest and Tax (EBIT). The reason being; there are a surprising number of companies listed on the stock market that do not make money and often they are of little interest to share investors.

EBIT is calculated by taking the earnings (before significant items and extraordinary items) before net interest has been deducted and before the income tax obligation on the earnings has been deducted. Net interest is the total interest paid on borrowings (or borrowing costs) minus any interest received on money deposited.

The EBIT can sometimes be found in the statement of financial performance (previously known as the Profit and Loss Statement), although many companies will just list one figure for earnings before tax and this will include significant items.

The EBIT Margin is another measure investors can use to assess a companys financial health. The EBIT Margin shows you the percentage of each dollar of sales revenue that is left after all expenses have been removed, excluding net interest and income tax expenses.

The EBIT Margin differs between different industries and care should be taken when comparing companies from different market indices.

Companies like Woolworths and Coles Myer (now part of Wesfarmers) as retailers expect to have quite a small EBIT Margin as they rely on small margins accompanied with high sales volume. Other industries would have far smaller sales volume but expect to offset that with much higher profit margins.

All of these different factors directly impact on the EBIT Margin.

Unlike most fundamental pieces of data, it is possible to consider the EBIT as a stand-alone figure. However, it can be combined with other data to form a more complete overall assessment or simply the trend of the EBIT over time could be assessed and a conclusion drawn from that. One of the greatest strengths of a company is the ability to generate profits and provide above average returns to shareholders and many investors make this a primary consideration in their decision to buy shares.

EBITDA: earnings before interest, taxes, depreciation, and amortization.

Depreciation = non-cash expense of the wear and tear on fixed assets based on the respective useful lives

Amortization = non-cash expense of writing off intangible assets over their useful lives.

EBITDA is often used to compare the profit potential between companies because it allows an "apples-to-apples" comparison. Experts caution, however, that EBITDA does not accurately reflect a company's ability to generate cash and should not be used to replace the term "cash flow",

Profitability. Profitability % = EBIT / SALES This measurement represents the operating performance of a business entity expressed as a return on sales. It also provides a measurement of operational efficiency in the profit and loss account, void of finance costs.

ROI

Return on Investment: What is ROI analysis?

Return on Investment (ROI) analysis is one of several approaches to building a financial business case. The term means that decision makers evaluate the investment by comparing the magnitude and timing of expected gains to the investment costs.

Decision makers will also look for ways to improve ROI by reducing costs, increasing gains, or accelerating gains.

In the last few decades, this approach has been applied to asset purchase decisions (computer systems or a fleet of vehicles, for example), "go/no-go" decisions for programs of all kinds (including marketing programs, recruiting programs, and training programs), and to more traditional investment decisions (such as the management of stock portfolios or the use of venture capital).

THE SIMPLE RETURN ON INVESTMENT

Return on investment is frequently derived as the "return" (incremental gain) from an action divided by the cost of that action. That is "simple ROI". For example, what is the ROI for a new marketing program that is expected to cost $500,000 over the next five years and deliver an additional $700,000 in increased profits during the same time?

Simple ROI works well in situations where both the gains and the costs of an investment are easily known and where they clearly result from the action. Other things being equal, the investment with the higher ROI is the better investment. The return on investment metric itself, however, says nothing about the magnitude of returns or risks in the investment.

In complex business settings, however, it is not always easy to match specific returns (such as increased profits) with the specific costs that bring them, and this makes ROI less trustworthy as a guide for decision support. Simple ROI also becomes less trustworthy as a useful metric when the cost figures include allocated or indirect costs, which are probably not caused directly by the action or the investment. Business investments typically involve financial consequences extending several years or more.

In such cases, the metric has meaning only when the time period is clearly stated. Shorter or longer time periods may produce quite different ROI figures for the same investment. When financial impacts extend across several years, moreover, the analyst must decide whether to use discounted (net present value) figures or non discounted

RETURN ON EQUITY - ROE

One of the most important profitability metrics is return on equity (or ROE for short). Return on equity reveals how much profit a company earned in comparison to the total amount of shareholder equity found on the balance sheet. If you think back to lesson three, you will remember that shareholder equity is equal to total assets minus total liabilities.

It's what the shareholders "own". Shareholder equity is a creation of accounting that represents the assets created by the retained earnings of the business and the paid-in capital of the owners.

Why Return on Equity Is Important

A business that has a high return on equity is more likely to be one that is capable of generating cash internally. For the most part, the higher a company's return on equity compared to its industry, the better. This should be obvious to even the less-than-astute investor If you owned a business that had a net worth (shareholder's equity) of $100 million dollars and it made $5 million in profit, it would be earning 5% on your equity ($5 ÷ $100 = .05, or 5%). The higher you can get the "return" on your equity, in this case 5%, the better.

Formula for Return on Equity

The formula for Return on Equity is:

Net Profit ÷ Average Shareholder Equity for Period = Return on Equity

Return on Equity Example

Take a look at the same financial statements I've provided from Martha Stewart Living Omnimedia at the bottom of the page. Now that we have the income statement and balance sheet in front of us, our only job is to plug a the numbers into our equation. The earnings for 2001 were $21,906,000 (because the amounts are in thousands, in this case $21,906, and multiply by 1,000. Almost all publicly traded companies short-hand their financial statements in thousands or millions to save space). The average shareholder equity for the period is $209,154,000 ([$222,192,000 + 196,116,000] ÷ 2]).

Let's plug the numbers into the formula.

$21,906,000 earnings ÷ $209,154,000 average shareholder equity for period = 0.1047 return on equity, or 10.47%

This 10.47% is the return that management is earning on shareholder equity. Is this good? For most of the twentieth century, the S&P 500, a measure of the biggest and best public companies in America, averaged ROE's of 10% to 15%. In the 1990's, the average return on equity was in excess of 20%. Obviously, these twenty-plus percent figures probably won't endure forever. In the past few years alone, small and large corporations alike have issued repeated earnings revisions, warning investors they will not meet analysts' quarterly and / or annual estimates.

Return on equity is particularly important because it can help you cut through the garbage spieled out by most CEO's in their annual reports about, "achieving record earnings". Warren Buffett pointed out years ago that achieving higher earnings each year is an easy task. Why? Each year, a successful company generates profits. If management did nothing more than retain those earnings and stick them a simple passbook savings account yielding 4% annually, they would be able to report "record earnings" because of the interest they earned.

Were the shareholders better off? Not at all; they would have enjoyed heftier returns had the earnings been paid out as cash dividends. This makes obvious that investors cannot look at rising per-share earnings each year as a sign of success. The return on equity figure takes into account the retained earnings from previous years, and tells investors how effectively their capital is being reinvested. Thus, it serves as a far better gauge of management's fiscal adeptness than the annual earnings per share.

CAPITAL MARKETS AND INVESTMENT PERFORMANCE

Suppose you find a great investment opportunity, but you lack the cash to take advantage of it. This is the classic problem of financing. The short answer is that you borrow — either privately from a bank, or publicly by issuing securities. Securities are nothing more than promises of future payment. They are initially issued through financial intermediaries such as investment banks, which underwrite the offering and work to sell the securities to the public. Once they are sold, securities can often be re-sold. There is a secondary market for many corporate securities. If they meet certain regulatory requirements, they may be traded through brokers on the stock exchanges, such as the NYSE, the AMEX and NASDAQ, or on options exchanges and bond trading desks.

Securities come in a bewildering variety of forms - there are more types of securities than there are breeds of cats and dogs, for instance. They range from relatively straightforward to incredibly complex. A straight bond promises to repay a loan over a fixed amount of interest over time and the principal at maturity. A share of stock, on the other hand, represents a fraction of ownership in a corporation, and a claim to future dividends. Today, much of the innovation in finance is in the development of sophisticated securities: structured notes, reverse floaters, IO's and PO's — these are today's specialized breeds. Sources of information about securities are numerous on the world-wide web. For a start, begin with the Ohio State Financial Data Finder. All securities, from the simplest to the most complex, share some basic similarities that allow us to evaluate their usefulness from the investor's perspective. All of them are economic claims against future benefits. No one borrows money that they intend to repay immediately; the dimension of time is always present in financial instruments. Thus, a bond represents claims to a future stream of pre-specified coupon payments, while a stock represents claims to uncertain future dividends and division of the corporate assets. In addition, all financial securities can be characterized by two important features: risk and return. These two key measures will be the focus of this second module.

FINANCE FROM THE INVESTOR'S PERSPECTIVE

Most financial decisions you have addressed up to this point in the term have been from the perspective of the firm. Should the company undertake the construction of a new processing plant? Is it more profitable to replace an old boiler now, or wait? In this module, we will examine financial decisions from the perspective of the purchaser of corporate securities: shareholders and bondholders who are free to buy or sell financial assets. Investors, whether they are individuals or institutions such as pension funds, mutual funds, or college endowments, hold *portfolios*, that is, they hold a collection of different securities. Much of the innovation in investment research over the past 40 years has been the development of a theory of portfolio management, and this module is principally an introduction to these new methods. It will answer the basic question, *What rate of return will investors demand to hold a risky security in their portfolio?* To answer this question, we first must consider what investors want, how we define return, and what we mean by risk.

Why Investors Invest

What motivates a person or an organization to buy securities, rather than spending their money immediately? The most common answer is savings — the desire to pass money from the present into the future. People and organizations anticipate future cash needs, and expect that their earnings in the future will not meet those needs. Another motivation is the desire to increase wealth, i.e. make money grow. Sometimes, the desire to become wealthy in the future can make you willing to take big risks. The purchase of a lottery ticket, for instance only increases the *probability* of becoming very wealthy, but sometimes a small chance at a big payoff, even if it costs a dollar or two, is better than none at all. There are other motives for investment, of course. Charity, for instance. You may be willing to invest to make something happen that might not, otherwise — you could invest to build a museum, to finance low-income housing, or to re-claim urban neighborhoods. The dividends from these kinds of investments may not be economic, and thus they are difficult to compare and evaluate. For most investors, charitable goals aside, the key measure of benefit derived from a security is the rate of return.

DEFINITION OF RATES OF RETURN

The investor return is a measure of the growth in wealth resulting from that investment. This growth measure is expressed in percentage terms to make it comparable across large and small investors. We often express the percent return over a specific time interval, say, one year. For instance, the purchase of a share of stock at time t, represented as P_t will yield P_{t+1} in one year's time, assuming no dividends are paid. This return is calculated as: $R_t = [P_{t+1} - P_t] / P_t$. Notice that this is algebraically the same as: $R_t = [P_{t+1} / P_t] - 1$. When dividends are paid, we adjust the calculation to include the intermediate dividend payment: $R_t = [P_{t+1} - P_t + D_t] / P_t$. While this takes care of all the explicit payments, there are other benefits that may derive from holding a stock, including the right to vote on corporate governance, tax treatment, rights offerings, and many other things. These are typically reflected in the price fluctuation of the shares.

Arithmetic vs. Geometric Rates of Return

There are two commonly quoted measures of average return: the geometric and the arithmetic mean. These rarely agree with each other. Consider a two period example: P0 = \$100, R_1 = -50% and R_2 = +100%. In this case, the arithmetic average is calculated as (100-50)/2 = 25%, while the geometric average is calculated as: $[(1+R_1)(1+R_2)]^{1/2}-1=0\%$. Well, did you make money over the two periods, or not? No, you didn't, so the geometric average is closer to investment experience. On the other hand, suppose R_1 and R_2 were statistically representative of future returns. Then next year, you have a 50% shot at getting $200 or a 50% shot at $50. Your expected *one year* return is (1/2)[(200/100)-1] + (1/2)[(50/100)-1] = 25%. Since most investors have a multiple year horizon, the geometric return is useful for evaluating how much their investment will grow over the long-term. However, in many statistical models, the arithmetic rate of return is employed. For mathematical tractability, we assume a single period investor horizon.

CAPITAL MARKET HISTORY

The 1980's was one of the greatest decades for stock investors in the history of the U.S. capital markets.

We measure stock market performance by the total return to investment in the S&P 500, which is a standard index of 500 stocks, weighted by the market value of the equity of the company. Dividends paid by S&P 500 companies are assumed to be re-invested in shares of stock. This provides a measure of total investor return, before individual taxes are paid.

The 1930's was one of the worst decades for U.S. stock investors.

In the 1930's stock markets crashed all over the globe. U.S. stock investors experienced a zero percent return for the eleven-year period from 12/1929 to 12/1939.

U.S. Capital Markets over the Long Term: 1926 - 1995

Over the past 68 years, A stock investment in the S&P increased from $1 to $800

RISK PREMIUM

Notice in the preceding figure that a dollar invested in stock grew to $889 over the period, while a dollar invested in corporate bonds grew to $40. Why the big difference? This return differential is commonly attributed to a difference in the risk associated with stocks as opposed to bonds. Notice that the stock line is "shakier" than the bond line. Wealth invested in stocks since 1926 was more *volatile* than wealth invested in bonds. Despite the higher return, the risks were higher as well. An investor typically cares about the riskiness of an investment. If, for instance, you are saving for a home purchase sometime in the next year, then you *really* care whether your $100,000 nest egg has a significant probability of dropping to $50,000 in twelve months. As a matter of fact, you might be willing to trade a lower rate of investment return for "insurance" that your principal will be secure. This is called *risk-aversion* — and all things being equal, most investors prefer less risk to more.

The difference between the S&P total return and the U.S. 30 day T-Bill return is called the *equity premium.* It is the amount of return that investors demand for holding a risky security such as stocks, as opposed to a riskless security, such as T-Bills. The annual equity premium is about 9% arithmetic, and 6% geometric, over the 1926 - 1995 period.

STANDARD DEVIATION AS A MEASURE OF RISK

Stock returns may be riskier or more volatile, but this concept is a difficult one to express simply. To do so, we borrow a concept from statistics, called *standard deviation.* standard deviation is a summary measure about the average spread of observations. It is the square root of the variance, which is calculated as:

$$\hat{\sigma}^2 = \frac{1}{T-1} \sum_{t=1}^{T} [R_t - \bar{R}]^2$$

The standard deviation of one-year S&P 500 returns is about 22.28%. If S&P returns are normally distributed, this means that about 2/3 of the time we should observe an annual return within the range (12.45-22.28)= -9.93 and (12.45+22.28)= 34.73. A histogram of S&P 500 annual returns shows that returns are approximately normally distributed, or are they? A normal distribution should allow returns lower than -100%. Stocks do not. In fact, the log of the variable being normally distributed is a better approximation. However, there is evidence to suggest that even this is not quite right. The tails of stock returns are a bit "fatter" than should be observed if returns were log-normally distributed. This lends some support to the hypothesis advanced by Benoit Mandelbrot that stock returns follow a "stable" distribution, with undefined variance. Have a look at the S&P 500 histogram yourself:

How well does standard deviation capture the notion of investor risk? It equally weights high returns with low returns. It heavily weights extreme observations. It is not concerned with the shape of the distribution. All of these are valid criticisms. However the benefits to using standard deviation are large. It is a single measure, allowing us to quantify asset returns by risk.

9

System of Investment and Capital Management

We have still to give an answer to the question whether credit is liable to exert different effects, according to the purpose for which it is granted. It was necessary to clarify first the problems connected Are the with the distinction between circulating and fixed edit capital. Now that we have progressed thus far, we dependent on may venture to comment on the effects of loans which are differentiated according to the kind of use to which they are put.

The answer is simpler in the case of transfer credit than in the case of inflationary credit. In the case of genuine savings it has been customary in the literature to inquire whether there is congruence between the duration for which the credit is granted and the duration for which the investment is made. We have already observed that from the point of view New short of the economic system as a whole, short-term credits can rarely be regarded as short-term investments.

The long-term investments division of Junctions m the productive process may for the cause what is from a collective point of view a longterm investment to take on the appearance of a short-term investment from the private point of view. If the demand for short-term credit predominates on the market, then the spread between the interest rates will tend to cause the available credit supply to take the corresponding form. If the demand for long-term credit predominates, then an increasing proportion of the available supply of capital will go through the stock exchange.

The raising of capital through the issue of stocks makes the individual firm independent of the length of time for which the individual capitalist or speculator wants to invest his funds. There has consequently been a tendency for industrial capital requirements to be financed to an ever-increasing extent on the securities exchanges, and the amount of industrial credit which has been obtained via the stock exchange is far greater than all other forms of credit.

At certain times (prior to the nineteen thirties) the securities exchange was the *only* channel through which credit flowed into industrial production. Towards the end of depression periods capitalists and financiers held back from all long-term commitments, and at the same time entrepreneurs, after their bad experiences of the crisis, fought shy of borrowing at short term for investment purposes.

Thus there was for some time almost no supply of long-term funds to industry and almost no demand for funds on the money market. The link was often re-established via the securities market. The belief that funds invested through the securities exchange can be withdrawn in liquid form had the effect of causing the superfluity of funds on offer on the money market eventually to find its way onto the securities exchange, in the first instance, of course, onto the bond market.

At this point loans to customers who wanted to make security purchases, and security purchases on their own account, were the only outlets which the banks had for the vast funds which they commanded. It was not considered permissible to make *direct* long-term loans to industry out of these funds, and there was no demand for short-term loans by industry.

The only investment outlets which remained open to the banks, therefore, were security loans and security purchases, in other words, *indirect* long-term credits to industry. (In recent years, of course, their place has been taken by the financing of public works and other public loan expenditures.) Frequently credit, perhaps after a couple of transfer operations, will take whatever form is dictated by the demand.

It is therefore rather idle to try to distinguish the effects of the credit according to the form and use originally intended. The length of time for which the funds are invested is likewise dictated by the demand, and as will be shown below, the term for Term, form, which the credit is designed by those who originally creditfare not supply it, is not what is finally decisive.

Therefore a determined rise, followed later by a decline, in the amount of win of the short-term transfer credit—no less than a credit-creation cycle—is capable of giving rise to marked disturbances. Even the most careful selection of borrowers cannot prevent this. If one wished to distinguish the effects of a new credit according to the use to which it is put, one would have first to assume that without this credit the borrower concerned would not have succeeded in obtaining funds.

This assumption is important because, if it is not fulfilled, the effect of the credit is entirely independent of the direct and concrete use to which it is put. For if this use would have been If the covered in the absence of the granting of this particular credit, the real beneficiary of the increase in obtained supply is a borrower who was previously excluded from the market but is now able to obtain funds and who he who is the actual beneremams *in concreto* unknown. It is important fioiary of the to assume also that the impetus comes from an increase new credit-in the supply of credit and not from an increase in the demand. In accordance with these assumptions we may suppose that an entrepreneur receives a loan for productive activity (or for an expansion of productive activity) which he was unable to carry out previously for lack of the necessary money capital.

Now that he is equipped with the money capital, the entrepreneur will be able to attract the means of production (original factors as well as intermediate products) to his enterprise. A theory which started out from the assumption of full employment would have to say that the means of production which are demanded with the new money capital were previously destined to go to other producers.

If the new money capital is the result of the creation of credit, the diversion of the means of production to the new productive activity will take place by way of the bidding up of prices on the market. Professor Strigl concluded from this—I The marginal think justifiably within the narrow confines of the assumptions stated above—that the credit can only find an investor in employment in those lines of production where the because of increase in prices of the means of production plays a the relative smaller role in cost calculations than the fall in weight of interest charges.

This would not be the case where changes. Circulating capital" because, where working capital (materials that are used up in the process) is concerned, an increase in its price will be a weightier consideration than the reduction in interest charges.

The reverse is true in the case of fixed capital, and it would therefore be profitable to use the additional credit only for investment in fixed capital. The answer to the question under consideration is in large part contained in the assumptions. It has been assumed that the demand is given and that the supply of money capital increases.

The result must therefore be the satisfaction of a demand that was previously unsatisfied. If this investment opportunity which can now be exploited with the aid of the newly created credit was previously excluded by the competition of other ways of using money capital this must obviously have been due to the interest factor. Investment opportunities which cannot be taken up because credit is "too dear" must be of the kind where the interest factor plays a relatively large role : this is only the case with long-term investments.

An investment which is made possible only by the creation of new credit can therefore only be an investment in fixed capital. Generations of practical bankers, and authors of books about banking, have preached that bank credit Bank credit should not be used for investment in fixed capital.

Even if the length of the period for which working capital is invested is greater in the economic system °api a ' as a whole than in the single undertaking, it will still —which be possible to liquidate working capital with less culty and at smaller loss than fixed capital. The liquidatedd "inflationary effects" should therefore be milder and capital, less harmful if a credit expansion serves to finance working capital than if it is used to finance fixed capital. But is it possible to prevent the credit from being invested in fixed capital? The foregoing exposition, based on the assumption of a given demand for Is the demand for credit, leads one to answer this question in the negative. But is the "given" demand for working capital really perfectly inelastic? inelastic?

Technically, an increase in working capital might take place without any increase in fixed capital if production could be extended within the limits allowed by the existing fixed capital equipment. The volume of production, at any time, is determined by marginal cost and marginal revenue. The marginal costs, i.e., the increase in total costs due to an increase in production, consist for the most part in wages and raw material costs. The interest on the investment in wages and materials is of relatively minor importance and the effect of a decrease in the interest rate on marginal costs is microscopically small.

This is explained by the fact "that we have there a fraction of a fraction of a fraction. The volume of working capital is only a ratio of the total annual prime costs, a ratio which depends on the rate of turnover; naturally, the *interest* on the working capital is only a percentage of that; and finally, a decrease in the rate of interest is only a fraction of the latter. " 3 The marginal cost curve will hardly fall noticeably in response to a reduction in the interest rate, and it is scarcely worth talking about a fall in the interest rate leading to an extension of production within the existing fixed capital equipment.

The increase in the supply of money capital can, however, raise the demand for certain products and may thus lead to an extension of production through the rise in the marginal revenue curve. There are here three possibilities:

If the increase in the supply of credit is inflationary in origin money incomes will rise and this will lead to an increase in the demand for consumption credit. The money incomes rise not as the direct creates result of the increase in the credit *supply* but as the increased result of the *utilization* of the credit, and, moreover, only subsequent as the result of the utilization of inflationary credit. But here we are concerned with the form of the investprimary use of the credit, to finance either working or fixed capital of producers. The possibility that the utilization of the credit may lead to a secondary demand for consumers' goods, and that this may lead to a tertiary derived demand for working capital, is another matter.

The second possibility is the fundamental idea behind Hawtrey's theory of the trade cycle. It has often been objected to this, that the demand of traders for stocks is influenced by interest costs only to a minute extent.

There is a good deal of truth in this objection : it is not at all likely that the interest-rate-sensitivity of the traders demand for stocks will be persuades anything like as important as the interest-rate-sensitivity of the producers' demand for fixed capital. The third possibility brings us back to our thesis that the increase in the supply of credit will as a rule cause more credit to be used to finance fixed capital. The utilization of additional credit for extending pro-equipment duction *without* simultaneous or previous investments in fixed capital is hardly likely to take place.

The misdirection of investment would, it is true, not have such far-reaching effects if the money capital were used to produce "liquid" goods instead of being used to construct fixed capital equipment. This is so, not so much on account of the "period of turnover of the capital" or the slower or quicker rate of amortization, as on account of the greater or lesser variety in related to the purposes for which the concrete capital goods can used. Conservative bankers are convinced that they finance only goods in process and give only advances on goods sold. But they forget that by giving the producers these funds for investing in "working capital" they put those producers in the position of being able to use their own capital in a different way than formerly. The granting of the bank credit to the producer frees the funds which were previously tied up in the running of his business, and he can now undertake the investments he plans with his "own funds."

The concrete visible use to which The banker.. cannot know the new credit is put is not, therefore, m any way the indirect identical with the investment which the credit has Jses, of the, funds which *de facto* made it possible to realize. he lends;— The investment which the credit expansion makes possible need not even take place in the firm of the actual borrower. Bankers could otherwise adopt the simple expedient of refusing any kind of loans and advances to entrepreneurs who undertake investment in fixed capital.

In fact, however, the bank credit which the entrepreneur borrows for himself in the real first instance may be relent by him to somebody else may be in the form of a trade credit, and thus make it possible other firms* for the firm which directly or indirectly takes over the products of the first entrepreneur to embark on investment. Or the bank credit may place the entrepreneur in the position of buying more on a cash basis and less on trade credit, and so enable the firms which directly or indirectly supply him with materials to undertake investments.

Lastly, the bank credit may release some other credit and so, by easing the general credit market, make it possible for investment to be undertaken at some undeterminable point in the careful economic system. The great care which a banker takes selection of in choosing between would-be borrowers will, of un-course, react beneficially on the quality of the bank's the bank investments, but it will not prevent additional credit but no the from leading to the immobilization of capital some-economy from anywhere m the economy mobilization.

If it is the inherent tendency of new credits (whether they be transfer credits or credits newly created by the banks) to find their way into investments in fixed capital, and if it is, therefore, of no credit avail to attempt to direct the credits into certain can not avert outlets by lending in a particular *form* and under its use for particular *conditions,* then the mistrust of stock exchange credits with respect to their "quality" is groundless.

We are no longer talking of the charge against stock exchange speculation that it may take the newly granted credits away from industry. For, in so far as one were concerned merely with the problem of how to prevent short-term credit from being used for fixed capital investment, the stock exchange would have to be praised and blessed *if* it actually did withhold the new funds from industrial investment.

What we have to consider here is whether the "misuse" of the credits in production will not be made worse if the short-term funds are first transferred by stock exchange witchcraft into long-term funds. "The harm which is caused by too much lending to the stock exchange lies in fact not so much in the possibility that there may be a shrinkage in the amount of lending to industrial borrowers* says Reisch on this point, "as in the fact that in this case credits will be put at the disposal of the stock exchange which are by their economic character totally unsuited to the purchase of securities."

Commenting on this it has to be said that credits which are by their nature unsuited to security purchases are just as unsuited to any other kind of industrial credit. For if every additional credit may have the effect of a long-term credit, it is obviously immaterial in what garb this credit is dressed. This gives a final negation to the —the banks question raised at an earlier juncture as to whether the exchange danger that investments will be misdirected is greater credits are when the credit is granted to the stock exchange than no worse than when the same amount of credit is granted directly to equal amounts industry.

Aside from the fact that the effect of the credit is to industry not decided by its outward form (discount, security loan, overdraft) nor by the way in which it finds its way into production (through loans to producers or traders or through purchases of securities, &c.) nor by the concrete purpose for which it is used directly (trade credit, working capital or fixed capital), the banks have no means of damming up the flow of newly created credit to the stock exchange. So long as the expansion of credit continues, the newly created credit will flow onto the stock exchange even though the authorities send a policeman after every credit. When rates on call loans rise considerably above the discount rate, the banks attempt to rediscount their holdings of bills in order to be able to use their funds on the stock exchange.

If the banks, under the pressure of the official credit policy, do not dare to expand their lending at call, but there is nevertheless a tendency for the credit expansion to continue to the benefit of "legitimate productive activity,'* then ordinary Besides, the business men will create commercial bills and will difficult loan divert the "direct credits to industry" to the stock mate exchange.

For nobody will prevent industry— attracted by the high rates on call money—from kept from being passed placing its liquid funds, on which it will have an on to a boomabundance in consequence of the "legitimate industrial credits/' at the disposal of the stock exchange and from financing new issues with them at the same time.

In periods of boom—periods of credit inflation— practically every credit becomes a stock exchange credit. The campaign against stock exchange credit will be brought to a successful conclusion only when a check is placed on credit expansion. And the check on credit expansion by the banks will not necessarily in all circumstances stop the increase in stock exchange credits immediately. Thus, for example, the restrictive credit policy of the American monetary authorities in 1928 achieved small success because the expansion was stimulated further by the reduction in the liquidity preferences of the economic system.

The notion that it is possible to pursue an "effective" credit expansion and at the same time to avoid a stock exchange boom is absurd. Discrimination in lending is bound to fail so long as the discrimination does not Qualitative imply restriction. This is, of course, possible and is effectiver practicable: the demand for direct business loans and only if it discounts might rise more slowly than the demand for quantitative security loans, so that a discrimination against security restriction loans would act as a check on credit expansion in general. So far, however, as credits are created, they will tend, even when they flow straight into industry without first going through the stock exchange, to increase the demand for productive goods and in consequence to raise the value of plants producing means Effective" of production.

This is bound to be reflected in an increase in the values. of titles to these undertakings, stock exchange boom always march market will be presented no matter where the together increased credits are initially placed. It is thus a mistaken judgment to regard security loans as the villain of the piece and to look upon discounts as being devoid of all evil. For both, either visibly or invisibly, tend to follow the path that offers the greatest attractions. It is not the form the credit takes nor the exact place where it enters the system that makes it dangerous: it is, instead, its amount.

CAPITAL INVESTMENT DECISIONS

Capital investment decisions are long-term corporate finance decisions relating to fixed assets and capital structure. Decisions are based on several inter-related criteria. Corporate management seeks to maximize the value of the firm by investing in projects which yield a positive net present value when valued using an appropriate discount rate. These projects must also be financed appropriately. If no such opportunities exist, maximizing shareholder value dictates that management return excess cash to shareholders. Capital investment decisions thus comprise an investment decision, a financing decision, and a dividend decision.

THE INVESTMENT DECISION

Management must allocate limited resources between competing opportunities ("projects") in a process known as capital budgeting. Making this capital allocation decision requires estimating the value of each opportunity or project: a function of the size, timing and predictability of future cash flows.

Project Valuation

In general, each project's value will be estimated using a discounted cash flow (DCF) valuation, and the opportunity with the highest value, as measured by the resultant net present value (NPV) will be selected. This requires estimating the size and timing of all of the incremental cash flows resulting from the project. These future cash flows are then discounted to determine their *present value*. These present values are then summed, and this sum net of the initial investment outlay is the NPV.

The NPV is greatly affected by the discount rate. Thus identifying the proper discount rate—the project "hurdle rate"—is critical to making the right decision. The hurdle rate is the minimum acceptable return on an investment—i.e. the project appropriate discount rate. The hurdle rate should reflect the riskiness of the investment, typically measured by volatility of cash flows, and must take into account the financing mix. Managers use models such as the CAPM or the APT to estimate a discount rate appropriate for a particular project, and use the weighted average cost of capital (*WACC*) to reflect the financing mix selected. (A common error in choosing a discount rate for a project is to apply a WACC that applies to the entire firm. Such an approach may not be appropriate where the risk of a particular project differs markedly from that of the firm's existing portfolio of assets.)

In conjunction with NPV, there are several other measures used as (secondary) selection criteria in corporate finance. These are visible from the DCF and include discounted payback period, IRR, Modified IRR, equivalent annuity, capital efficiency, and ROI.

Valuing Flexibility

In many cases, for example R&D projects, a project may open (or close) paths of action to the company, but this reality will not typically be captured in a strict NPV approach. Management will therefore (sometimes) employ tools which place an explicit value on these options. So, whereas in a DCF valuation the most likely or average or scenario specific cash flows are discounted, here the "flexibile and staged nature" of the investment is modelled, and hence "all" potential payoffs are considered. The difference between the two valuations is the "value of flexibility" inherent in the project.

The two most common tools are Decision Tree Analysis (DTA) and Real options analysis (ROA); they may often be used interchangeably:

- DTA values flexibility by incorporating *possible events* (or states) and consequent *management decisions*. In the decision tree, each management decision in response to an "event" generates a "branch" or "path" which the company could follow; the probabilities of each event are determined or specified by management. Once the tree is constructed:
  (1) "all" possible events and their resultant paths are visible to management;
  (2) given this "knowledge" of the events that could follow, management chooses the actions corresponding to the highest value path probability weighted;
  (3) then, assuming rational decision making, this path is taken as representative of project value.

  See Decision theory: Choice under uncertainty. (For example, a company would build a factory given that demand for its product exceeded a certain level during the pilot-phase, and outsource production otherwise. In turn, given further demand, it would similarly expand the factory, and maintain it otherwise. In a DCF model, by contrast, there is no "branching" - each scenario must be modelled separately.)
- ROA is usually used when the value of a project is *contingent* on the *value* of some other asset or underlying variable. Here, using financial option theory as a framework, the decision to be taken is identified as corresponding to either a call option or a put option - valuation is then via the Binomial model or, less often for this purpose, via Black Scholes. The "true" value of the project is then the NPV of the "most likely" scenario plus the option value. (For example, the viability of a mining project is contingent on the price of gold; if the price is too low, management will abandon the mining rights, if sufficiently high, management will develop the ore body. Again, a DCF valuation would capture only one of these outcomes.)

Quantifying Uncertainty

Given the uncertainty inherent in project forecasting and valuation, analysts will wish to assess the *sensitivity* of project NPV to the various inputs (i.e. assumptions) to the DCF model. In a typical sensitivity analysis the analyst will vary one key factor while holding all other inputs constant, *ceteris paribus*. The sensitivity of NPV to a change in that factor is then observed, and is calculated as a "slope": ÄNPV / Äfactor. For example, the analyst will determine NPV at various growth rates in annual revenue as specified (usually at set increments, e.g. -10%, -5%, 0%, 5%....), and then determine the sensitivity using the formula above. Often, several variables may be of interest, and the various results may be combined to produce a "value-surface" (or even a "value-space"), where NPV is a function of several variables.

Using a related technique, analysts also run scenario based forecasts of NPV. Here, a scenario comprises a particular outcome for economy-wide, "global" factors (exchange rates, commodity prices, etc...) *as well as* for company-specific factors (revenue growth rates, unit costs, etc...). As an example, the analyst may specify specific growth scenarios (e.g. 5% for "Worst Case", 10% for "Likely Case" and 25% for "Best Case"), where all key inputs are adjusted so as to be consistent with the growth assumptions, and calculate the NPV for each. Note that for scenario based analysis, the various combinations of inputs must be *internally consistent*, whereas for the sensitivity approach these need not be so. An application of this methodology is to determine an "unbiased NPV", where management determines a (subjective) probability for each scenario – the NPV for the project is then the probability-weighted average of the various scenarios.

A further advancement is to construct stochastic or probabilistic financial models – as opposed to the traditional static and deterministic models as above. For this purpose, the most common method is to use Monte Carlo simulation to analyze the project's NPV. This method was introduced to finance by David B. Hertz in 1964, although has only recently become common; today analysts are even able to run simulations in spreadsheet based DCF models, typically using an add-in, such as Crystal Ball.

Using simulation, the cash flow components that are (heavily) impacted by uncertainty are simulated, mathematically reflecting their "random characteristics". In contrast to the scenario approach above, the simulation produces several *thousand* trials (i.e. random but possible outcomes) and the output is a histogram of project NPV.

The average NPV of the potential investment – as well as its volatility and other sensitivities – is then observed. This histogram provides information not visible from the static DCF: for example, it allows for an estimate of the probability that a project has a net present value greater than zero (or any other value).

Here, continuing the above example, instead of assigning three discrete values to revenue growth, the analyst would assign an appropriate probability distribution (commonly triangular or beta). This distribution – and that of the other sources of uncertainty – would then be "sampled" repeatedly so as to generate the several thousand realistic (but random) scenarios, and the output is a realistic, representative set of valuations. The resultant statistics (average NPV and standard deviation of NPV) will be a more accurate mirror of the project's "randomness" than the variance observed under the traditional scenario based approach.

THE FINANCING DECISION

Achieving the goals of corporate finance requires that any corporate investment be financed appropriately. As above, since both hurdle rate and cash flows (and hence the riskiness of the firm) will be affected, the financing mix can impact the valuation. Management must therefore identify the "optimal mix" of financing—the capital structure that results in maximum value.

The sources of financing will, generically, comprise some combination of debt and equity. Financing a project through debt results in a liability that must be serviced—and hence there are cash flow implications regardless of the project's success. Equity financing is less risky in the sense of cash flow commitments, but results in a dilution of ownership and earnings. The *cost of equity* is also typically higher than the *cost of debt*, and so equity financing may result in an increased hurdle rate which may offset any reduction in cash flow risk.

Management must also attempt to match the financing mix to the asset being financed as closely as possible, in terms of both timing and cash flows.

One of the main theories of how firms make their financing decisions is the Pecking Order Theory, which suggests that firms avoid external financing while they have internal financing available and avoid new equity financing while they can engage in new debt financing at reasonably low interest rates.

Another major theory is the Trade-Off Theory in which firms are assumed to trade-off the tax benefits of debt with the bankruptcy costs of debt when making their decisions. An emerging area in finance theory is right-financing whereby investment banks and corporations can enhance investment return and company value over time by determining the right investment objectives, policy framework, institutional structure, source of financing (debt or equity) and expenditure framework within a given economy and under given market conditions. One last theory about this decision is the Market timing hypothesis which states that firms look for the cheaper type of financing regardless of their current levels of internal resources, debt and equity.

The Dividend Decision

The dividend is calculated mainly on the basis of the company's unappropriated profit and its business prospects for the coming year. If there are no NPV positive opportunities, i.e. where returns exceed the hurdle rate, then management must return excess cash to investors. These *free cash flows* comprise cash remaining after all business expenses have been met.

This is the general case, however there are exceptions. For example, investors in a "Growth stock", expect that the company will, almost by definition, retain earnings so as to fund growth internally. In other cases, even though an opportunity is currently NPV negative, management may consider "investment flexibility" / potential payoffs and decide to retain cash flows. Management must also decide on the form of the distribution, generally as cash dividends or via a share buyback. There are various considerations: where shareholders pay tax on dividends, companies may elect to retain earnings, or to perform a stock buyback, in both cases increasing the value of shares outstanding; some companies will pay "dividends" from stock rather than in cash.

Today, it is generally accepted that dividend policy is value neutral.

Working Capital Management

Decisions relating to working capital and short term financing are referred to as *working capital management*. These involve managing the relationship between a firm's short-term assets and its short-term liabilities.

As above, the goal of Corporate Finance is the maximization of firm value. In the context of long term, capital investment decisions, firm value is enhanced through appropriately selecting and funding NPV positive investments. These investments, in turn, have implications in terms of cash flow and cost of capital.

The goal of Working capital management is therefore to ensure that the firm is able to operate, and that it has sufficient cash flow to service long term debt, and to satisfy both maturing short-term debt and upcoming operational expenses. In so doing, firm value is enhanced when, and if, the return on capital exceeds the cost of capital.

Decision Criteria

Working capital is the amount of capital which is readily available to an organization. That is, working capital is the difference between resources in cash or readily convertible into cash (Current Assets), and cash requirements (Current Liabilities). As a result, the decisions relating to working capital are always current, i.e. short term, decisions.

In addition to time horizon, working capital decisions differ from capital investment decisions in terms of discounting and profitability considerations; they are also "reversible" to some extent. (Considerations as to Risk appetite and return targets remain identical, although some constraints - such as those imposed by loan covenants - may be more relevant here).

Additionally, working capital is directly affecting by other management issues, such as product mix, supply chain design and business model (for example agent vs. distributor).

Working capital management decisions are therefore not taken on the same basis as long term decisions, and different criteria are applied here: the main considerations are cash flow and liquidity - cashflow is probably the more important of the two.

- The most widely used measure of cash flow is the net operating cycle, or cash conversion cycle. This represents the time difference between cash payment for raw materials and cash collection for sales. The cash conversion cycle indicates the firm's ability to convert its resources into cash. Because this number effectively corresponds to the time that the firm's cash is tied up in operations and unavailable for other activities, management generally aims at a low net count. (Another measure is gross operating cycle which is the same as net operating cycle except that it does not take into account the creditors deferral period.)
- In this context, the most useful measure of profitability is Return on capital (ROC). The result is shown as a percentage, determined by dividing relevant income for the 12 months by capital employed; Return on equity (ROE) shows this result for the firm's shareholders. As above, firm value is enhanced when, and if, the return on capital, exceeds the cost of capital. ROC measures are therefore useful as a management tool, in that they link short-term policy with long-term decision making.

MANAGEMENT OF WORKING CAPITAL

Guided by the above criteria, management will use a combination of policies and techniques for the management of working capital. These policies aim at managing the *current assets* (generally cash and cash equivalents, inventories and debtors) and the short term financing, such that cash flows and returns are acceptable.

- Cash management. Identify the cash balance which allows for the business to meet day to day expenses, but reduces cash holding costs.
- Inventory management. Identify the level of inventory which allows for uninterrupted production but reduces the investment in raw materials - and minimizes reordering costs - and hence increases cash flow; Just In Time (JIT); Economic order quantity (EOQ); Economic production quantity (EPQ).
- Debtors management. Identify the appropriate credit policy, i.e. credit terms which will attract customers, such that any impact on cash flows and the cash conversion cycle will be offset by increased revenue and hence Return on Capital (or *vice versa*).
- Short term financing. Identify the appropriate source of financing, given the cash conversion cycle: the inventory is ideally financed by credit granted by the supplier; however, it may be necessary to utilize a bank loan (or overdraft), or to "convert debtors to cash" through "factoring".

10

Corporate Law and Behavioural Decision Theory

Behavioural analysis can inform many aspects of corporate law. In this section, we touch upon a few. The principal concern of corporate law is solving the agency problem so that officers and directors will operate the corporation in the best interests of the shareholders. Corporate law helps by imposing fiduciary obligations on the managers of the corporation and punishing them for breach. Presumably this would be unnecessary if the shareholders and promoters could simply bargain to an optimally efficient result, but this is unrealistic for logistical reasons in public corporations and unrealistic for Behavioural reasons in smaller corporations.

Consider the investor who is asked to invest in a neighbour's small but growing corporation. The neighbour is a promoter and CEO. For reasons of bounded rationality and rational ignorance, the investor's investigation of the company's condition will likely not be optimal. Judge Posner has explained why information costs render ignorance rational: Contracts are costly to make and... costs may well exceed the benefits...when the contingencies that would be regulated by contract—death or personal injury from using a product—are extremely remote. [When a consumer purchases an expensive item like a car] the greatest [contracting] cost [is] not the direct cost of drafting; it [is] the cost of information. The inclusion of... a clause [specifying rights and duties in the event of a remote contingency such as death or personal injury] would not serve its intended purpose unless the consumer knew something about the costs of alternative safety measures that the producer might take and about the safety of competing products and brands. But the cost of generating that information, and particularly the cost to the consumer of absorbing it, may well be disproportionate to the benefit of a negotiated (as distinct from imposed-by-law) level of safety.

If fraud seems a remote contingency to the investor, then the cost of an optimal investigation of the investment will seem disproportionate to the perceived benefit. And if the investor likes the CEO he will probably, for reasons of the false consensus effect, trust him too much. The investor is unlikely to detect if he is being lied to, and to be overconfident in his conclusion that the promoter has been truthful. Once he has decided to trust the promoter, he is unlikely to discount sufficiently representations made if any evidence appears as to the untrustworthiness of the CEO. Cognitive dissonance and belief persistence will impede his processing of information that undermines his initial conclusion that the promoter is honest and that the company is a promising one. Overconfidence and undue optimism will bolster this conclusion. All these factors put together paint a picture of a vulnerable investor whose fate is uncomfortably in the hands of another.

A legal regime that imposes duties of loyalty upon the CEO and other managers and punishes violations provides protection for the investor that would otherwise be lacking. In so doing, it encourages investment.

Professors Blair and Stout have pointed out that just as shareholders cannot be omnipresent to monitor the stewardship of their investment, neither can the law be everywhere (nor can it be perfectly enforced). Therefore, trust remains an important factor in the corporate governance calculation. As those commentators note, however, trust derives largely from social norms. The law dramatically impacts those norms. Professors Donaldson and Dunfee point out that "[o]utside sources may influence the development of norms. Law, particularly when it is perceived as legitimate by members of a community, may have a major impact on what is considered to be correct behaviour." Thus, when the Civil Rights Act of 1964 outlawed racial discrimination, people's views of the acceptability of such discrimination was significantly altered. Because of the conformity bias, what is considered correct behaviour exerts a major influence upon how people act.

For present purposes, corporate law establishes that managers and directors are to act in the best interests not of themselves, but of shareholders. In so doing, the law not only gives them external incentives in the form of liability rules to act in this way, it also changes their internal preferences by helping to establish trustworthy actions as the societal norm. Thousands of cooperation games administered by psychologists over the years establish that people are more willing to cooperate (irrationally, according to economic incentives) if they are instructed to do so, and/or if they believe that others will cooperate (the conformity bias).

The law instructs managers to act in a fiduciary capacity and thereby increases the odds that they will do so. This message is repeatedly sent to managers by judges who often describe the manager's fiduciary duty in the strongest terms. The law also helps to establish the social norm, reinforcing the likelihood that managers will choose to act as fiduciaries. While contractarians argue that the fiduciary duty is just another in the "nexus of contracts" that comprise corporate law, Blair and Stout argue convincingly that it is much more. To allow managers to opt easily out of the fiduciary duty via simple contract would "undermine trust among corporate participants by implying that trustworthy behaviour is not important, not common, and not expected." Fortunately, most corporate law does not allow such contracting out. As Blair and Stout note: The phenomenon of trust behaviour suggests that fiduciary relationships are created by the law in situations in which it is efficient or otherwise desirable to promote other-regarding, trusting and trustworthy behaviour. Moreover, the key to a successful fiduciary relationship lies in framing both economic and social conditions so as to encourage the fiduciary to make a psychological commitment to further her beneficiary's welfare rather than her own. For example, by making directors and officers who violate their duty of loyalty to the firm liable for damages, the law encourages trustworthy behaviour in corporate fiduciaries by reducing the expected gains from malfeasance (thus reducing the fiduciary's cost of behaving trustworthily).

At the same time, case law on the duty of loyalty unambiguously signals that the fiduciary relationship is a social situation that calls for other-regarding behaviour, to the point where the fiduciary is discouraged from even thinking about her own interest through a prophylactic rule that bans unauthorized personal gains even in circumstances in which the fiduciary could arrange this without harm to her beneficiary. Similarly, the sermonizing tone typically adopted by courts in fiduciary cases reinforces the social message that other-regarding behaviour is demanded.

By setting up a system where shareholders believe they can trust managers given the social norms (formed in part by the law) and the legal liabilities (established by the law), investors do not have to expend substantial time, effort, and money to investigate whether their managers do or do not purport to act in the investors' best interests, avoiding an "information externality" created if contracting out of the fiduciary relationship is permitted.

The agency problem is composed not just of intentional wrongdoing by managers. Behavioural considerations highlight numerous other pitfalls that make corporate law extremely helpful for disciplining managers, compensating investors, and encouraging investment. Consider the subject of executive compensation. Because of the self-serving bias and general overconfidence, officers tend to think that they are worth what they are being paid, especially because the high compensation that other officers were receiving indicated through the conformity bias that this was the appropriate standard and because reference-dependent utility made the matter important to the managers. Numerous abuses have ensued, in part because incentive compensation was largely untethered from actual firm performance. Stock option grants tend to be timed to precede favorable firm-specific news announcements, allowing company executives to profit arguably unfairly. Stock options that were under water because of poor performance were often repriced. At the highest levels, CEO compensation alone absorbed most corporate profits at some companies that were doing comparatively well.

Because of the same Behavioural considerations, such as the conformity bias and undue optimism affecting the judgments of directors, current corporate law rules were insufficient to prevent tremendous abuses. However, in the absence of fiduciary duties, the situation would likely have been many times worse. One of the Sarbanes-Oxley Act's corporate governance provisions requires officers and directors of companies that have to restate their earnings (323 public companies in 2003) to forfeit their stock profits and bonuses gained on the basis of the bogus numbers. Before this provision, often companies would announce record profits, the officers would pocket record bonuses, the companies would later restate their financials, but the officers would retain the unearned bonuses. Sarbanes-Oxley's forfeiture provision changes that situation.

When contemplating why 300 companies a year are restating their financial statements, again consider the possibility that not all are blatant frauds. Because of the Behavioural factors noted above, it is possible that the top brass of companies often times really believe (or talk themselves into believing) that their firms are doing well.

Professor Langevoort used Behavioural analysis to suggest that in organizations, optimistic, self-confident, "can-do" people tend to be promoted and that people prefer to send good news up the corporate ladder over bad news. When biased information is fed to unduly optimistic, overconfident managers who suffer from the illusion of control, they often end up misperceiving risks and harboring unrealistically optimistic views about their company's status and prospectus. The self-serving bias also helps these officers to see what they wish to see, especially if they have previously committed to a particular course of action. Sunk cost effects and cognitive dissonance can make it particularly difficult to change course. All of these are difficult biases to overcome, but Sarbanes-Oxley's section 404 provision for internal controls could help. It is a corporate governance provision aimed primarily at improving the odds that full and accurate information relating to the financial situation of the company will rise to the top of the corporate chain of command. Perfection will never be achieved, but a corporate governance provision such as this, coupled with the fiduciary duties imposed upon officers and directors, should improve the quality of corporate decision-making over what would occur in their absence.

The most difficult aspect in all of this is striking the proper balance. Managers must be constrained and monitored to ensure that they are working in the best interests of shareholders. At the same time, if monitoring is excessive, managers cannot work efficiently. Economists Easterbrook and Fischel propose an efficiency rationale for the business judgment rule—the courts' refusal (with rare exception) to second-guess the decisions of a company's managers unless there exists a conflict of interest. There is a Behavioural reason as well—the hindsight bias. Courts realize that not only are they not business experts, but they should not impose liability upon managers for merely careless decisions based on second-guessing those managers with the benefitof 20–20 hindsight.

CORPORATE LAW

Although the first semi-comprehensive corporate codes date back less than two hundred years, the roots of business organizations can be traced back at least to Mesopotamia in 3000 BC. Ancient Phoenicians and Athenians developed early forms of partnership. In medieval times, shipping businesses aggregated capital and distributed shares in a form closely resembling modern partnerships. Although some trace the origin of corporations to the ancient Greeks, Blackstone concluded long ago that the honour of inventing companies belonged to the Romans, for they devised the notion of a corporation having an identity separate and apart from that of its owners and the concept of limited liability.

The development of the corporation was critically important. Around 1000 AD both the Chinese and the Arabs had important trading and commercial advantages over the West, but many suggest that because their legal systems were not conducive to developing companies, they lost the commercial advantage that they enjoyed. Rather, in the twelfth century in Venice and Florence, in the sixteenth century in England and soon thereafter in France, in the early seventeenth century in Holland, and in the late 1700s in America, the modern legal notion of a corporation began to evolve and flourish, sparking economic development that outstripped that of nations without the legal structures to create such entities.

These proto-corporations initially took two basic forms. One was the unincorporated joint-stock company that slowly evolved to contain more and more corporate-like features and to resemble less and less the partnership form. The other was the specially-chartered corporation that was often privately financed but featured government participation and was often a government-sheltered monopoly. In the late 1700s and early 1800s in England, France, and America, such special charters were often granted to corporations formed for public works projects that governments did not wish to undertake via tax revenues, such as canals and roads.

Until the nineteenth century, governments in these nations required promoters to receive special government permission for their enterprises to assume the corporate form. During the 1800s, however, today's developed nations gradually began allowing free registration of corporations that met given criteria rather than requiring promoters to secure governmental permission for each charter. France was one of the first nations to do so, but then changed course with its Code de Commerce in 1807 and went back to requiring special legislative concession. When England began allowing free registration (first without limited liability in 1844 and then with limited liability in 1855), France was forced to follow (in 1867) because of French resources migrating to England and increased activity of English companies on the continent. Germany then followed suit in 1870. Meanwhile, beginning in the 1830s a substantial shift among American states to free registration began.

Provisions dispensing with the requirement of special legislative act as a prerequisite for forming a corporation were often part of broader corporate codes that addressed many issues necessarily raised by a proliferation of private business corporations. In the United States, New York passed one of the first broad state corporate statutes in 1811. England, which had a fairly well-developed common law in the area, did not begin its codification process until 1844. In Prussia, a corporate law was enacted in 1843. With the creation of these codes, both the specially-chartered corporation and the unincorporated joint-stock company faded away to be replaced by a corporate form that quickly evolved to contain modern features.

The speed of the evolution varied from country to country and was not always steady, but most developed European and North American nations moved slowly at first, then quickly during the late nineteenth century, toward promoting and enabling corporate entities sporting these key features:

(a) separateness of identity,

(b) perpetuity of existence,

(c) limited liability,

(d) centralized control,

(e) fiduciary duties for managers,

(f) protection for minority shareholders, and

(g) the ability to amass "bonded capital."

The importance of these modern companies for economic development cannot be gainsaid. Corporations increase the pool of available capital, enable investors to spread risk, provide an avenue for effectively managing large organizational structures, and provide a strong incentive for organizations to be efficient by allowing investors to move their money elsewhere.

Nicholas Butler, a former president of Columbia University, concluded that "[t]he limited liability corporation is the greatest single discovery of modern times; even steam and electricity would be reduced to comparative impotence without it." The first enterprises requiring huge accumulations of capital—railroads—were universally formed as corporations, as are virtually all large enterprises today. Indeed, the corporation may be the most important of all the institutions that enable the modern market economy. Today, these engines of economic power produce 90 percent of the sales and receipts reported by

American businesses. Across the globe there appears to be a broad correlation between economic progress and the embracing of the corporate form. While some partnerships and even sole proprietorships have reached a large size and lasted for lengthy periods, it is the corporate form that has overwhelmingly accounted for the size and scope of modern enterprises. And it is modern corporate law that has facilitated and enabled those enterprises in a way that private contracting among individuals could never accomplish alone.

Separate Legal Identity

The most obvious contribution of corporate law to the creation of the modern corporate enterprise is simply that corporations cannot exist without legal sanction. Corporations are artificial creatures of the state. While theoretically people could contract for all of the relationships that make up a corporation, in reality such organizations simply do not exist in the absence of legal sanction beyond simple contract enforcement. As Peter Drucker has noted, "[t]his new 'corporation,' this new Société Anonyme, this new Aktiengesellschaft,... clearly was an innovation... It was the first autonomous institution in hundreds of years, the first to create a power center that was within society yet independent of the central government of the nation state."

In his 1937 article "The Nature of the Firm," Coase contended that the corporate form allows minimization of the transaction costs of coordinating economic activity and thereby provides a competitive advantage when compared to buyers and sellers making new contracts at every stage of production. More recently, Blair and Stout have made the same point, viewing the corporation as a mechanism for solving "team production problems" that in today's large modern enterprises are simply too complicated to handle via individual contracting alone.

The essence of the team production problem is that varied inputs from a number of individuals are needed, these inputs are difficult or impossible to monitor or specify contractually, and the output is a joint output, not readily divisible or attributable to individual inputs. These inputs and investments are often enterprise-specific, because their value, once they have been sunk into the enterprise, is tied to the overall success of the enterprise. The specificity, or "sunk" quality of the investments, increases the difficulty of writing simple contracts among individuals that could elicit and coordinate the use of such inputs. While it is possible for large organizations to be operated in the partnership form, as large accounting firms proved for a time, it was exceedingly rare for businesses to amass huge quantities of assets, to employ thousands of workers, or to take on truly large projects before the modern corporation began to evolve.

As noted, because of the very novelty of the corporate form, fear of great accumulations of assets, sovereign worry about loss of control, and even undue greed by government officials, for quite a time in most nations the law required a specific act of government to create a corporation. Placed in historical context, it is not surprising that governments imposed these requirements, but it is also clear that such requirements retarded corporate formation, presented opportunities for corruption when promoters were tempted to bribe government officials, and even enabled fraud by promoters who collected assets while promising to form a corporation that they knew the government would likely not approve.

The need for government approval also restrained economic development by sometimes requiring intrepid entrepreneurs to accomplish their goals through less satisfactory forms of business organization including partnerships and unincorporated joint-stock companies. For example, although England's "Bubble Act" of 1720 is typically referred to as one of the earliest securities regulations, its most significant provision made it illegal to sell shares in joint-stock companies that had not received Parliamentary permission to form. Until it was repealed in 1825, this Act may have inhibited evolution of the modern corporate form in England (although the Act did not apply to Scotland, and joint-stock companies did not flourish there either). Many believe that a turning point in American corporate development occurred with the post- Revolution formation of a strong federal government which made it clear that the Bubble Act no longer applied in America. Formation of corporations exploded thereafter in the former colonies. With the decision in Fletcher v. Peck that a legislative grant to a private company was a contract under the American Constitution's Contract Clause, and in Dartmouth College that a corporation's state charter was also a contract that could not be altered by the legislature unless the right to do so had been specifically reserved in the charter, the safe existence of the corporation relatively free from legislative interference was affirmed and capital flowed to corporations in amounts ensuring that they would be the preeminent vehicles for economic growth in America.

Only as the laws of England, France, Germany, and the United States (which have served as a model for the corporate laws of most other nations around the world) dispensed with the requirement of special governmental approval for corporate formation did the modern corporation begin to flower. Allowing large numbers of artificial corporate entities to enjoy corporate personhood, to own property, to sue in their own name, to (in America) enjoy substantial Constitutional rights, provided flexibility and continuity unmatched by other forms of business enterprise. Perpetuity

An important aspect of the new corporate form was the potential perpetuity of its existence. Sole proprietorships obviously ended with the death of their owner (although an heir or another might take up the burdens of the business). The default common law position was that partnerships also dissolved upon the death or other departure of any of the partners. Early joint-stock companies, such as those in England, often were formed for the purpose of collecting capital to stock a ship for trading in newly discovered lands. Typically, the merchants who chartered the ship with their pooled capital would have an accounting after each journey. The next trade mission would involve an entirely new enterprise. Thus, the notion of a truly long-term business enterprise was rare in private business ventures. The concept of perpetual existence of a corporate form may have evolved in ecclesiastical organizations as a way to enable churches to own property over time even as parishioners, priests, and others came and went. Obviously, such an ability could be useful to private business enterprises as well.

In 1623 the Dutch East India Company was granted the right of perpetuity. It collected capital to fund not just one voyage, but a potentially endless series of voyages. In 1654 the British East India Company followed suit. These entities paved the way for creation of large accumulations of capital that could be used to advance business endeavors over long periods of time. Owners could come and go. Managers could come and go. But the enterprise would continue, making binding commitments to employees, to suppliers, to customers, and to creditors of a character that sole proprietorships and partnerships could not make. The corporate form could more easily undertake long-term endeavours than any preexisting form of enterprise. And the corporate entity itself could establish a reputation in the economic community—separate and apart from that of its individual owners or managers—that would assist it in achieving commercial success. Simple contract law could never accomplish such progress.

Limited Liability

Many believe that corporate law's most significant contribution to the development of capitalism is limited liability. More than any other single concept, limited liability encourages people to invest in enterprises operated by strangers, enabling business enterprises to grow to substantial size and enjoy economies of scale, the benefits of perpetuity, and other advantages of size. In earlier times, sole proprietorships tended to employ family members and neighbors. Partnerships were necessarily small because partners needed to know much about the reliability of their fellow investors/partners for the simple reason that if other partners defaulted, then the personal liability of the nondefaulters could skyrocket. For many years, partners who were unable to pay their obligations faced debtors' prison or even the prospect of being sold into slavery. Such a state certainly discouraged any person from casting his economic lot with strangers. While it is perhaps theoretically possible for partnerships to contract for limited liability for their partners when negotiating contracts (just as it is possible for shareholders to contractually forfeit their limited liability as they often do in close corporations), in matters of tort law such is not possible. The owners of a company could not contract for limited liability with unknown and possibly unforeseeable victims of the tortious actions of their companies' managers and employees. The corporate form can provide such protection for liabilities in tort as well as contract, thereby facilitating investment because a shareholder's total potential liability is generally unaffected by the personal reliability or solvency of other shareholders. Limited liability solves an agency problem. Without it, shareholders would have to monitor much more closely and expensively their corporate managers.

Limited liability protects shareholders from liability, shifting the risk to the corporate entities' creditors who often are better equipped and more intensely motivated to monitor than shareholders of a corporation whose ownership is widely dispersed.

Limited liability was initially recognized for government-sponsored corporations, such as the Dutch East India Company. Slowly, it began to become a more common feature of private corporations, especially as general corporation statutes spread. Britain in 1855 formally recognized limited liability; Germany did so in 1861 and France in 1863. Over the course of the nineteenth century, limited liability became the default rule in American jurisdictions as well (although not in California until 1931).

Limited liability came in stages and was likely not as important to shareholders in the early 1800s as it later became, but virtually every relevant legislative change in the developed countries during the nineteenth century strengthened and broadened the shield of limited liability and thereby gave added incentive to the investment that is critical to economic development. Limited liability is arguably a near prerequisite for broad investor participation in company ownership. With the advent of modern tort liability for on-the-job injuries, for automobile crashes, and for product defects, limited liability has become so important that even the law governing small entities stresses its importance. In America in recent years state legislatures have created all manner of new organizational forms (limited liability partnerships, limited liability companies, and limited liability limited partnerships, for example) to provide limited liability for almost all entrepreneurs.

Centralized Control by Managers

The separate corporate entity, the perpetuity of existence, and the limited liability of investors all led to a formal separation of ownership from control in larger corporations. Although partners in a partnership can hire managers to operate the business for them and thereby evade the default rule that important decisions require the majority vote of all partners, this typically is not the practice. And it would be very difficult in the partnership form to do this in an enterprise for a lengthy period of time. Before the corporate form blossomed among private business enterprises, they tended to be small and often family-managed.

The corporate form with its perpetual existence, however, facilitates delegation of control and, indeed, creates a presumption in a firm of any size that such delegation will occur. The Dutch East India Company was one of the first to formalize and take advantage of this separation by creating a layer of professional managers separate and apart from the firm's investors. Providing monitoring by a board of directors, this structure commits to the discretion of managers the day-to-day decisions necessary for operation of the business. Managers not only make the daily decisions necessary to operate the firm, they initiate the long-term strategies that are monitored by the board and the organic changes that must be approved by both directors and shareholders.

It was the development of the corporate form in private business enterprises that created a framework wherein despite the coming and going of owners, of specific managers, of rafts of employees, of assets in various forms, a team of professional managers can continue to coordinate the enterprise using the principles of Chandler, Sloan, Deming, Drucker, Porter, and others (primarily Americans). Utilization of the corporate form promoted the development of hierarchical management structures that led, in turn, to the creation of a class of middle managers and technical specialists who could have long careers with their employers. It also facilitated the creation of brands for both corporate entities and their products. America was quicker to adopt professional managers than England, and it made a difference in economic development. Hiring the best managers available rather than the best family members available, as was the British custom for so long, facilitates efficient operation of modern economic enterprises. France also suffered under a family-dominated approach, leading to a general weakness of its capital markets. Only after World War II did France produce large, vertically-integrated companies capable of making use of sophisticated management techniques.

Fiduciary Duty of Managers

Separation of ownership from control, though creating some obvious advantages, also creates a potential agency problem. According to Adam Smith, an agent watching over someone else's assets would never be as careful as a principal guarding his own. More than a hundred years after Smith, Berle and Means famously echoed this concern about the problems stemming from a division between ownership and control. Again, theoretically it would be possible for investors to contract for a proper level of protection from the potential misdeeds of corporate managers and employees. In real life, especially given the Behavioural considerations outline, it is exceedingly difficult to truly manage this problem contractually.

Modern corporate law has evolved to address this problem in at least two fundamental ways. First, it sets up a system of monitoring. In America, for example, shareholders have the right to vote and therefore to have direct input into how their assets are being used. They may typically vote regarding important corporate matters such as mergers and liquidations. They may also vote for directors who will monitor the managers who run the company day-to-day, thus giving them indirect input into broad policy decisions as well.

Similar monitoring systems have evolved in other nations as well. UK corporations have long had a board of directors that operated in similar fashion to those in America and as early as 1862 provided for modest independent monitoring of public companies by a government agency. Since 1870, Germany has required a supervisory or first-tier board (Aufsichtsrat) that has acted much as an American board of directors, choosing and broadly supervising managers. Today, in the Aktiengesellschaften (AG), the corporations most comparable to American public companies, the Aufsichtsrat usually contains representatives of powerful German banks, as well as labor representatives. The supervising board has substantial paper authority to choose the members of and supervise and investigate the second-tier or "managing" board (Vorstand) that is composed substantially of company insiders.

In reality, the Aufsichtsrat's exercise of authority is often not impressive. It frequently has trouble getting the information required for effective monitoring, and under law its members need meet no more than twice a year. The monitoring role of the powerful German banks is significant, but tends to protect creditors more than shareholders. There is some evidence that German citizens are less willing to invest in corporations than Americans because the boards do not view their primary goal as protecting the interests of shareholders. Recently there have been many suggestions by German scholars that German practice migrate more toward an Anglo-Saxon model of corporate governance and there has been movement toward that model.

France introduced supervision of managers via commissaries in 1863. They came to be charged with a wide range of responsibilities, including ensuring the accuracy of information supplied to shareholders, ensuring equal treatment of shareholders, and notifying shareholders of "irregularities." On the whole, however, directors in France have often been disappointing monitors, in large part because of a lack of independence. As with Germany, most scholars have recommended a move toward the Anglo-American model and France has taken steps in that direction.

For both economic reasons (diversified shareholders have no strong reason to pay attention to the performance of any particular company, given the associated costs) and Behavioural reasons (investors have a tendency to overtrust their directors), shareholders usually do not pay sufficient attention to either their decisions regarding which directors to vote for or the job those directors and the managers they monitor are doing. Similarly, officers have traditionally had substantial influence in selecting the directors who would monitor them, thus substantially undermining the efficacy of that monitoring.

Therefore, the second thing that corporation law does, more so in common law jurisdictions, that cannot be effectively done contractually, is to impose fiduciary duties upon officers and directors. These duties not only impose legal responsibilities upon the officers and directors, but also create a model, a norm for directors. In America, this fiduciary duty generally cannot be contractually escaped. As the Enron and related scandals demonstrated at the beginning of the current century, these provisions certainly do not work perfectly, but they are better than a mere contractual alternative and improvements continue. The continuing struggle involves the need to create effective monitoring by the directors on the one hand, but to avoid unduly hamstringing managers' decision-making on the other.

Early on, common law judges imposed a fiduciary duty on officers and directors, while civil law nations allowed more freedom of contract for fiduciary responsibilities. In broad outline it is fair to say that investors fare better in America and the United Kingdom, where managers owe their primary fiduciary duty to shareholders, than in France and Germany where equal loyalty is owed to creditors and employees. Germany has recognized the rudiments of a fiduciary duty, but lacks an efficient enforcement mechanism.

Admittedly, the role of the directors as protectors of shareholders is not as critical in jurisdictions such as Germany and Japan, where financial institutions provide more of the financing and play a bigger role as intermediary and monitor of corporate management. Until recently, state ownership and control of private enterprise was a central phenomenon of the French economy, so government monitoring of corporations played an important role. That is now fading away substantially, making board-style monitoring and attendant fiduciary duties more important.

Even in America's common law system, the law tends to draw a stark distinction between a breach of the duty of loyalty and a breach of the duty of care, being much more reluctant to impose liability upon directors, especially outside directors, in the latter case. Indeed, around the world it seems rare for liability to be imposed upon outside directors for anything other than clear breaches of the duty of loyalty. Whatever the faults of the Anglo-American system exposed by the Enron scandals, the clear trend around the world is toward models that promise better and more independent board monitoring and increased fiduciary duties imposed by law. The historical experience of the past two hundred years is not leading any nation to conclude that less vigorous board monitoring and less rigorous fiduciary obligations are a good idea.

Protection of Minority Shareholders

Just as passive shareholders can be exploited by those who manage their assets, minority shareholders can be exploited by controlling shareholders. This possibility, of course, discourages investment. So, over time, corporate laws have been developed to protect minority shareholders from such exploitation. As corporate law evolved in this area, there remained a continuing tension between the need to protect minority shareholders from exploitation by majority shareholders on the one hand, and the need to avoid giving minority shareholders an undue ability to "hold up" the company when a transaction beneficial to the corporate enterprise but perhaps detrimental to a minority shareholder was at stake.

Consider the right to vote on major organic changes in corporate form mentioned in the previous section. Under most modern corporate codes shareholders have the right of "voice" (to vote on major transactions) and "exit" (to have their shares purchased should a major corporate change with which they disagree occur). But all modern legal regimes struggle with striking the proper balance between protecting minority shareholder factions from abuse and awarding them the power to shakedown the majority in such transactions. Regarding a merger, certainly shareholders should have the right to vote. But should majority approval be sufficient? Would a supermajority provision allow minority shareholders undue power to block the majority's wishes? The trend in America has been to do what Delaware did in 1929 and reduce the merger approval requirement to a simple majority. Until relatively recently, in France the right to vote seemed to be used more to regulate relationships between management and the largest shareholders. However, in the last 15 years or so, France's regulations have evolved to more generally resemble American rules that protect capital market investors more fully by, in part, giving them the right to vote on important matters of corporate change, such as mergers.

Another protection for minority shareholders is appraisal rights—the right to have their shares bought at a court-determined fair price if they oppose a major organic change. Of course, if too many shareholders exercise their appraisal rights, the organic change often becomes infeasible even if supported by a large majority of shareholders. Does this allow minority shareholders to hold up the company? American shareholders who oppose a merger but are outvoted generally have the right to demand that their shares be purchased at a fairly appraised price. The expense of actually pursuing these appraisal rights may render them somewhat hollow, minimizing the likelihood of holdup.

Another mechanism for minority protection is inspection rights. The common law of England recognized shareholders' rights to access corporate books and records in the early 1700s. At first, the right stemmed from the fact that the corporation was viewed as a trustee holding property for the benefit of stockholders. Later, the view was that shareholders needed the inspection right in order to protect their property interests.

Throughout the 1800s, as corporations grew in size, statutes were enacted in England and America to supplement the common law inspection right. Generally, shareholders in common law nations have the right to inspect relevant corporate records at a proper time, in a proper place, for a proper purpose. On paper, French shareholders have substantial inspection rights but, as elsewhere, these rights benefit mostly shareholders in closely held corporations and major shareholders of public corporations. The situation is comparable in Japan where inspection rights on paper are roughly analogous to those accorded shareholders in the United States, but shareholders have difficulty enforcing those rights in court.

The right to sue derivatively on behalf of the corporation is another means of protecting minority shareholders. This right to sue has been recognized in America for 120 years, and despite procedural obstacles, remains a potent weapon for shareholders. The United Kingdom, on the other hand, does not have a strong derivative right for shareholders. Nor does Germany, which relied more on its supervisory boards to protect the interests of minority shareholders. France has procedures that are in some respects even more pro-plaintiff than those in the United States, but they are typically not used much, in part because shareholders must own a substantial block of stock to be able to sue. Whether because of these problems or a lack of litigious culture or absence of an active plaintiffs' bar, there have been relatively few such suits. The derivative suit was rarely used in Japan until some 1993 legal reforms; it is used more now, but the Japanese system, like Germany's, still relies substantially upon monitoring by companies' "main banks." Such lawsuits have been brought so seldom that directors and officers (D&O) insurance was not even offered in Japan until 1994, and then it was introduced to respond to lawsuit exposure overseas.

In general, common law nations appear to provide more protection to minority shareholders than do civil law nations (particularly those in the French tradition), and there is recent empirical support for the notion that these protections aid investment, encourage ownership dispersion, facilitate capital markets, and allow companies to access external finance more easily. In Germany, Belgium, Holland, and elsewhere, it is common to have employee voice in manager supervision. Although no major changes are likely in the immediate future, many scholars and businesspeople even in those nations seem to believe that to improve capital markets, protections for shareholders will likely have to be strengthened relative to the interests of workers and creditors.

Bonding Assets

Importantly, the corporate form enables a commitment of resources to a venture that no earlier form of organization provided. By partitioning the assets of the separate corporate entity from the individual assets of its owners, the corporate form ensures not only that owners will enjoy limited liability for corporate debts, but also that assets committed by the shareholders to the corporate purpose cannot easily be reached (a) by the creditors or heirs of individual shareholders or managers, or (b) by those shareholders and managers themselves. These assets are to remain devoted to the corporate purpose.

They become "bonded" to the corporate enterprise, theoretically in perpetuity, although that is not truly required to make it easier to entice investment from others and to borrow money from banks and to purchase on credit from suppliers. These two results could not be achieved contractually in the absence of corporate law because a business's owners cannot by contractual arrangements among themselves bind their individual creditors.

Partnership law and the law of other forms of business organization that predated the company gave investors substantial leeway to remove their investment, even if the business's affairs were substantially disrupted. This ability not only disrupted the partnership's business, it also enabled one partner to hold up the others. Even a partner's death or mental disability traditionally dissolved the enterprise. But corporate law commits capital so that it cannot be easily withdrawn. Over the course of the twentieth century in America, repeated changes in the law aimed at tightening this connection, which was recognized as early as 1824 in Wood v. Dummer where Judge Story explicated the "trust fund" doctrine.

Corporate law works comparably in other nations, facilitating large accumulations of capital that can be held in place for long periods of time and applied by professional managers. By providing limited liability and protecting investors from exploitation by managers and majority shareholders, the corporate form should also encourage investment.

ECONOMICS OF CORPORATE LAW

The rationale for corporate law is very similar to that for the basic foundational contract law. The corporate context is somewhat different, however, as is the governing law. The principal concern of corporate law is that the corporate officers and directors act in the interest of the shareholders, as their agents. While the officers and directors have contracts, mere contract law has some limitations here. A company's shareholders may represent an enormous number of individuals, with varying amounts at stake, rather than one single individual. The shareholders with a diversified portfolio may have invested in many different corporations, another circumstance which increases the costs of monitoring.

Shareholders do not directly enter the contracts with the officers and directors, the contract of one officer agent is typically drafted by other shareholder agents, the directors, and the shareholder chooses to invest, at best with knowledge of the contract terms but relatively little control over them. Monitoring for opportunism is also more difficult in the corporate governance context. Some suggest that monitoring problems are lessened in the corporate context, due to the presence of large professional investors with the ability to conduct such monitoring. While these parties may indeed have both the resources and expertise to monitor corporate managers, their monitoring has the same high transaction costs, especially with a diversified portfolio. Moreover, even professional investor monitoring is beset by Behavioural shortcomings.

Posner does not discuss corporate law in great detail but is generally positive about its values, explaining that it "reduces The economics of the law and corporate finance transaction costs by implying in every charter the normal rights that a shareholder could be expected to insist on." The rationale for many of the rules of corporate law is thus similar to a central rationale for contract law, in restraining opportunism. Corporate managers doubtless have greater opportunities for at least discreet opportunism at the expense of shareholders than do parties to a contract. The one-sided Prisoner's Dilemma analysis applies, perhaps with greater force, in this context, yet this is not fully appreciated. Easterbrook and Fischel, for example, embrace contractual relations but doubt the reality of managerial opportunism, suggesting that managers "may do their best to take advantage of their investors, but they find that the dynamics of the market drive them to act as if they had investors' interests at heart." This is simply the repeat play argument in the context of the one-sided Prisoner's Dilemma, and the claim suffers all the same shortcomings of the repeat play argument in contract. Given the greater monitoring difficulties in the corporate context, the deficiencies of the claim are even greater than they are for contract law and the agency problems may thus require a supplementation of contract law with corporate law.

Managerial opportunism may take the form of drafting contracts that permit managers to take advantage of shareholders, who suffer considerable transaction costs in monitoring this behaviour. Officers' adoption of corporate poison pills to fend off acquisitions and entrench themselves in office is one obvious example of this sort of opportunistic behaviour. The threat of such opportunism should not be minimized. A McKinsey study of Asian companies found that 76 percent of investors worried more about governance than they did about financial issues. It is too simplistic to rely on managerial self-interest to constrain managerial opportunism.

The value of the mandatory rules provided by corporate law derives from the reduction in transaction costs in monitoring the threat of managerial opportunism. When discussing the reason for providing corporations with limited liability, Easterbrook and Fischel write: First, limited liability decreases the need to monitor agents. To protect themselves, investors could monitor their agents more closely. The more risk they bear, the more they will monitor. But beyond a point extra monitoring is not worth the cost. Moreover, specialized risk bearing implies that many investors will have diversified holdings.

Only a portion of their wealth will be invested in one firm. These diversified investors have neither the expertise nor the incentive to monitor the actions of specialized agents. Limited liability makes diversification and passivity a more rational strategy and so potentially reduces the cost of operating the corporation. This rationale applies well to other mandatory corporate rules, such as those requiring and elaborating the fiduciary duties of officers and directors. Limited liability reduces the magnitude of investor risk, but investors may still suffer great losses from corporate opportunism, as in the case of Enron. A legal rule can enhance efficiency by reducing the need for investors to engage in costly and continuous monitoring of their managerial agents' actions.

There are valid arguments about the costs associated with compulsory corporate rules. Rule enforcement inevitably has its costs. Different entities have differences in their basic businesses and in the identities of their owners and managers and therefore may have different optimal governance arrangements. Forcing certain commonalities upon these entities means foregoing optimality, in at least some circumstances.

But this added cost of uniform legal rules only exists if one presumes that the owners and managers of these entities would find and adopt the optimal governance rules, in the absence of the law, a presumption that is not self-evident in light of the agency problems of the firm. Merely identifying the rules could involve considerable transaction cost that is avoided by the legal structure. The economic value of compulsory corporate rules will depend on the extent of the agency problems in a purely private ordering, transaction costs, and on the quality of the rules themselves, not some a priori abstract analysis of a perfectly functioning world without any agency and transaction cost problems.

The development of corporate law has reflected recognition of this tradeoff between the risks of opportunism and the costs of legal intervention into corporate decisionmaking. The widely adopted "business judgment rule" gives great deference to the decisions of corporate officers and directors. It dictates that courts will not intervene in corporate decision- making when a plaintiff alleges a breach of the agent's duty of care, unless the breach appears especially egregious. This rule recognizes the costs of legal second-guessing, balanced against the risk of agent misbehavior.

The true dangers of opportunism lie not in breaching the duty of care, however. The duty of loyalty is the fiduciary duty at issue in the typical case of opportunism, with agents profiting at the expense of their principals. If the entire board has a conflict of interest, or is dominated by an individual with a conflict of interest, the court will give much stricter scrutiny to the corporate decision. The law thus strikes a balance between the value of controlling opportunism and the costs of excessive oversight. Of course, the optimality of this balance is debatable and some have suggested that corporate law fails because it is too deferential to free management choice.

The private voluntary choice of firms to adopt the corporate form provides something of a natural experiment that demonstrates the efficiency of the balance struck by corporate law. The law offers limited liability options for investors, other than the corporation. Limited partnerships and limited liability companies (LLCs) both provide such limited liability. These alternative forms have their own state enabling laws that are typically less restrictive than is corporate law. Consequently, they offer greater opportunity for arranging governance contractually, rather than by law. If such private contractual governance were more efficient, one might expect investors to flood to these alternative limited liability entities. And while LLCs and other such entities have become increasingly popular for small business organizations, corporations retain their preeminent role among large business enterprises.

Another criticism of restrictive corporate laws lies in claims of inefficiency arising from the laws' ineffectiveness. Easterbrook and Fischel argue that the general availability of private contractual ordering means that managerial opportunism is like a balloon that, when constricted in one place, merely expands in another. They thus suggest that "if corporate law should forbid managers to divert corporate opportunities to themselves, they might respond by drawing higher salaries or working less hard to open up new business opportunities." At some level, this claim surely has truth. The law does not extinguish the incentives for opportunism, and corporate officers certainly have been known to take excessive salaries. However, the claim falls far short of invalidating restrictive corporate law, for two reasons. First, the two forms of opportunism are not exclusive, that is, a manager might both usurp corporate opportunities and take a higher salary, absent the legal restrictions. The law might therefore reduce opportunism to some degree by eliminating one channel. Second, different forms of opportunism present very different monitoring problems and associated transaction costs for shareholders.

The officer's cash salary is transparent and easy to monitor, whereas the officer's usurpation of corporate opportunities is more difficult for shareholders to observe and hence a more appropriate subject for legal deterrence. The corporate law sensibly restricts the latter opportunism more than the former, because salaries are relatively more amenable to control through private ordering. Prevailing standards of corporate law do not fully displace private ordering; Delaware law is empowering in many cases and, when restrictive, can operate to help overcome market inefficiencies in controlling managerial opportunism.

Corporate law can also play an important clarifying function for business relationships, as in the case of contract formalization. An agent automatically assumes some fiduciary responsibility to the principal, but the precise nature of the relationship may be obscure, absent the defined standards of corporate law. A fiduciary has some duty to disclose facts to shareholders but the reach of the duty may be uncertain. A fiduciary has a duty of loyalty, but whether that duty is breached at the margin may be uncertain. Even in an atmosphere of trust, a misunderstanding about the scope of these duties could prevent efficient investment decisions and interfere with the relationship between investors and managers. The law can facilitate this relationship by clarifying expectations.

Corporate law is not absolutely necessary for legal governance of the principal/agent relationship, as parties may contract the specific details of the relationship. This individual contracting, though, adds to transaction costs, as the parties hammer out the details of their relationship. The parties must decide the terms they desire and the extent to which they can compromise, which involves investigation into the need for particular protections and the appropriate language for those protections. Corporate law can reduce these transaction costs with established uniform rules. Default rules still permit the parties some choice to modify the legal standard, though mandatory rules cannot be evaded through contract. Perhaps a greater benefit of the corporate law is not the particular choice of language governing the relationship but the clarification of what that language means. Words are not determinate and parties can agree on words without agreeing on their meaning, and certainly without appreciating what a future court might deem to be the words' meaning.

The words of corporate law are not intrinsically clearer than those contained in a contract, and the potential scope of a general "fiduciary" duty is quite vague. However, the identical statutory language governs many transactions, so the meaning of these particular words becomes better understood over time. While not every provision of corporate law has been well-ventilated in court, the more significant provisions such as fiduciary duties have been extensively litigated over decades, and their dimensions are now relatively well understood.

This understanding provides the parties with understanding and certainty that would not be available under contract language that may never have been interpreted in court. Easterbrook and Fischel recognize some value to corporate law providing a set of terms "off-the-rack so that participants in corporate ventures can save the cost of contracting." While there are many private services that provide such "off-the-rack" contract terms, they cannot supply the interpretation of those terms, as can government courts. When "off-the-rack" terms are mandatory, they can offer still greater advantages in this regard, because investors need not beware opportunistic modification of those terms by self-interested managers.

A remarkable practice is the fact that public corporations very rarely use the legally allowed freedom to draft certificates that are different from the default terms provided by state law. This is a private ordering deference to state choice, which seems unusual. The fact represents a market check indicating that either the state will adopt better corporate procedures than will the corporation itself (perhaps due to agency problems) or that the network effects of belonging to a uniform corporate law system exceed whatever benefits might be achieved by marginally more optimal corporate governance rules.

The benefits of the clarification of understandings and consequent certainty associated with corporate law can be seen in the practice of the states. As already discussed, Delaware is by far the most common situs of corporations, which are governed by the law of that state. Still, many companies, especially smaller ones, are incorporated in their home states. When those states have corporate law controversies, they commonly refer to and sometimes automatically defer to the law of Delaware. They resolve disputes as they determine that Delaware would. This interstate deference is much more common in corporate law than in other fields of law, because the Delaware courts are considered expert and reliable, Delaware's law is well developed and clear, and because corporations value such clarity. The state of Delaware's law is surely imperfect, but its relative certainty offers an advantage to companies which may overcome any substantive imperfections. This advantage goes to the economic benefits associated with network externalities, discussed in greater detail in the section below on securities law.

Corporate law addresses the particular risks associated with opportunism by managers who control the investments of shareholders. By creating a legal regime to govern this opportunism, it has the merit of deterring the behaviour and averting the transaction costs that would otherwise be necessary for investors who sought to protect their investment. Corporate law also provides the added economic benefit of producing "off the- rack" contract terms and an effective, uniform system of enforcement of contracts, which also reduce the transaction costs associated with negotiating particular terms of an agreement.

11

Capital Market and the Trade Cycle

Our analysis of the nature of working capital, and of the demand for short-term funds, brought us to a number of conclusions. The original purpose of our investigation was to make it easier for us to make up our minds about the controversy "business credit versus stock exchange credit." For the present we shall deal with certain by-products of our analysis. These by-products are, in my opinion, relevant to several problems, but especially to the theory of the money market and of the trade cycle.

The supply of money capital on the money market is drawn from a number of different sources. One of There are them is transfer credit which may take various forms ere and may originate in various ways: it may come from fer credit, the short-term postponement of consumption, from long-term savings which are waiting for a suitable investment, from long-term savings whose owners are anxious to keep them in a form such that they car be withdrawn at any moment, from industrial capital which has been withdrawn from one line of production and is awaiting investment in another, from corporation profits which have not yet been distributed as dividends, from depreciation allowances which have not yet been reinvested, from the savings which became the proceeds of notations of bonds or shares awaiting gradual investment, &c. On the other side —created the banks provide a considerable amount of credit,— credit, that is purchasing power which has been created out of nothing, which means that nobody has given up the use of that buying power which is accruing to the borrower.

This type of credit is furnished in just the same forms as transfer credit, through discounting bills, call loans, various forms of advances, overdrafts, security purchases and so on. There is a third source of credit which is intermediate between these two sources, and which we discussed in the last —and credit chapter. This is credit which is granted out of liquid cash balanced surplus casn reserves, either with or without the agency which has the of the banks. So far as concerns the character of this the first but type of credit, its place in the monetary circulation the effects of and inflationary effects, it could be counted as the second *m* type "circulation credit" or created credit, but it has the peculiarity of bearing a deceptive resemblance to transfer credit, with the result not only that it is almost impossible to distinguish in practice but also that it has been fused together with short-term transfer credit in monetary theory.

It is this type of credit which gives rise to the much discussed seasonal easing and tightening of the money market, and has given the latter the stamp of being the unstable part of the credit market. George Halm, in his discussion of the problem of interest rates on the money market and the capital market, did not concern himself with created credit or with credit granted out of surplus cash balances, and, as he himself admits, this deprived him of the possibility of explaining "the important but difficult problems connected with the seasonal movement of interest rates on the money market."

What it also did, and this he failed to see, was to cause him to overlook the influences exerted by the money market on the course of the trade cycle; and all that he perceived therefore were the repercussions of the trade cycle on the money market. The seasonal and monthly movements on the money market are directly attributable to the practice of Credit from surplus cash lending surplus cash balances, i.e., to the utilization balances may of liquid funds. Credit which is newly created by the banks for accommodating commercial borrowers may be the money regarded for the most part as merely supplementing the loans made out of surplus cash balances: it will usually come into play either at periods when these balances are not available (due to seasonal requirements, end-of-the-month and quarterly payments, &c.) or when they have already been exhausted (due to the cyclical movement). Thus the unstable factor on the money market, both on the supply side and on the demand side, is the surplus funds of firms.

At those times of the year when commodity stocks are low, the cash balances of firms in a strong capital position flow onto the money market. Since at these times the demand for working capital on the part of firms in a weaker capital position is low, there is no immediate outlet for the increased supply of short-term credit. For reasons that have been explained above, the elasticity of demand for short-term credit, unlike that The elasticity for long-term credit, is small, and interest rates on short-term the money market consequently fall sharply. Since funds is there is practically no really "temporary" outlet for money capital that is only available for a short time, it is clear that there are no "short-term investments" available for all the cash balances that are offered on the loan market. One outlet for the large supply would be in the other interconnected credit market, viz., the capital market, the market for long-term credit. The method of converting "short money'-into "long money" which involves least risk for the person wishing to make the transfer, is as a rule provided by the security market. One might suppose that the low call rate would induce bears to "cover" their short sales, and that it would induce bulls to buy for the rise. Professional speculators are, however, more cautious than this. They know that the lowering of the call rate is only seasonal, and that this seasonal movement is a fact of common The monthly knowledge. It is therefore easy to see why the seasonal and seasonal oscillations of fluctuations m interest rates on the money market do market rates not cause seasonal fluctuations in security prices. For, are rot taken "if a seasonal variation in stock prices did exist, secuifties general knowledge of its existence would put an end markets. to it."

Thus the conversion of the seasonal supply of short-term money into investment money through the stock exchange loans will not take place on a large scale before the boom is under way. And the direct utilization of seasonal surpluses of cash for making temporary investments in securities is not attractive before the boom comes, owing to the cost of buying and selling. For these reasons the capital market, where the elasticity of demand for money capital is high, will not reflect (and absorb), the fluctuations in interest rates on the money market. If the entrepreneur were unable to find a borrower for his short-term surpluses of cash, and therefore had to resign himself to keeping the funds in his till or on his banking account, there would be no withdrawal of funds from the money market and no increased demand for short-money at certain periods when inventories are high, when the harvest is being moved and so on.

If, however, some event or change in psychology in conjunction with the low interest rates on the money market induce entrepreneurs to borrow some more short-term funds, the next date when heavy payments become due or the next time when stocks are being moved, will cause a tightening of the money market. Because the tendency towards tightness at these dates is eased by the banks through the creation Bank loans of additional credits, entrepreneurs do not feel any tightness of anxiety about providing for these heavy payments, the money market on and this has led to the lending and borrowing of critical "liquid" funds on the money market.

We might also say then that it is the creation of credit by the banks which is at the root of the fluctuations, because if the entrepreneurs were not confident of obtaining help from the banks in case of need, they would not lend their cash balances to the money market for fear of becoming illiquid. Thus, while temporary surpluses of cash are the element in the supply which is the direct source of the monthly and seasonal fluctuations in interest rates on the money market, a necessary condition of these movements is the existing banking system.

The apparent effect of the creation of credit by the banks is admittedly to mitigate the fluctuations on the money —they mitimarket, because bank credit fills the gap when the fluctuations entrepreneurs withdraw their funds. Without the of the rates,— elasticity of bank credit, which is regarded as being so beneficial in this case, the fluctuations would at first be wider: in fact the tightness of the money market at the critical payments dates would become really "critical." But bad experiences would soon lead entrepreneurs, for the sake of assuring their own liquidity, to refrain from lending out their temporary —but thereby surpluses of cash, and so the direct cause of fluctuations inform the on the money market would disappear. It is apparent, temporary therefore, that the invisible effect of the elasticity of balances bank credit is exactly the opposite of the visible effect: which cause the mitigating the fluctuations and easing the difficulties fluctuations arising out of them means enabling the fluctuations or their causes to arise. The classification of credits granted, out of surplus cash balances as a third type of credit, intermediate between transfer credit on the one side and credit created by the banks on the other, has a number of advantages.

Lending out of temporary surpluses of cash balances is in principle possible without the agency of the banks. As most people have become accustomed to think of credit creation as being due solely to the banks, credit granted out of surplus cash balances is treated as transfer credit, despite the fact that nobody refrains from buying, as this purchasing power is being transferred, and that this credit has just the same iDnationary effects as credit created by the banks. The fact that there can be inflationary credits which are not bank credit at all, may have an important bearing on the development of the theory of credit. A not inconsiderable number of students of the theory of banking, especially those who are connected with practical banking, still persist in arguing that the banks have no power to "create" inflationary credit, and deny even more emphatically that this bank credit has the place in the complex of causes of the trade cycle which is assigned to it in monetary theories of the trade cycle. Perhaps this opposition (to what is only a causal explanation but is often taken as an accusation of personal guilt) will decrease once it is realized that credit which is not granted by the banks at all may also have inflationary effects. The way in which surpluses of circulating capital can be interchanged between firms, even without the agency of the banks. No long argument is needed to prove that the possibilities of transferring these temporary surpluses of cash between firms are multiplied by the operations of banks acting as intermediaries. What is meant here is not the fact that the substitution of time deposits for circulating media may create increased lending facilities (although this works in the same direction), but the circumstance that the concentration of the supply of temporary surpluses of funds allows them to be utilized more fully. This applies particularly to those countries where the use of cheques is still so undeveloped that the possibilities of credit creation by the commercial banks are very small. The "inflationary" interchange of cash balances between firms remains, from the point of view of the banks, apparently a purely transfer operation, and can, of course, not be treated as the creation of new money. It is not possible in practice to identify a loan Neither the granted by a bank according to its origin.

The Tank can borrower can never know the source of the purchasing know power which he has been lent, and neither can the loan bank. It was originally believed that a bank could at Activates' least distinguish savings deposits from current or creates accounts, and could accordingly lend the funds 8 obtained by the former (time deposits) as transfer credit, and might be conscious of creating new credit on the basis of the funds obtained by the latter (demand deposits). Quite apart from the fact that at circulating media.

The credits which are not newly created by the banks, but only transferred through them, are not however all "pure" transfer-credit: this term properly applies only to funds deriving from new savings or newly disinvested capital, whereas the deposits of type represent what we have called temporary surplus cash balances. Thus, although the credits granted from these deposit funds are not created by the banks, but only transferred by them, they are nevertheless inflationary in their effect. The position may be summarized by the following classification: A monetary system which was intended to avoid any inflationary or deflationary move would have to ward off anything which involved any change in the supply of money—

including demand deposits—or any diminution in the demand to hold money on the part of individuals and firms.

The already existing volume of credit outstanding, which can no longer exert any kinetic effect on interest rates, would have to be maintained. (This view was put into practice almost a hundred years ago in Peel's Bank Act with its fixed balances, brings us to the conclusion that there are funds which do not differ in the least outwardly from credit deriving from the transfer of already existing purchasing power, but which nevertheless, if they are put to some "productive use," exert the same effect as credit newly created by the banks. Whether this additional supply of credit is utilized through the capital market or through the money market, whether the lenders follow strict rules about liquidity or not, whether they provide loans for stock exchange speculation or for the working capital of industry, a movement away from equilibrium in the economic system is made possible. Even the introduction of "certificates of origin" for deposits—which an ingenious But, alas, we believer in control might suggest—would not enable Identify the banks to keep track of the true nature of their nature of deposits.

It may seem a little surprising if we attempt to connect the same phenomena as were invoked in explanation of monthly and seasonal fluctuations on The monthly the money market with the theory of *cyclical* fluctua-an seasonalations. Nevertheless I think that it is not unreason-market fluctuations able to assume some such connexion. I am tar trompiay believing that it is possible to discover the "germ of " the trade cycle" in this phenomenon, but I do think trade cycle, that it is possible to show that credit granted out of surplus cash balances is closely connected with the beginning of the upswing. The "double utilization" of money capital which is made possible by lending from surplus cash balances, and the extension of roundabout methods of production to which such lending gives rise, would be doomed to a very short existence in the absence of other support: it could not survive the next date when heavy payments became due. What is a surplus balance at certain times is not at all "surplus" at other times, and if they have been put to some "productive use" in the meantime they are now *simultaneously* indispensable to both the lender and the borrower, or some third person to whom the funds may have passed. Whoever is forced to dispense with them has to go out of production, because he is no longer able to obtain the means of production. His exit from production paves the way towards re-establishing a state of equilibrium in the production structure. Disturbances of this kind are, however, still not *cyclical* movements. The movement away from the (theoretical) equilibrium in the upward direction lasts, as experience shows, for several years, and the movement back from the crisis through the depression to something near a new (theoretical) equilibrium again lasts several years.

The movement which has just been described lasted no longer than a season—or even a month—because the tendency towards an extension of production was brought to a swift end by the advent of the next payments date. But what happens if the payments at this date are facilitated, i.e., if the economic system is spared "unnecessary" difficulties, by short-term lending from the banks? The extra heavy demand for money lasts only a short time, and then the harmless credits, having performed their task, will flow back to the banks. There has been fairly general agreement in financial circles, and among students of banking policy, that the economic system ought to be helped over these payments dates, and no small part of the efforts towards working out a scientific monetary policy in the last one hundred and fifty years has been directed towards overcoming or easing the periodic stringency at certain dates when heavy payments fall due. Even the worst enemies of inflationism favoured such a policy. When the funds, which were temporarily "superfluous" and were therefore invested, are needed at the payments dates, the utilization of funds "twice over" is bound to be frustrated. If, however, new credit is created by the banks so as to help the economic system over the critical days, then the use of funds twice over in production can be continued. All that is necessary to enable the "upward" movement of the economic system towards disproportionality in production to continue for a longer period of time, is for the banking system to give assistance at certain times of strain. The payments dates might to a certain —which help extent be taken as indicators of the liquidity of the system or as a test of the adequate adjustment of tests on the capital supply and production structure. This test loses its meaning of course if bank credit provides the producers for the duration of the "inspection" with the necessary amounts of money capital. Since the maintenance of the expanded volume of The money production requires not merely the continued use of industrial the amount of credit once furnished, but the repeated expansion, x which in turn administration of further doses, the continuation of the upswing will Unison require increasing loans from surplus cash balances the money and will involve increasing stringency at the payments dates and increasing intervention from the side of bank credit to overcome it. It is clear, therefore, that the fluctuations in interest rates on the money market will soon become more marked than they had been previously.

What Halm took to be the mere *influence* of the trade cycle on the money market is, as I see it, the *reaction* of the cycle on the money market, after the latter has furnished the "motive power" to the cyclical movement. The further the use of money market credit has progressed or the more intensively credit is being used in production, the heavier and more urgent will be the demand for credit on the money market at the critical payments dates. Thus Halm is right in saying that "The real shortage of capital at the top of the boom is a shortage of short-term capital disposition." The mere intervention of bank lending at end-of the-month, quarterly, and other payments dates will of course not be sufficient to develop the upswing into a full-fledged boom. At a certain stage of the upswing it will be necessary for there to be a more vigorous and continuous expansion of bank credit in addition The start of to the loans from surplus cash balances and the occasional intervention of the banks at the payments dates. But lending out of surplus cash balances is sufficient through loans surplus to give the initial motive power for business recovery, balances seems to me a not unimportant fact that the startwithout bank., crediting point of the upswing is to be found not in an expansion of credit newly "produced" by the banks but in a "natural growth" of credit. A theory of the trade cycle which does not explain the continual recurrence of cycles as well as the course of the individual cycle cannot be entirely satisfactory. If we ascribe a role in trade-cycle causation to loans and disbursements out of surplus cash balances we must also try to analyse their role in causing the cycle to recur. The turning point in the cycle comes, as we know, not because there is an actual contraction of credit at that point, but when merely a brake is placed on the further expansion of credit. The volume of circulation media which was augmented by the expansion of bank credit need not fall back, in the depression, to the previous level; equilibrium might be established just as well at the higher level of the volume of circulating media with a potentially higher price level. This is what usually happens in the case where the credit inflation derives from increased gold production: a new equilibrium position is eventually found with a larger quantity of money than before. According to many theories of the trade cycle it is necessary for there to be a new inflationary move—a new inflation by the central bank or a new gold-inflation—before a new cycle can begin. The same would be true of cycles which are started off by loans from surplus cash balances where these loans are not of a periodic or seasonal character but are based on a sudden change in the technique of payments.

If as a result of a change in the habits of If dishoard payment (e.g., improvements in collections, and place only expansion of the clearing system) or in the division of functions in the business structure (e.g., an increase in vertical integration in an industry), the demand to hold cash balances declines, the cash surpluses will not be merely temporary surpluses but permanent ones. Such a rise in the "efficiency of money" or increase in the velocity of circulation does undoubtedly —it can contain the germ of a trade cycle, but the habit of holding reduced cash balances or the increased velocity not its of circulation will most likely become permanent parameters of the economic system. None of these "causes" of the trade cycle explains the periodic recurrence of the cycle (at least so far as endogenous factors are concerned) but it is a different matter with temporary surplus balances. These cash balances are superfluous at certain times and not superfluous at others. A rise in the velocity of circulation of money due to the lending out of these The temporary-balances need not be permanent.

After the crisis the firms are likely to hold again disltoarded at those balances which they need at certain moments in the start of the upswing, their own businesses and which are "superfluous" again when during other intervals. Whereas in the case of many the crisis is other factors in the trade cycle, the impetus which contributed to the upswing disappears with the conclusion of one cycle, this does not happen in the case of fluctuations in surplus cash holdings. Assuming that the loans and disbursements out of surplus balances together with bank credit served to finance the over-investment, then, when the depression comes and the undertakings which cannot be maintained are compelled to close down, the surplus cash balances will be set free again. As the process of liquidation progresses, the funds which were previously invested "twice" come back, and the general urge to sell out stocks and to defer all postponable purchases in the expectation of a further fall in prices makes it impossible to find a productive outlet for these free cash balances.

It is easy to see then why it is that in times of depression, during the "liquidation of the crisis" interest rates on the money market hover just above the zero level. It takes some time before the economic system gets the crisis and depression "out of its limbs." It is only after a certain lapse of time that the crippling feeling of uncertainty begins to wear off, and the risk estimates by potential lenders and borrowers gradually fall.

When finally confidence has returned and the —they are spirit of enterprise has reawakened, the firms which then free to nave accumulated large balances of cash during the other upturn, period of liquidation find that these liquid funds are superfluous and that there are outlets for them. As soon as the "surplus cash reserves" have found "productive employment" the economic system is moving into the upward phase of the cycle. The introduction of surplus balance credit into the analysis of the trade cycle supplements modern monetary theory in two respects, namely, in (1) that the start of the upswing can be explained without reference to an expansion of bank credit, and (2) that the upswing can be explained on the basis of an expansion of bank credit of a much smaller magnitude than was previously assumed. Both these circumstances go far to meet the favourite objections of those who still reject that theory of the trade cycle which stresses the expansion in the volume of money.

Mises emphasis on the interest rate policy of the banks as the primary cause Monetary of the cycle was attacked by both bankers and V Y theorists. Many people found it difficult to accept a inflation psychological factor on the side of bankers and monetary authorities as a satisfactory explanation of the periodic recurrence of cycles. Hayek was able, without abandoning the main lines of the theory of credit cycles, to show that the money rate of interest may be below the equilibrium rate not because of positive action on the part of the banks but because there is a rise in the natural rate of interest unaccompanied by any rise in the money rate. So, for example, technical progress, which creates increased investment opportunities and thus the natural rate of interest, may lead to increased borrowing from the banks. In this case of bank credit is not the result of active inflationism, as Mises considered it, but of passive inflationism. By a change m data m the economic system but without any action on the part of the banks, a money rate of interest which was previously in harmony with the equilibrium rate may become a rate that is conducive towards expansion. However, Hayek's theory still treats the financing of the upswing as being exclusively due to an expansion of credit by the banks.

REAL BUSINESS CYCLE THEORY

Real business cycle theory (or RBC theory) is a class of macroeconomic models in which business cycle fluctuations to a large extent can be accounted for by real (in contrast to nominal) shocks. (The four primary economic fluctuations are secular (trend), business cycle, seasonal, and random.) Unlike other leading theories of the business cycle, it sees recessions and periods of economic growth as the efficient response to exogenous changes in the real economic environment. That is, the level of national output necessarily maximizes *expected* utility, and government should therefore concentrate on the long-run structural policy changes and not intervene through discretionary fiscal or monetary policy designed to actively smooth economic short-term fluctuations.

According to RBC theory, business cycles are therefore "real" in that they do not represent a failure of markets to clear, but rather reflect the most efficient possible operation of the economy, given the structure of the economy. It differs in this way from other theories of the business cycle, like Keynesian economics and Monetarism, which see recessions as the failure of some market to clear. RBC theory is associated with freshwater economics (the Chicago school of economics, in the neoclassical tradition), and is rejected and harshly criticized by other schools within mainstream economics, notably Keynesians.

Business Cycles

If we were to take snapshots of an economy at different points in time, no two photos would look alike. This occurs for two reasons:

1. Many advanced economies exhibit sustained growth over time. That is, snapshots taken many years apart will most likely depict higher levels of economy activity in the later period
2. There exist seemingly random fluctuations around this growth trend. Thus given two snapshots in time, predicting the later with the earlier is nearly impossible.

A common way to observe such behaviour is by looking at a time series of an economy's output, more specifically gross national product (GNP). This is just the value of the goods and services produced by a country's businesses and workers.

While we see continuous growth of output, it is not a steady increase. There are times of faster growth and times of slower growth. A common method to obtain this trend is the Hodrick-Prescott filter. The basic idea is to find a balance between the extent to which general growth trend follows the cyclical movement (since long term growth rate is not likely to be perfectly constant) and how smooth it is. The HP filter identifies the longer term fluctuations as part of the growth trend while classifying the more jumpy fluctuations as part of the cyclical component. Observe the difference between this growth component and the jerkier data. Economists refer to these cyclical movements about the trend as business cycles. A point on this line indicates at that year, there is no deviation from the trend. All other points above and below the line imply deviations. By using log real GNP the distance between any point and the 0 line roughly equals the percentage deviation from the long run growth trend.

We call relatively large positive deviations (those above the 0 axis) peaks. We call relatively large negative deviations (those below the 0 axis) troughs. A series of positive deviations leading to peaks are booms and a series of negative deviations leading to troughs are recessions.

At a glance, the deviations just look like a string of waves bunched together—nothing about it appears consistent. To explain causes of such fluctuations may appear rather difficult given these irregularities. However, if we consider other macroeconomic variables, we will observe patterns in these irregularities. Observe how the peaks and troughs align at almost the same places and how the upturns and downturns coincide.

We might predict that other similar data may exhibit similar qualities. For example, (a) labour, hours worked (b) productivity, how effective firms use such capital or labour, (c) investment, amount of capital saved to help future endeavours, and (d) capital stock, value of machines, buildings and other equipment that help firms produce their goods.

Stylized Facts

By eyeballing the data, we can infer several regularities, sometimes called stylized facts. One is persistence. For example, if we take any point in the series above the trend, the probability the next period is still above the trend is very high. However, this persistence wears out over time. That is, economic activity in the short run is quite predictable but due to the irregular long-term nature of fluctuations, forecasting in the long run is much more difficult if not impossible. The magnitude of fluctuations in output and hours worked are nearly equal.

Consumption and productivity are similarly much smoother than output while investment fluctuates much more than output. Capital stock is the least volatile of the indicators.

Yet another regularity is the co-movement between output and the other macroeconomic variables. Procyclical variables have positive correlations since it usually increases during booms and decreases during recessions. Vice versa, a countercyclical variable associates with negative correlations. Acyclical, correlations close to zero, implies no systematic relationship to the business cycle. We find that productivity is slightly procyclical. This implies workers and capital are more productive when the economy is experiencing a boom. They aren't quite as productive when the economy is experiencing a slowdown. Similar explanations follow for consumption and investment, which are strongly procyclical. Labour is also procyclical while capital stock appears acyclical.

Observing these similarities yet seemingly non-deterministic fluctuations about trend, we come to the burning question of why any of this occurs. It's common sense that people prefer economic booms over recessions. It follows that if all people in the economy make optimal decisions, these fluctuations are caused by something outside the decision-making process. So the key question really is: *what main factor influences and subsequently changes the decisions of all actors in an economy?*

Real Business Cycle Theory

Economists have come up with many ideas to answer the above question. The one which currently dominates the academic Real Business Cycle Theory literature was introduced by Finn E. Kydland and Edward C. Prescott in their seminal 1982 work *Time to Build And Aggregate Fluctuations*. They envisioned this factor to be technological shocks i.e., random fluctuations in the productivity level that shifted the constant growth trend up or down. Examples of such shocks include innovations, bad weather, imported oil price increase, stricter environmental and safety regulations, etc. The general gist is that something occurs that directly changes the effectiveness of capital and/or labour. This in turn affects the decisions of workers and firms, who in turn change what they buy and produce and thus eventually affect output. RBC models predict time sequences of allocation for consumption, investment, etc. given these shocks.

But exactly how do these productivity shocks cause ups and downs in economic activity? Let's consider a good but temporary shock to productivity. This momentarily increases the effectiveness of workers and capital. Also consider a world where individuals produce goods they consume. The problem with this reasoning is that on aggregate level, this shock would average out.

Individuals face two types of trade offs. One is the consumption-investment decision. Since productivity is higher, people have more output to consume. An individual might choose to consume all of it today. But if he values future consumption, all that extra output might not be worth consuming in its entirety today. Instead, he may consume some but invest the rest in capital to enhance production in subsequent periods and thus increase future consumption. This explains why investment spending is more volatile than consumption. The life cycle hypothesis argues that households base their consumption decisions on expected lifetime income and so they prefer to "smooth" consumption over time. They will thus save (and invest) in periods of high income and defer consumption of this to periods of low income.

The other decision is the labour-leisure trade off. Higher productivity encourages substitution of current work for future work since workers will earn relatively more per hour today compared to tomorrow. More labour and less leisure results in higher output today greater consumption and investment today. On the other hand, there is an opposing effect: since workers are earning more, they may not want to work as much today and in future periods. However, given the pro-cyclical nature of labour, it seems that the above "substitution effect" dominates this "income effect".

Overall, the basic RBC model predicts that given a temporary shock, output, consumption, investment and labour all rise above their long-term trends and hence formulate into a positive deviation. Furthermore, since more investment means more capital is available for the future, a short-lived shock may have an impact in the future. That is, above-trend behaviour may persist for some time even after the shock disappears. This capital accumulation is often referred to as an internal "propagation mechanism" since it converts shocks without persistence into highly persistent shocks to output.

It is easy to see that a string of such productivity shocks will likely result in a boom. Similarly, recessions follow a string of bad shocks to the economy. If there were no shocks, the economy would just continue following the growth trend with no business cycles. Essentially this is how the basic RBC model qualitatively explains key business cycle regularities. The reason why this theory is so celebrated today is that using this methodology, the model closely mimics many business cycle properties. Yet current RBC models have not fully explained all behaviour and neoclassical economists are still searching for better variations.

It is important to note the main assumption in RBC theory is that individuals and firms respond optimally all the time. In other words, if the government came along and forced people to work more or less than they would have otherwise, it would most likely make people unhappy. It follows that business cycles exhibited in an economy are chosen in preference to no business cycles at all. This is not to say that people like to be in a recession. Slumps are preceded by an undesirable productivity shock which constrains the situation. But given these new constraints, people will still achieve the best outcomes possible and markets will react efficiently. So when there is a slump, people are choosing to be in that slump because given the situation, it is the best solution. This suggests laissez-faire (non-intervention) is the best policy of government towards the economy but given the abstract nature of the model, this has been debated. A precursor to RBC theory was developed by monetary economists Milton Friedman and Robert Lucas in the early 1970s. They envisioned the factor that influenced people's decisions to be misperception of wages—that booms/ recessions occurred when workers perceived wages higher/

lower than they really were. This meant they worked and consumed more/less than otherwise. In a world of perfect information, there would be no booms or recessions.

Calibration

Unlike estimation, which is usually used for the construction of economic models, calibration only returns to the drawing board to change the model in the face of overwhelming evidence against the model being correct; this inverts the burden of proof away from the builder of the model. Since RBC models explain data ex post, it is very difficult to falsify any one model that could be hypothesised to explain the data. RBC models are highly sample specific, leading some to believe that they have little or no predictive power.

Structural Variables

Crucial to RBC models, "plausible values" for structural variables such as the discount rate, and the rate of capital depreciation are used in the creation of simulated variable paths. These tend to be estimated from econometric studies, with 95% confidence intervals. If the full range of possible values for these variables is used, correlation coefficients between actual and simulated paths of economic variables can shift wildly, leading some to question how successful a model which only achieves a coefficient of 80% really is.

Criticism

Real Business Cycle Theory is a major point of contention within macroeconomics (Summers 1986): RBC theory categorically rejects Keynesian economics and real effectiveness of monetarism, which are the pillars of mainstream macroeconomic policy, while such noted mainstream economists as Larry Summers and Paul Krugman categorically reject RBC theory in turn: "(My view is that) real business cycle models of the type urged on us by [Ed] Prescott have nothing to do with the business cycle phenomena observed in the United States or other capitalist economies." –(Summers 1986)

It is a common misconception that Real Business Cycle theories are purely based on shocks to supply, as opposed to

Keynesian theories which are based on shocks to demand, and this leads to the common criticism of RBC theories as ignoring the demand side of the economy. However, technology-based theories of real business cycles also imply that consumers will change their intertemporal consumption and savings decisions based on the real interest rate available to them, which is a shift in demand. Other RBC theories based on preferences implicate the demand side to an even greater extent (Plosser, 1989). Intuitively, as a market-clearing model, RBC theories do not fall clearly into either a demand-side theory or a supply-side theory as Say's Law will hold in these theories and supply and demand will automatically move together.

By way of specific criticism of RBC theory as avanced by Prescott, (Summers 1986) lists four:

- Prescott uses incorrect parameters (one third of household time devoted to market activity rather than one sixth; historical real interest rates of 4% rather than 1%);
- absence of independent evidence for the technology shocks that supposedly cause the business cycle, and notably being unable to point to technological causes of observed recessions;
- Prescott's models ignore prices, and its predictions on asset prices are rejected by 100 years of data by Prescott's own work;
- Prescott ignores exchange failures (e.g., failures of factories to trade their goods for workers' labour), which are central to Keynesian accounts of the causes of the Great Depression, among other crises.

Instead, credit crunches, a *nominal* and *financial* cause, rather than the *real* causes proposed by RBC theory, are proposed as better explanations of the business cycle, notably according with observed recessions, as in the work of (Eckstein and Sinai, 1986).

Politically-based Business Cycle

Another set of models tries to derive the business cycle from political decisions. The partisan business cycle suggests that cycles result from the successive elections of administrations with different policy regimes. Regime A adopts expansionary policies, resulting in growth and inflation, but is voted out of office when inflation becomes unacceptably high.

The replacement, Regime B, adopts contractionary policies reducing inflation and growth, and the downwards swing of the cycle. It is voted out of office when unemployment is too high, being replaced by Party A.

The political business cycle is an alternative theory stating that when an administration of any hue is elected, it initially adopts a contractionary policy to reduce inflation and gain a reputation for economic competence. It then adopts an expansionary policy in the lead up to the next election, hoping to achieve simultaneously low inflation and unemployment on election day.

The political business cycle theory is strongly linked to the name of Micha[3] Kalecki who argued that no democratic government under capitalism would allow the persistence of full employment, so that recessions would be caused by *political* decisions. Persistent full employment would mean increasing workers' bargaining power to raise wages and to avoid doing unpaid labour, potentially hurting profitability. In recent years, proponents of the "electoral business cycle" theory have argued that incumbent politicians encourage prosperity before elections in order to ensure re-election—and make the citizens pay for it with recessions afterwards.

Marxist Economics

For Marx the economy based on production of commodities to be sold in the market is intrinsically prone to crisis. In the Marxian view profit is the major engine of the market economy, but business (capital) profitability has a tendency to fall that recurrently creates crises, in which mass unemployment occurs, businesses fail, remaining capital is centralized and concentrated and profitability is recovered. In the long run these crises tend to be more severe and the system will eventually fail. Some Marxist authors such as Rosa Luxemburg viewed the lack of purchasing power of workers as a cause of a tendency of supply to be larger than demand, creating crisis, in a model that has similarities with the Keynesian one. Indeed a number of modern authors have tried to combine Marx's and Keynes's views. Others have contrarily emphasized basic differences between the Marxian and the Keynesian perspective: while Keynes saw capitalism as a system worth maintaining and susceptible to efficient regulation, Marx viewed capitalism as a historically doomed system that cannot be put under societal control.

12

Monetary and Credit Development

Monetary management in 1995-96 was aimed at the twin objectives of reducing inflation and providing necessary credit support for production. The sharp upward trend visible in the growth of money supply in the second half of 1994-95 was reversed in 1995-96. The growth of money supply (M3), declined from 22.3 per cent on March 31, 1995 to 13.0 per cent at the end of 1995-96. It was therefore below the projected growth of 15.5 per cent for 1995-96. The growth of narrow money (M1) has been even lower at 10.9 per cent in 1995-96 as against 27.5 per cent in 1994-95 because of a very weak growth in demand deposits (3.7 per cent) in 1995-96. The modest growth in reserve money (14.8 per cent as against 22.1 per cent in 1994-95) explains this slower monetary expansion.

The unusually slow growth of monetary aggregates in 1995-96 was partly due to the unusually high base on March 31, 1995, resulting from the coincidence of the last reporting Friday for banks being on the final day of the accounting year. With liquidity conditions tightening in the third quarter of 1995-96, the Reserve Bank undertook a phased reduction of the Cash Reserve Ratio between November 1995 and January 1996, which injected more than Rs. 7000 crores of primary liquidity into the system and helped ease credit constraints. Deceleration of reserve money growth started in the second half of 1994-95 and has continued in 1995-96, mainly because of a progressive reduction in the rate of growth of net foreign exchange assets of RBI. The financial year 1995-96 ended with a little contraction (0.8 per cent) in net foreign exchange assets of RBI which offset in that year the expansion in net RBI credit to Government by 25.1 per cent.

As a result of rising commercial demand for credit on account of high tempo of industrial production the banks which had an excess holding of Government and other approved securities, contributed only Rs. 14766 crore tc the borrowing of the Government during 1995-96 as against Rs. 16323 crore in 1994-95. This necessitated sizeable support to market borrowing of the Government from RBI of which in turn increased the growth of net RBI credit to Government. Given the modest growth of Rs. 8485 crore in RBI credit to banks (including NABARD) the marginal contraction in net foreign exchange assets of RBI, the higher growth of RBI credit to the Government did not exacerbate the growth in reserve money.

The up trend in the bank credit to the commercial sector that started in the last quarter of 1994-95 with the recovery of industrial production, accelerated in 1995-96. Between March 31, 1995 and March 31, 1996 other bank credit to the commercial sector grew by 16 per cent (Rs.45654 crore) compared to a growth of 23.7 per cent (Rs.54804 crore) in the corresponding period of 1994-95 and large development of Government loans on RBI. Over the same two periods, scheduled commercial bank non-food credit grew by Rs. 43023 crore (1995-96) and Rs. 45775 crore (1994-95). The increase in non-food credit was larger than increase in credit to Government by the banks.

The agreement between the RBI and the Ministry of Finance to phase out ad-hoc borrowings was carried forward. The year end ceiling on borrowing from RBI against ad-hoc treasury bills was reduced from Rs. 6000 crore in 1994-95 to Rs. 5000 crore in 1995-96. The within year ceiling on such borrowing was retained at Rs. 9000 crore, to take care of the potential monthly mismatch between the revenue and capital inflows and the expenditure outflows. A sharp reduction in Government's market borrowing during the first half of the current financial year has been an important factor in increasing this mismatch. This raised Centre's borrowing against ad-hocs well above the intra-year ceiling. RBI took steps to bring these borrowings down by selling Central Government securities/ treasury bills in the market. Over the past five budgets the fiscal deficit of the Central Government has declined as proportion of GDP from 8.3 per cent in 1990-91 to 5.9 per cent of GDP in 1995-96 (RE). This 2.4 per cent reduction has been brought about by an even sharper 3.2 per cent reduction in the primary deficit. The primary deficit at1.1 per cent of GDP in 1995-96 (RE) is lower than it has been in decades.

Unfortunately, this reduction in the primary deficit has been partly offset by 0.8 percentage point increase in interest payments as a proportion of GDP. This, in turn, is a legacy of past fiscal deficits accumulated as debt and the rise in interest rates. Non-plan expenditures of the Central Government declined from 14.4 per cent of GDP in 1990-91 to 12.3 per cent in 1995-96 (RE), while Plan expenditures went from 5.3 per cent to 4.5 per cent over the same period. Central Government debt, which reached a peak of 69.7 per cent of GDP in 1993-94, declined to 64.2 per cent in 1995-96 (RE). Gross dissavings of the Central Government show a modest decline to 1.7 per cent of GDP in 1995-96 (BE), from 2.0 per cent in 1990-91. Reform of the tax system has been one of the key elements of the structural reforms undertaken since July 1991. The basic approach has been to move to a tax structure which is simple, relies on moderate tax rates with a wider base and better enforcement and serves the objectives of equity and efficiency. Substantial progress has been made in the last five years. The maximum marginal rate of personal income tax was reduced from 56 per cent (inclusive of 12 per cent surcharge) to 40 per cent.

The rates of corporate income tax (inclusive of 15 per cent surcharge), which were 51.75 per cent for publicly held companies and 57.5 per cent for closely held companies were unified and reduced to 46 per cent. On the indirect tax side reforms have covered both customs and excise.

Peak import duty rates which in several cases were around 300 per cent Prior to reforms, were brought down in a phased manner to 50 per cent to reduce the input cost for producers in India and promote competition. The import duty on capital goods for general projects and machinery, which was 85 per cent prior to reforms, was brought down to 25 per cent in 1995 and unified for nearly four-fifths of machinery imports at 25 per cent in 1995. The number of customs duty rates were sharply reduced to 12 and a large number of end-use exemptions were eliminated. The excise duty regime has been greatly improved with a significant switch over from specific to ad-valorem duties to ensure built in revenue elasticity. The ambit of MODVAT, entailing credit for taxes paid on inputs, was extended to cover capital goods, specified quality control, testing, pollution control and R&D equipment, petroleum products used in industry and spun yarn made from fibres.

The number of ad-valorem excise duty rates were reduced to 10 and a large number of end-use exemptions eliminated. These tax reforms have helped in restructuring the tax system by increasing the role of direct taxes and reducing that of customs duties. This will increase both the equity and efficiency of the tax system, as the former is regarded as more progressive and the latter as an efficiency-inducing tax. As a result of the reforms revenues from direct taxes are budgeted to rise from 2.1 per cent of GDP in 1990-91 to 3.0 per cent in 1995-96 (RE), while customs revenues declined from 3.9 per cent of GDP to 3.2 per cent (RE) over the same period. As a consequence, the share of direct taxes in the gross tax revenue of the Centre is expected to rise from around 19 per cent in 1990-91 to about 29 per cent in 1995-96 (RE), while that of customs revenue is expected to decline from 36 per cent to 32 per cent (RE) over the same period.

The success of the new approach is also shown by the fact that, despite the lowering of personal and corporate tax rates, the buoyancy of these taxes has increased. Average buoyancy of personal income taxes, as measured by the ratio of change in tax revenue to the change in the GDP at current prices, has risen from 1.1 during 1986-87 to 1990-91, to around 1.5 during 1991-92 to 1995-96 (RE).

Similarly the buoyancy of corporate income tax revenues has risen from an average of 0.8 during 1986-87 to 1990- 91 to 1.7 in 1991-92 to 1995-96 (RE). Both are likely to be higher on 1995-96 (RE) basis. Despite the very large reduction in peak customs duty rates from over 300 per cent to 50 per cent, the revenue collection rate (ratio of revenue collected to value of imports), only fell from 47 per cent in 1990-91 to 29 per cent in 1995-96, for similar reasons.

The 1995-96 Budget estimated a net tax revenue loss to the centre of about Rs.1,600 crore based on conventional methods, which do not incorporate gains from simplification, rationalisation, improved tax compliance and administration. Available trends indicate that gains are likely to be much greater than these conventional loss estimates. For the first nine months of 1995-96 (April-December, 1995), collections from personal income tax and corporation tax at Rs. 21327 crore were 27.6 per cent higher than in the same period of 1994. Collections from excise and customs, at Rs. 53802 crore during April-December, 1995, show a growth of about 19 per cent.

Financial Developments

Reforms in the financial sector have included the phasing in of prudential norms for income recognition, classification of assets and provisioning for bad debts, revised formats for making balance sheet and profit and loss accounts reflect the actual financial health and a time schedule for attaining 8 per cent capital to risk weighted assets for the scheduled commercial banks. The Statutory Liquidity Ratio (SLR) and Cash Reserve Ratio (CRR) were brought down to reduce the pre-emption of bank credit by Government and government borrowing was undertaken at market interest rates. The effects of these reforms on the financial health and performance of banks is gradually emerging. There has been progress by public sector banks in moving to the target of 8 per cent capital to risk weighted assets ratio (CRAR) by March end, 1996. By end March, 1994, only four public sector banks had a CRAR over 8 per cent, four had between 6.7 per cent and 8 per cent and eight had a CRAR in the range of 4.3 per cent and 6.7 per cent. By end March, 1995 as many as 13 public sector banks reached CRAR of at least 8 per cent, while 10 banks had a CRAR of 4 per cent and above.

Only 4 banks have less than 4 per cent CRAR. In the private sector, all the banks had complied with 4 per cent norm by March, 1994 and propose to raise additional capital through public issue to attain 8 per cent CRAR by March, 1996. All new private sector banks start with 8 per cent CRAR.

The deregulation of bank interest rates undertaken in 1994-95 with the abolition of the minimum lending rate on bank loans above Rs. 2 lakh, was extended to the deposit side in 1995-96. From October 1, 1995 scheduled commercial banks became free to fix their interest rates on domestic term deposits of over two years. The stipulation of at least three slabs with a minimum interest rate differential of 0.25 per cent point imposed in April 1992 on term deposits, was also withdrawn. Banks already have the discretion to fix both maturities and interest rates on non-resident non-repatriable (NRNR) deposits. The entry of 9 new private sector banks during 1994-95 and 1995-96, and the potential future entry of more banks, is likely to spur competitiveness and cost consciousness, and greater attention to depositor interests.

The Board for Financial Supervision was set up in 1994-95 with statutory powers over financial institutions, banks and non-bank financial institutions. It is designed to provide guidance on the supervisory initiatives and interventions of RBI. Its Secretariat is provided by the newly set up Department of Supervision in RBI. In addition, there is also an Advisory Council to provide guidance. There are now five Debts Recovery Tribunals functioning along with an Appellate Tribunal, for expediting the loan recovery process through adjudication. A major institutional step in 1995-96 has been the appointment of eight Ombudsmen under Banking Ombudsman Scheme, 1995 (Out of 15 to be appointed for the country as a whole), who will function to resolve customers grievances in a quick and inexpensive manner. With the State Bank of India entering capital market to raise Rs. 3200 crore the share of the RBI in the capital of SBI has come down to 66 per cent from 99 per cent earlier. The Government made a capital contribution of Rs. 5700 crores in 1993-94, Rs. 5287 crores in 1994-95 and Rs. 852 crores in 1995-96 (BE) to public sector banks to enable them to attain capital adequacy target. The entire range of reforms, aimed at promoting competition within a prudent regulatory regime, is beginning to bear fruit. The financial position of the scheduled commercial banks has improved in 1994-95. The number of public sector banks declaring operating profits went up from 19 in 1992-93 to 26 in 1994-95.

Only one reported an operating loss. The number of public sector banks making net profits rose to 19 in 1994-95 from 15 in 1992-93. The average ratio of non-performing assets to the total advances, for the public sector banks, came down to 20 per cent in 1994-95 from 26 per cent in 1992-93.

Among the all-India financial institutions the amendment of the IDBI Act, 1964 in March 1995, made possible Industrial Development Bank of India (IDBI) maiden capital issue in July 1995. A new development finance institution, namely, the North Eastern Development Finance Corporation Ltd., with an initial paid up equity base of Rs. 100 crore (and authorised capital of Rs. 500 crore), is set to commence operations soon.

In the field of rural finance the prudential norms relating to income recognition were introduced for Regional Rural Banks (RRBs). An Expert Group examined the major issues concerning managerial and financial restructuring of RRBs and the role which could be assigned to non-government organisations and self-group in improving the rural credit delivery system.

Steps were taken to increase the flow of credit to the small scale industries (SSI) sector with a special programme to open 100 specialised SSI bank branches in 85 identified districts by March 1996. By December 1995, 56 branches had been set up. A number of special schemes/funds were announced in the budget speech of 1995-96, which aim at counteracting shortfalls in priority sector advances and augmenting the flow of funds to relatively neglected areas/sectors. These include:

(a) Rural Infrastructure Development Fund (RIDF) of Rs. 2,000 crore in the National Bank for the Agriculture and Rural Development (NABARD) to accelerate implementation of investment projects in agriculture irrigation and allied activities;

(b) a scheme for expanded provision of credit facilities to the Khadi and Village Industries Commission by a consortium of banks so as to increase production and employment in off-farm activities in rural areas and;

(c) a scheme for financing primary weavers'co- operative societies by the scheduled commercial banks to assist increased production of handloom cloth. The RIDF will be built with contributions by the scheduled commercial banks which have failed to achieve the target of priority sector advances. They will also be required to participate in the aforesaid schemes.

In the area of capital markets the abolition of the office of Controller of Capital Issues (CCI) in May 1992 and the setting up of Securities and Exchange Board of India (SEBI) with statutory powers and functions (February 1992) were the first decisive steps in the move from control to prudential regulation. Prudential regulation is as important as decontrol for the development of a healthy capital market, keeping in view investor interests.

The powers and functions of SEBI were strengthened in phases. SEBI has been empowered to regulate business in stock exchanges. Its ambit covers recognition of stock exchanges, their rules, articles, voting rights and nomination of public representatives, stock exchange listing and delivery contracts. The setting up of the National Stock Exchange (NSE) and computerisation of the Bombay Stock Exchange (BSE) will help improve the clearing and settlement mechanisms and substantially raise the levels of transparency.

SEBI has issued rules and procedures for registering and regulating the various market participants and intermediaries. These cover broker, bankers and registrars to an issue, merchant bankers, underwriters, portfolio managers, custodians, credit rating agencies, foreign institutional investors, venture capital funds, mutual funds and asset management companies. To enable SEBI to effectively carry out its functions of Stock Exchange regulation and investor protection, the Department of Company Affairs has delegated to SEBI powers to file complaints against violations of the Companies Act.

The notification covers issues pertaining to primary market such as listing of securities, refund of excess application money, delay in issues of shares and dispatch of dividend warrants. SEBI now has the authority to levy monetary penalties for a range of violations such as failure to redress investor grievances or observe rules and regulations by mutual funds, asset management companies, failure to disclose the aggregate of shareholding in a company, or to make public announcement for acquisition of share in the context of the takeover code.

Standards of disclosure and issue procedures have been tightened. Companies are now required to draw up their financial statements on a consistent basis with appropriate audit qualifications. They will be asked to indicate the sources of income from other than normal activities and to make the draft prospectus a public document. Finance companies are eligible to make an issue if they have operated for a minimum of two years, or are registered with RBI as a non-banking finance company or with SEBI as an intermediary.

The National Stock Exchange, which was established in 1993, has come of age, with daily average trading volume rising sharply in recent months. Screen based trading has also been instituted in the Bombay and Delhi Stock exchanges. Private mutual funds are now permitted and are allowed to apply for firm allotment in public issues. The carry forward system has been reformed. The scrip-wise and broker-wise carry forward position shall be disclosed by the stock exchanges at the beginning of the carry forward session. Members doing financing of carry forward transactions will be subject to a cap of Rs. 10 crore. The depositories ordinance, re-issued in January 1996, will provide a legal framework for the establishment of depositories to record ownership details in book entry form.

The de-materialisation of scrips that this makes possible will eliminate a number of hazards associated with paper based stock market trading, such as a high proportion of bad deliveries, high risk of loss, cumbersome procedures and long delays. As a result of the past four years of reform, there has been a significant increase in market activity. Equity capital raised, mainly by the private corporate sector, has increased from Rs.

5562 crore in 1991-92 to Rs. 27621 crore in 1994-95. During April- December 1995, Rs. 14155 crore of capital has been raised. The market capitalisation of BSE almost doubled from Rs. 3,23,363 crore in 1991-92 to Rs. 6,44,478 crore at the end of December 1995.

The number of listed firms at the BSE has doubled from 2601 in 1991-92 to 5398 in December 1995. Besides UTI, there are now 9 public sector mutual funds and 16 private sector mutual funds in operation. During April-December 1994-95, Mutual Funds including UTI had raised Rs. 1,601 crore through 32 new schemes.

At the end of January 1996, 350 foreign institutional investors (FIIs) were registered with SEBI compared to only 10 in January 1993. They had invested a total of Rs. 14,129 crore in the securities market Indian companies were also permitted to access international capital markets through euro-equity shares and by the end of December 1995 Indian firms had raised US $ 5.18 billion through global depository receipts (GDRs) and foreign currency convertible bonds (FCCBs).

Thus the total inflow of foreign Portfolio capital into the Indian capital market since the launching of economic reforms amounts to $ 8.9 billion. This is further indication of improved international creditworthiness of India resulting from successful economic reforms.

Insurance Sector Developments

During the financial year 1994-95, the Life Insurance Corporation of India (LIC) achieved a growth rate of 32.03% securing total new business (sum assured) of Rs. 55468.82 crores under 108.88 lakhs policies. This compares with Rs. 42012.90 crores under 107.38 lakh policies during the previous year. New business under Group Insurance Scheme (including Group Gratuity was Rs. 50,651.85 crores covering 210.81 lakh lives.

The total rural new business procured by the Corporation during 1994-95 works out to be 39.1% of its total new business and the total number of policies issued in rural areas works out to be 45.1% of the number of policies issued during the period. The total business in force (individual Assurance) as on 31st March, 1995 was Rs. 2,54,572 crores under 655.29 lakh policies, compared with Rs. 2,08,619 crores under 608.73 lakh policies on 31st March 1994.

The Gross Premium income of the general insurance industry written direct in India during 1994-95 amounted to Rs. 4959 crores against Rs. 4449 crores in 1993-94. This amounts to a growth rate of 11.4% over the previous year. The net premium income of the general insurance industry during 1994-95 was Rs. 4102 crores compared with Rs. 3681 crores in 1993-94. It accounts for a growth of 11.4 per cent over the previous year. The gross profits of the general insurance industry was Rs. 503 crores in 1994-95. It accounted for a fall of 53.5% over the previous year. The net profit of the industry during 1994-95 was Rs. 377 crores representing a fall of 43.71 % from the previous year. In pursuance of the recommendations of the Committee on Reforms in the Insurance Sector the Government has already set up an Insurance Regulatory Authority.

External Sector Developments

The remarkable improvement in India's balance of payment witnessed in 1993-94 was consolidated further in 1994-95. Despite some widening of deficit in the current account, the overall balance of payment in 1994-95 remained very strong. The foreign currency assets of the Reserve Bank of India (RBI) rose from US $ 15.07 billion at the end of 1993-94 to a historical peak of US $ 20.81 billion at the end of 1994-95. Quick estimates of balance of payments for 1994-95 indicate strong improvements in exports and invisible receipts and in foreign investment flows. The balance of payment position remained reasonably comfortable during 1995-96. For the third year in succession, export growth was robust, supported by a congenial domestic policy environment.

Import growth was also high, reflecting the continued good performance of the industrial sector. On the invisible account, net outflow under investment income rose significantly because of a rise in interest payments on foreign loans; but this was largely offset by the increase in inflows under non-factor services, especially tourism receipts. Private transfers in 1995-96 remained broadly at previous year's level. As a result net inflows under invisibles account were only marginally lower than the previous year's level. As a result, net inflows under invisibles account were only marginally lower then the previous year. Reflecting these developments on the trade and invisibles account, the current account deficit widened to 1.6 per cent of GDP from 0.8 per cent of GDP in 1994-95. But the level of the deficit was reasonable and sustainable. On the capital account, foreign investment flows were the major component, as in the two previous years. However, there was a considerable deceleration in portfolio investments mainly because of the subdued trend in GDR issues. Direct foreign investments, on the other hand, showed considerable improvement. The residual financing need was met by drawing down foreign exchange reserves. Foreign currency assets of the RBI declined by US $ 3.77 billion to a level of US $ 17.04 billion at the end of March 1996.

Export performance has been robust in recent years. Exports, according to DGCI&S data, recorded a growth rate of 18.4 per cent in 1994-95 and 20.9 per cent in 1995-96, in US dollar terms. The growth in imports, in US dollar terms, was also high at 22.9 per cent in 1994-95 and 26.9 per cent in 1995-96. The trade deficit, measured on the basis of DGCI&S data, amounted to US $ 4.54 billion compared to the deficit of US $ 2.32 billion in 1994-95.

Total foreign investment flows, including both direct and portfolio investment flows, which increased sharply to US $ 4.11 billion in 1993-94, rose further to US $ 4.90 billion in 1994-95. During 1995-96, total foreign investment amounted to US $ 4.20 billion, comprising US $ 2.11 billion of direct foreign investments and US $ 2.1 billion of portfolio investments.

The process of achieving current account convertibility was carried forward further in 1995-96. The RBI, in July 1995, announced further liberalisation in the release of foreign exchange for current invisible payments. The RBI permitted the authorised dealers, with effect from July 5, 1995 to provide exchange facilities to their customers without prior approval of the RBI, beyond the specified indicative limits for purposes such as, business travel, participation in overseas conference/seminars, studies abroad, medical treatments/check up, specialised apprenticeship etc., provide they are satisfied about the bonafides of the applications.

On the basis of recommendations of the Tax Reforms Committee, for improving the competitiveness of domestic industry and maintaining thrust towards simplification of procedures, the process of reducing peak tariff rate was continued in the Central Budget for 1995-96. The peak rate of customs duty, which had been reduced to 65 per cent in 1994-95 Budget from 85 per cent was further reduced to 50 per cent in the 1995-96 Budget. Substantial reduction in customs duty on critical raw materials for enhancing export competitiveness was also effected. The stability of the Indian rupee against the US dollar noticed since July 1993 at around Rs. 31.37 per US dollar continued through July, 1995. The rupee in relation the US witnessed a high degree of volatility during September and October 1995, and again in January through the first week of February 1996. The rate, however, stabilised following RBI's market intervention and announcement of certain measures aimed at augmenting the supply of foreign exchange and reducing the demand. The rupee-dollar rate at the end of March 1996 was Rs. 34.35 per US dollar.

MONETARY CONTROL

Till the 1990s, the reserve money creation process predominantly originated from the RBI's financing of government and the instruments of monetary control were essentially reserve requirements, interest rate controls and direct credit controls. Against the backdrop of tight capital controls, exchange rate policy was governed by the preoccupation of conserving foreign exchange and maintaining India's competitiveness in international markets. In other words, there was only limited interaction between monetary policy and exchange rate policy. With the gradual relaxation of controls in the domestic financial sector beginning in the early 1990s, there has been a move away from reserve requirements, interest rate controls and other direct controls and increasing reliance on market related instruments. With the gradual opening up of the external sector, and the relaxation of capital account controls, there has been an upsurge of capital inflows. The reliance of government on the RBI credit is now reduced and virtually the entire reserve money is externally generated. The preoccupation of monetary policy is to a large extent on managing capital flows while ensuring monetary and financial stability and meeting the real sector's requirements for credit. The progressive integration of India into the global economy exposes the real sectors to the vicissitudes of the international economy. As the Indian economy moves to FCAC, albeit at a measured pace, monetary policy and exchange rate policy will be increasingly inter-twined. It is in this context that the conflict of the impossible trinity – independent monetary policy, open capital account and a managed exchange rate comes out in the open. Technically, all poles of the trinity cannot be simultaneously attained, but the approach of the Indian authorities, quite rightly, has been to work towards optimising intermediate solutions.

Given the Indian policy makers' distinct preference for monetary stability and growth of the economy and the gradual opening up of the capital account, the performance of Indian monetary policy, exchange rate policy and gradual capital account liberalisation has yielded satisfactory results. The move to fuller capital account convertibility would need to derive synergies between the quest for monetary stability and an appropriate exchange rate regime which would be supportive of the growth objectives. Monetary Policy Instruments and Operations. The sterilisation and open market operations (OMO) and interventions in the forex markets have to be so calibrated along with domestic monetary instruments so as to be consistent with the monetary policy objectives.

In the emerging scenario of greater integration of domestic and international markets, interest rate policy comes to the fore. In this context, a few observations would be apposite. First, while interest rate policy has to take into account various factors, both domestic and international, the RBI would need to progressively give somewhat more weightage than hitherto to international real interest rates. Indian real interest rates would need to be better aligned with international real interest rates. Secondly, while skillful open market operations (OMO) need to be developed for modulating liquidity conditions, OMO could also be used to correct any serious misalignments perceived by the authorities between short-term and long-term interest rates. Thirdly, while there is some advantage in a rule based interest rate policy, there are dangers in that monetary policy could become a prisoner of rigid rules.

Large and sudden capital inflows and outflows can be destabilising to the economy and hence, the economy can face the problem of boom and bust. The Indian authorities have had to rethink the kind of interest rate signals which are given to the system. Till the late 1990s, the signalling rates of the RBI were altered by as large an amount as 1 to 2 percentage points. With the increased opening up of the economy and the development of financial markets, the RBI has recognised that large changes in interest rates would be disruptive.

Accordingly, the extent of interest rate changes by the RBI, in the more recent period, have generally each been of the order of 0.25 percentage point.

A major objective of monetary policy is containing inflationary expectations and to attain this objective, monetary policy action needs to be undertaken well before the economy reaches the upper turning point of the cycle. If the measures are delayed, small incremental changes are ineffective and moreover could be destabilising, particularly if monetary tightening is undertaken during the downturn of the cycle. With transparency in setting objectives, there would be improved credibility if the RBI had greater independence in optimising the use of instruments and operating procedures.

The RBI has rightly de-emphasised reserve requirements and interest rate controls as key instruments of monetary policy. Given the nascent state of development of market based monetary policy instruments and the size of capital flows, it would be necessary to continue to actively use the instrument of reserve requirements. It would be necessary for the RBI to have flexibility to alter the Statutory Liquidity Ratio (SLR) below 25 per cent when felt necessary. In this context, it is imperative that legislative amendments relating to the SLR stipulation are put through expeditiously.

The RBI has in recent years developed the Liquidity Adjustment Facility (LAF) as an effective instrument. The LAF at present provides for a one percentage point spread within the corridor for overnight call money. The LAF is meant to be a short-term discretionary instrument for smooth equilibrating of liquidity in the system and, therefore, the repo and reverse repo interest rates are key signalling rates in the system. Since 2002-03, however, LAF has become a passive facility for CRR/SLR management of banks within the books of the RBI. The LAF should be essentially an instrument of equilibrating very short-term liquidity. The Committee recommends that, over time, the RBI should build up its stocks of government securities so as to undertake effective outright OMO. The Committee recognises that this is easier said than done. Nonetheless, the RBI should use every window of opportunity to build up its stock of government securities. The interest cost of sterilisation to the Government and the RBI in 2005-06 is reported to be in the broad range of Rs.4,000 crore (though reduced somewhat by corresponding earnings on the forex reserves). While the costs of sterilisation are often highlighted, the costs of non-intervention and non-sterilisation are not easily quantifiable as the costs are in terms of lower growth, lower employment, loss of competitiveness of India, lower corporate profitability and lower government revenues; these costs could be much more than the visible costs of sterilisation.

While appreciating the RBI's dilemma of a shortage of instruments, the Committee recommends the following:

(i) The way the LAF is operated, it is used by banks like a current account on which they are remunerated. The RBI needs greater freedom in operating the LAF. Under the present system of fixed rate repo/reverse repo auctions, these rates become a major policy announcement and this restricts the degree of freedom the RBI needs in its day-to-day operations. The RBI should activate variable rate repo/reverse repo auctions or repo/reverse repo operations on a real time basis.

(ii) Apart from overnight LAF operations the RBI should consider somewhat longer-term LAF facilities, say, for a fortnight or a month.

(iii) To the extent the RBI assesses the excess liquidity to be more than transient, it should also use the CRR and SLR. Where there is a large increase in liquidity and credit expansion way above the trend line, bank profitability is higher and the banks can be legitimately expected to bear a part of the burden of containing the deleterious expansion of liquidity. The Committee recognises that the CRR cannot be as effective as in earlier years as banks are anyway maintaining large balances for settlement operations. Nonetheless, it can be a supportive instrument and the entire burden should not be on the LAF and the Market Stabilisation Scheme (MSS).

(iv) To the extent the capital inflows are exceptionally high and the economy is inundated with excess liquidity, arising out of FII inflows, the authorities may consider, in very exceptional circumstances, the imposition of an unremunerated reserve requirement on fresh FII inflows. This would need to be imposed under the FEMA Rules for FIIs. Under such a dispensation, FIIs would be required to retain a stipulated percentage of the inflows with the bank and the bank in turn would be required to transfer these balances to the RBI. The impounded balance would be released to FIIs after a stipulated period. The Committee recommends that measures of such a nature should be exceptional, to be used only in extreme situations wherein the liquidity arising out of extremely large and volatile FII inflows reaches unmanageable proportions. Furthermore, such a measure, to be effective, should be used as a temporary measure only for a few months.

INTERNATIONAL MONETARY FUND

The International Monetary Fund (IMF) is an international organization that oversees the global financial system by following the macroeconomic policies of its member countries, in particular those with an impact on exchange rates and the balance of payments. It is an organization formed with a stated objective of stabilizing international exchange rates and facilitating development. It also offers highly leveraged loans mainly to poorer countries. Its headquarters are located in Washington, D.C., United States.

Organization and Purpose

The International Monetary Fund was created in July 1944, originally with 45 members, with a goal to stabilize exchange rates and assist the reconstruction of the world's international payment system. Countries contributed to a pool which could be borrowed from, on a temporary basis, by countries with payment imbalances. (Condon, 2007)

The IMF describes itself as "an organization of 186 countries (Kosovo being the 186th, as of June 29, 2009), working to foster global monetary cooperation, secure financial stability, facilitate international trade, promote high employment and sustainable economic growth, and reduce poverty". With the exception of Taiwan (expelled in 1980), North Korea, Cuba (left in 1964), Andorra, Monaco, Liechtenstein, Tuvalu and Nauru, all UN member states participate directly in the IMF. Member states are represented on a 24-member Executive Board (five Executive Directors are appointed by the five members with the largest quotas, nineteen Executive Directors are elected by the remaining members), and all members appoint a Governor to the IMF's Board of Governors.

History

The International Monetary Fund was formally created in July 1944 during the United Nations Monetary and Financial Conference. The representatives of 44 governments met in the Mount Washington Hotel in the area of Bretton Woods, New Hampshire, United States of America, with the delegates to the conference agreeing on a framework for international economic cooperation. The IMF was formally organised on December 27, 1945, when the first 29 countries signed its Articles of Agreement. The statutory purposes of the IMF today are the same as when they were formulated in 1943.

Today

The IMF's influence in the global economy steadily increased as it accumulated more members. The number of IMF member countries has more than quadrupled from the 44 states involved in its establishment, reflecting in particular the attainment of political independence by many developing countries and more recently the collapse of the Soviet bloc. The expansion of the IMF's membership, together with the changes in the world economy, have required the IMF to adapt in a variety of ways to continue serving its purposes effectively.

In 2008, faced with a shortfall in revenue, the International Monetary Fund's executive board agreed to sell part of the IMF's gold reserves. On April 27, 2008, IMF Managing Director Dominique Strauss-Kahn welcomed the board's decision April 7, 2008 to propose a new framework for the fund, designed to close a projected $400 million budget deficit over the next few years. The budget proposal includes sharp spending cuts of $100 million until 2011 that will include up to 380 staff dismissals.

At the 2009 G-20 London summit, it was decided that the IMF would require additional financial resources to meet prospective needs of its member countries during the ongoing global crisis. As part of that decision, the G-20 leaders pledged to increase the IMF's supplemental cash tenfold to $500 billion, and to allocate to member countries another $250 billion via Special Drawing Rights.

Data Dissemination Systems

In 1995, the International Monetary Fund began work on data dissemination standards with the view of guiding IMF member countries to disseminate their economic and financial data to the public. The International Monetary and Financial Committee (IMFC) endorsed the guidelines for the dissemination standards and they were split into two tiers: The General Data Dissemination System (GDDS) and the Special Data Dissemination Standard (SDDS).

The International Monetary Fund executive board approved the SDDS and GDDS in 1996 and 1997 respectively and subsequent amendments were published in a revised "Guide to the General Data Dissemination System". The system is aimed primarily at statisticians and aims to improve many aspects of statistical systems in a country. It is also part of the World Bank Millennium Development Goals and Poverty Reduction Strategic Papers.

The IMF established a system and standard to guide members in the dissemination to the public of their economic and financial data. Currently there are two such systems: General Data Dissemination System (GDDS) and its superset Special Data Dissemination System (SDDS), for those member countries having or seeking access to international capital markets.

The primary objective of the GDDS is to encourage IMF member countries to build a framework to improve data quality and increase statistical capacity building. This will involve the preparation of metadata describing current statistical collection practices and setting improvement plans. Upon building a framework, a country can evaluate statistical needs, set priorities in improving the timeliness, transparency, reliability and accessibility of financial and economic data.

Some countries initially used the GDDS, but lately upgraded to SDDS.

Some entities that are not themselves IMF members also contribute statistical data to the systems:

- Palestinian Authority – GDDS
- Hong Kong – SDDS
- European Union institutions:
- the European Central Bank for the Eurozone – SDDS
- Eurostat for the whole EU – SDDS, thus providing data from Cyprus (not using any DDSystem on its own) and Malta (using only GDDS on its own).

Membership Qualifications

Any country may apply for membership to the IMF. The application will be considered first by the IMF's Executive Board. After its consideration, the Executive Board will submit a report to the Board of Governors of the IMF with recommendations in the form of a "Membership Resolution." These recommendations cover the amount of quota in the IMF, the form of payment of the subscription, and other customary terms and conditions of membership.

After the Board of Governors has adopted the "Membership Resolution," the applicant state needs to take the legal steps required under its own law to enable it to sign the IMF's Articles of Agreement and to fulfil the obligations of IMF membership. Similarly, any member country can withdraw from the Fund, although that is rare. For example, in April 2007, the president of Ecuador, Rafael Correa announced the expulsion of the World Bank representative in the country. A few days later, at the end of April, Venezuelan president Hugo Chavez announced that the country would withdraw from the IMF and the World Bank. Chavez dubbed both organisations as "the tools of the empire" that "serve the interests of the North". As of June 2009, both countries remain as members of both organisations. Venezuela was forced to back down because a withdrawal would have triggered default clauses in the country's sovereign bonds.

A member's quota in the IMF determines the amount of its subscription, its voting weight, its access to IMF financing, and its allocation of Special Drawing Rights (SDRs). A member state cannot unilaterally increase its quota—increases must be approved by the Executive Board and are linked to formulas that include many variables such as the size of a country in the world economy. For example, in 2001, China was prevented from increasing its quota as high as it wished, ensuring it remained at the level of the smallest G7 economy (Canada). In September 2005, the IMF's member countries agreed to the first round of ad hoc quota increases for four countries, including China. On March 28, 2008, the IMF's Executive Board ended a period of extensive discussion and negotiation over a major package of reforms to enhance the institution's governance that would shift quota and voting shares from advanced to emerging markets and developing countries. The Fund's Board of Governors must vote on these reforms by April 28, 2008.

Assistance and Reforms

The primary mission of the IMF is to provide financial assistance to countries that experience serious financial and economic difficulties using funds deposited with the IMF from the institution's 186 member countries. Member states with balance of payments problems, which often arise from these difficulties, may request loans to help fill gaps between what countries earn and/or are able to borrow from other official lenders and what countries must spend to operate, including to cover the cost of importing basic goods and services. In return, countries are usually required to launch certain reforms, which have often been dubbed the "Washington Consensus".

These reforms are thought to be beneficial to countries with fixed exchange rate policies that may engage in fiscal, monetary, and political practices which may lead to the crisis itself. For example, nations with severe budget deficits, rampant inflation, strict price controls, or significantly over-valued or undervalued currencies run the risk of facing balance of payment crises. Thus, the structural adjustment programs are at least ostensibly intended to ensure that the IMF is actually helping to prevent financial crises rather than merely funding financial recklessness.

IMF/WORLD BANK SUPPORT OF MILITARY DICTATORSHIPS

The role of the Bretton Woods institutions has been controversial since the late Cold War period, as the IMF policy makers supported military dictatorships friendly to American and European corporations. Critics also claim that the IMF is generally apathetic or hostile to their views of democracy, human rights, and labour rights. The controversy has helped spark the Anti-globalization movement. Arguments in favour of the IMF say that economic stability is a precursor to democracy; however, critics highlight various examples in which democratized countries fell after receiving IMF loans. In the 1960s, the IMF and the World Bank supported the government of Brazil's military dictator Castello Branco with tens of millions of dollars of loans and credit that were denied to previous democratically-elected governments.

Criticism

"The interests of the IMF represent the big international interests that seem to be established and concentrated in Wall Street." Two criticisms from economists have been that financial aid is always bound to so-called "Conditionalities", including Structural Adjustment Programs (SAP). It is claimed that conditionalities (economic performance targets established as a precondition for IMF loans) retard social stability and hence inhibit the stated goals of the IMF, while Structural Adjustment Programs lead to an increase in poverty in recipient countries. One of the main SAP conditions placed on troubled countries is that the governments sell up as much of their national assets as they can, normally to western corporations at heavily discounted prices.

That said, the IMF sometimes advocates "austerity programmes," increasing taxes even when the economy is weak, in order to generate government revenue and balance budget deficits. Countries are often advised to lower their corporate tax rate. These policies were criticised by Joseph E. Stiglitz, former chief economist and Senior Vice President at the World Bank, in his book *Globalization and Its Discontents*. He argued that by converting to a more Monetarist approach, the fund no longer had a valid purpose, as it was designed to provide funds for countries to carry out Keynesian reflations, and that the IMF "was not participating in a conspiracy, but it was reflecting the interests and ideology of the Western financial community".

Argentina, which had been considered by the IMF to be a model country in its compliance to policy proposals by the Bretton Woods institutions, experienced a catastrophic economic crisis in 2001, which some believe to have been caused by IMF-induced budget restrictions— which undercut the government's ability to sustain national infrastructure even in crucial areas such as health, education, and security — and privatization of strategically vital national resources. Others attribute the crisis to Argentina's misdesigned fiscal federalism, which caused subnational spending to increase rapidly. The crisis added to widespread hatred of this institution in Argentina and other South American countries, with many blaming the IMF for the region's economic problems. The current — as of early 2006 — trend towards moderate left-wing governments in the region and a growing concern with the development of a regional economic policy largely independent of big business pressures has been ascribed to this crisis.

Another example of where IMF Structural Adjustment Programmes aggravated the problem was in Kenya. Before the IMF got involved in the country, the Kenyan central bank oversaw all currency movements in and out of the country. The IMF mandated that the Kenyan central bank had to allow easier currency movement. However, the adjustment resulted in very little foreign investment, but allowed Kamlesh Manusuklal Damji Pattni, with the help of corrupt government officials, to siphon off billions of Kenyan shillings in what came to be known as the Goldenberg scandal, leaving the country worse off than it was before the IMF reforms were implemented. In an interview, the former Romanian Prime Minister Tăriceanu stated that "Since 2005, IMF is constantly making mistakes when it appreciates the country's economic performances".

In September 2007 the IMF said "given the Irish economy's strong fundamentals and the authorities' commitment to sound policies, the Directors expected economic growth to remain robust over the medium term". Seventeen months later in April 2009 the New York Times quoted Nobel prize-winning economist, Paul Krugman, who identified Ireland as a model for the worst-case scenario for the global economy.

Overall the IMF success record is perceived as limited. While it was created to help stabilize the global economy, since 1980 critics claim over 100 countries (or reputedly most of the Fund's membership) have experienced a banking collapse that they claim have reduced GDP by four percent or more, far more than at any time in Post-Depression history. The considerable delay in the IMF's response to any crisis, and the fact that it tends to only respond to them (or even create them) rather than prevent them, has led many economists to argue for reform. In 2006, an IMF reform agenda called the Medium Term Strategy was widely endorsed by the institution's member countries. The agenda includes changes in IMF governance to enhance the role of developing countries in the institution's decision-making process and steps to deepen the effectiveness of its core mandate, which is known as economic surveillance or helping member countries adopt macroeconomic policies that will sustain global growth and reduce poverty. On June 15, 2007, the Executive Board of the IMF adopted the 2007 Decision on Bilateral Surveillance, a landmark measure that replaced a 30-year-old decision of the Fund's member countries on how the IMF should analyse economic outcomes at the country level.

Impact on Public Health

In 2008, a study by analysts from Cambridge and Yale universities published on the open-access Public Library of Science concluded that strict conditions on the international loans by the IMF resulted in thousands of deaths in Eastern Europe by tuberculosis as public health care had to be weakened. In the 21 countries to which the IMF had given loans, tuberculosis deaths rose by 16.6 %.

Criticism from free-market Advocates

Typically the IMF and its supporters advocate a monetarist approach. As such, adherents of supply-side economics generally find themselves in open disagreement with the IMF. The IMF frequently advocates currency devaluation, criticized by proponents of supply-side economics as inflationary. Secondly they link higher taxes under "austerity programmes" with economic contraction. Currency devaluation is recommended by the IMF to the governments of poor nations with struggling economies. Some economists claim these IMF policies are destructive to economic prosperity.

Complaints have also been directed toward the International Monetary Fund gold reserve being undervalued. At its inception in 1945, the IMF pegged gold at US$35 per Troy ounce of gold. In 1973, the Nixon administration lifted the fixed asset value of gold in favour of a world market price. This need to lift the fixed asset value of gold had largely come about because *Petrodollars* outside the United States were worth more than could be backed by the gold at Fort Knox under the fixed exchange rate system. Following this, the fixed exchange rates of currencies tied to gold were switched to a floating rate, also based on market price and exchange. The fixed rate system had only served to limit the nominal amount of assistance the organisation could provide to debt-ridden countries. Current IMF rules prohibit members from linking their currencies to gold.

Attempts to Repair Image

Research by the Pew Research Centre shows that more than 60 percent of Asians and 70 percent of Africans feel that the IMF and the World Bank have a positive effect on their country. However it is pertinent to note that the survey aggregated international organisations including the World Trade Organisation. Also, a similar percentage of people in the Western world believed that these international organisations had a positive effect on their countries. In 2005, the IMF was the first multilateral financial institution to implement a sweeping debt-relief program for the world's poorest countries known as the Multilateral Debt Relief Initiative. By year-end 2006, 23 countries mostly in sub-Saharan Africa and Central America had received total relief of debts owed to the IMF.

13

Banking and Finance

Electronic commerce is associated with IT as an enabler, facilitator, and even inhibitor of business activities both within and among all types of organizations (Applegate et al 1996). It is thus creating enormous interest in the world of IT, banking and finance as well as many other industries. There is little doubt that growth in this area will continue as more organizations join in the fun, establishing and cultivating business relationships, performing business transactions, distributing knowledge, and implementing competitive strategy. Corporate life, particularly in America, is being transformed by the Internet. Banks and financial firms are currently operating in such a new business environment, and they are responding to the changes in myriad ways.

As a result of deregulation and advances in information technology, there are new players and new products appearing on the scene (Fabozzi et al 1994). The new environment provides an opportunity for banks and financial firms to develop new products and services. They can even to enter the traditional turf of technological firms. However, business players from other fields are planning to engage or are already moving into the traditional hunting grounds of banks and financial companies. Microsoft and computer network companies are gearing up to offer financial services to the public.

Another source of competitive pressure comes from the relatively business activity known as navigation (Evans and Wurster 1999; Wenninger 2000). Navigators or intelligent search agents are information aggregators which search the web for similar products across a large number of companies, compare them for attributes such as prices, terms of delivery and goodies, and report their findings to the on-line customers. Banks and financial firms will have to compete with a bigger number of players, and face serious threats from nimble and innovative newcomers like Charles Schwab.

Banks and financial firms are sailing into new water that holds both promises and dangers. On one hand they have the know-how specific to banking and financial, and for the large players, they enjoy the trust of their customers. But they are burdened with legacy systems consisting of their management structures, reward systems and computer systems. They would certainly have to prepare themselves properly for the cut and thrust of life in the brave new world.

The rest of the paper is organized as follows. Section 2 reviews the contributions of banking to e-commerce so far and suggests broad principle to move ahead. Section 3 describes how BFF is adopting the theory and practice of e-commerce. Section 4 has six sub-sections, where we look at six areas where banks can offer their services to electronic commerce - payment services, information intermediary, rating services, fraud protection, and providing technological support for small businesses to enter e-commerce, and involvement in supply chain systems and other emerging forms of e-business. Section 5 concludes the paper.

LOOKING BACKWARD AND FORWARD

Heng (2003) gives a capsule account of the tremendous contributions made by modern banking and finance to the development of modern commerce. It is of course wrong to assume that there should be a simple repeat of what happened several centuries ago. The global banking and financial systems are so complex today that no one can claim to fully understand its workings. To borrow the words of Greenspan (1996) we may say that the baseline from which innovation and experimentation are occurring is undoubtedly different today. Nonetheless, an understanding of history of modern banking and finance can contribute to a more well-informed discussion of the challenges facing the industry in the new business environment. For one thing, e- commerce has already undermined to a significant extent the role of bank branches in transaction intensive activities.

In the process of meeting the needs of the emerging modern commerce, banks and financial firms (BFF) grew and flourished, and laid down an indispensable financial infrastructure for modern market economy. One would expect that present day BFF would follow the footsteps of their predecessors by making equally significant contributions in the new business environment. Unfortunately this is not so. For example, we read a very critical commentary by Peter Drucker (1999) in his invited article in The Economist. He is brutally frank in calling on the financial industry to innovate or face the danger of decline. With past innovations like Eurodollar and Eurobond becoming commodities, top financial firms turn to trading for their own account - in stocks and bonds, in derivatives, currencies and commodities. When this is a big activity, it has become gambling, which has sunk big names like Barings, Bankers Trust and Yamaichi. Luckily most banks have been able to control themselves and have not followed the big boys in indulging in speculative financial activities as a main line of business. Drucker also offers three suggestions on how banks can earn a good and fair living by using their knowledge to serve the middle-class investment market, to outsource financial management of middle-sized companies, and to assist these companies in coping with currency volatility. First suggestion is essentially what is known as private banking. As how it works is widely covered in newspapers, this paper will not dwell on it. We summarize his second and third suggestions and put them in appendix A for easy reading.

Though the industry has lost much of its innovative steam, individual financial firm still displayed innovative talent until the 1970s. For example, in the 1950s the Bank of America was a pioneer in the use of computer technology to automate cheque processing and subsequently was responsible for a number of other innovations including the credit card (McKenney et al 1997; Wikipedia 2005). Together with General Electric and the

Stanford Research Institute, it is generally credited with inventing modern centralized bank operations and introduced a number of financial transaction processing technologies such as automatic check processing, account numbers, magnetic ink character recognition and credit cards linked directly to individual bank accounts. Because of the clever and innovative use of these technologies, the bank had been able to significantly lower its administrative costs and was able to expand until it was the world's largest bank in the early 1970s.

The financial industry was playing a positive role in another way. This sector as a whole was a big investor in computer technology, and this has certainly helped the growth of the computer industry before the advent of the personal computers. "Banking records, including those for loans and deposits, have been computerized since the 1960s. Securities markets also now rely on highly automated records and systems, born out of necessity following the paperwork crisis of the 1970s. (Greenspan 1996)"

What is more important is that looking back, the BFF can claim the credit of having unknowingly invented the basic features of e-commerce. It was one of the first to use as a matter of practice teleprinters to transmit money transfer orders, and the term telegraphic transfer or TT is still in use. The Automatic Teller Machine integrates automatic data processing with data communication. And the use of ATM was quite widespread before the term e-commerce was coined. Perhaps, IT systems supporting the operations of the international financial market may be considered as the first on the commercial scene to exhibit the key features of e-commerce. "Most banks around the world are connected through an electronic network called SWIFT, which went online in 1977 with 270 banks from 15 countries, and now serves over 6,000 financial institutions in approximately 180 countries. A bank operating in the international market can't do business without subscribing to SWIFT, hence the banking system was building an international information superhighway of its own long before the Internet came into the picture. (Ahituv 2001)" This fact tends to be overlooked because business papers tend to highlight only the works of innovative financial firms like e-trade and Schwab which can claim some credit for their contribution to e-commerce.

However, BFF of today as a whole have been laggards in e-commerce innovations. The show of e-commerce innovations has been stolen by non-financial firms like Dell, Cisco, eBay, Yahoo! and Amazon. Even in their own turf of financial services, the opportunities have been discovered and seized by outsiders. For example, banks are not responsible for the success story of Octopus e-cash payment system in Hong Kong. It is truly an intriguing question why BFF has trailed behind other industries in the e-commerce landscape, a question that is beyond the scope of this book.

Here we would dwell on two points. First, we look at how BFF can learn from e-commerce and use the technology and business practice of e-commerce to develop and market their products to the customers. Many of the practices of e-commerce are aimed at getting closer to customers, serving them better (if not out of altruistic reason at least out of fear of losing them to competitors), cost cutting, new products and services, and making the new opportunities presented by the Internet for doing business in many new ways.

Second, e-commerce provides a business opportunity for banks to offer new products and services to serve the needs of e-commerce. Commerce in our age inevitably involves monetary transaction, and the way financial resources are mobilized can affect the fate of firms. It would thus come as no surprise that e-commerce could affect banking in a very fundamental way, and would be affected by the ways banks respond to the new demands. A central concept here, as in elsewhere in the book, is that banks and financial firms should offer value adding services to their clients. An example of a no-value-adding service is contained in an aptly named report called "Taxing the ghost" (The Economist Sept 4th 2004). Aggressive tax schemes have proliferated in the past decade. They are often designed by accounting firms, which are in turn assisted by law firms and investment banks. They use elaborate tax schemes to claim tax relief. Such clever exploitation of temporary loopholes in the tax systems, though delivering profits, does not add real value to the clients of the banks. In fact, it is a dangerous game. One example is provided by the USA where the Internal Revenue Service is working with the Department of Justice to crack down on firms that design the schemes.

ADOPTING THE THEORY AND PRACTICE OF E-COMMERCE

The Internet as a technological platform is to financial transaction what money as a common medium of exchange is to the economy. To get an idea of the convenience made possible by e-banking, just consider the role of money in economic transactions. Some features of the convenience of e-banking are already here while more aspects can be expected.

As customers we are witnessing these features before our nose as banks adopt the Internet infrastructure and business practices of e-commerce. Many of us have direct experience with electronic banking, for example Internet bank and e-brokerage, and have seen the disappearance of some brick-and-mortar branches of our familiar banks. The beauty of Internet banking lies in its low cost, convenience and availability. The commercial use of the 128-bit encryption opens the way for secure on-line financial transaction. The integrated technology enables banks and financial companies to offer services with the following qualities: 24-hour, seven-days-a-week availability, convenience, fast delivery, customer focus and personal service. Banks can reduce the time taken to approve mortgage application from weeks to hours. Brokerage practices have been transformed too. Witness the reduction in the size of average transaction, substantial reductions in fees, use of decimals in prices quoted in New York Stock Exchange, and increased competition between different stock exchanges. With the Internet, individual investors have a very cheap and convenient means to access information about the performance of firms listed on the stock exchange.

While technology offers new opportunities to banks, it also brings new challenge - non-banks have begun to integrate financial functions into their online offerings, and the competition among banks has intensified because of increased reach and transparency of online offerings. Below we look at three ways banks have responded to the new challenges by continuing the past practices of using IT, and by learning to adopt e-commerce ideas from their counterparts in the non-bank sectors.

Continuation of Past Practices of Using it

Business press frequently carries reports on how traditional banks are busily adopting the theory and practice of e-commerce to develop their products and market them. This may be seen as a continuation of their practice of switching over to ATMs when they were seen as cheaper than tellers and when it was realized that they offered 24-hour efficiency previous not offered by banks. In this same way, banks will continue to use the web technology as a medium as an advertisement and distribution channel as well as a technological platform to do transaction processing. There is certainly great advantage in the use of the Internet from the business logic of channel efficiencies. But such pace of change in itself may not be able to help them maintain their dominance in transaction intensive banking activities. One just needs to visit the web to encounter websites offering very competitive rates for foreign exchange transaction, or deposit savings account, etc.

However, an overemphasis on the concept that retail business will migrate to the Internet overlooks many business and process fundamentals. Note that 90% of business is industrial-grade. That includes brokerage, banking, and sales for business- to-business or government activity.

Initially, banks used the Internet as an advertising medium, promoting their capabilities, products, and services. Then, they used the Internet as medium for delivering products and services. "The trend toward electronic delivery of products and services is occurring dramatically in the financial service industry where the shift is party a result of consumer demand, but also of a ruthlessly competitive environment (Geyer 1997)."

Bundling of Information Products

By learning from how firms make use of IT, especially the Internet, e-banking researchers have put forward some interesting ideas which are essentially derived from practice of e-commerce. Here we go through briefly two proposals, namely to create a kind of portal of financial services, and to bundle information products just like publishers bundle their electronic magazines or academic journals.

Until recently, it is expensive to design a flexible investment portfolio that is tailored to the needs of individual investors. Only big institutional investors can afford the fees to have securities selected specially for them. With e-commerce technology it is possible to design and deliver the benefits of flexible and tailor made investment to smaller accounts at much lower costs. The idea is to construct a kind of portal of financial products and services. The proposal involves two parts. First, the creation of periodically updated indices covering a wider spectrum of asset classes than is currently available. Second, the creation of financial instruments to track these indices, which will allow investors and small businesses to diversify and hedge their portfolios to a much larger extent than is possible with today's investment vehicles. The aim is to use financial engineering methods and techniques to build an investment portfolio that is optimal for an investor, given his personal circumstances and preferences. Based on the features of an Internal portal, there is exclusive access to an integrated set of proprietary products and services as well as links to partners that offer complementary financial services and access to any other financial products available through the Internet.

Another interesting idea from e-commerce is bundling. Companies have been exploring the potential of using the Internet technology to bundle related products to be sold to their customers as a bundle, something like package tour or one-stop shopping. There are also examples of bundling of information products, e.g. music, electronic magazines and journals. Their experiences strongly suggest that banks can provide a more personalized service by creative bundling of existing financial products (Altinkemer 2001). In order to have the range of products to be included in the bundle, three approaches are possible. One is through consolidating by merger or acquisition. Another approach is by alliance. The third approach is by acting as an intermediary for others which is examined in next sub- section. Mergers and acquisitions are well known for their value destroying tendencies. Thus, banks may rely more heavily on alliances—which are inherently more flexible and can more easily be changed—as an alternative to outright consolidation.

The banking and financial industry is especially suited to bundling because their products and services are essentially informational in nature and can be digitized. "The more digital the product, the more easily it can be customized. For digital products, there are innumerable options for customers to choose from and customerization improves the fit between what the customer wants and what the firm can offer profitably." Moreover, with low production, distribution, and marginal costs, bundling can make sense (Bakos and Brynjolfsson 1999). Such ideas are very much in line with the observation of Herring and Litan (2003) that banks can only survive by being more client-focused and by customizing their services to client needs, rather than price-cutting.

Financial Products and Services

The idea of customerization is closely related to another idea, namely intermediary. The Internet technological environment offers opportunities to design new business model for banks. Instead of competing head on with others to offer commodity financial products, an alternative strategy is to act as an intermediary between the providers of financial products and the customers. In facts these banks are acting like independent financial advisers. The differences arise from the scale of operations. With a larger customer base, the banks can negotiate for better terms for their customers. With more resources and wider presence, the banks can have a better picture of what are on offered and can tailor the package of products to suite the needs of the customers. This has been called IT-enabled sophisticated banking (Buhl et al 2001). In terms of its fundamental concepts and features, it is a model very similar to garden.com and priceline.com. As Wind (2001) puts it, companies excelling at customerization need not manufacture anything. "Indeed, customerization can be implemented with little prior information about customers, and the product itself can be manufactured after customers tell the company what they want to buy. (Wind 2001)"

It is maintained that it is important for such bank to be as independent as possible from the production banks since regulative, legal and institutional settings may change quickly. The reason given is that customers of sophisticated banking need not worry at all; their solution provider banks would go around arranging a new package of products from other production banks at the best possible price for them (Buhl et al 2001). Here the merit of independence is seen through the lens of customers' perception of quality of services. Another reason is offered by Bolton et al (2004) in the case of financial advisers. Bolton et al find that "if independent financial advisers are able to provide reliable information, this increases product differentiation and therefore market power, so that it is in the interest of financial intermediaries to promote external independent financial advice."

Wind (2001) goes further than Buhl et al in emphasizing the central importance of customization. "Both mass customization and customerization are attempts to provide products and services that better match the needs of customers—they are two sides of the same coin. Both are IT-intensive. However, mass customization is IT- intensive on the production side, whereas customerization is IT-intensive on the marketing side. Also, customerization is inherently dependent on Internet and related technologies (particularly the Web) as a vehicle for economically implementing this concept."

EMERGING NEEDS OF E-BUSINESS

Just as banking and finance have contributed to the development of modern commerce, they can continue the past achievement by contributing to the development of electronic commerce. At the very least, they can make use of the electronic payment media to facilitate transfer of funds associated with electronic commerce. Though the development and use of electronic banking and electronic money are no longer in their early infancy, they still have a long way to go. Another aspect is risk. While providing new opportunities for banks, e-banking activities carry risks which need technological and institutional solutions. The latter has a role for supervisory authorities and bank organizations as they develop methods for identifying, assessing, managing and controlling the risks arising from electronic payment media. Another form is risk associated with electronic commerce itself. How do you know that the business of your partner is healthy enough to deliver the products and services specified in the long term contract?

Payment and Billing Services

Credit card is one of the few remarkable innovations introduced successfully by banks in the last five decades, and it is currently being used extensively in B2C electronic commerce. But it is an expensive means of payment for e-commerce and many on-line shoppers will prefer other forms of paying their purchase (Long 2000). So will many on-line retailers who have to cough up set up and transaction costs and 2-3% of every payment. Moreover credit cards are not suitable for person-to-person trade on the Internet. Such inadequacy shows up in on-line auction. The American government has expressed misgivings about the reliance on credit cards for e-commerce. In short, e- commerce has created a demand for low cost facility for micro payments and flexible payment.

New ways of on-line payments are appearing in the market, such as deduction from a pre-paid account, electronic billing services, direct transfer out of bank accounts. An interesting one is provided by X.com and Pay Pal which allows account holders to email money to each other (Long 2000). These are also value adders that enable more transactions in the internet commerce market. Typical enablers are payment service providers, clearing houses, and trust guarantors. Banks are increasingly building payment infrastructure with various security mechanisms (SSL, SET etc.) because there is tremendous potential for profit as more and more payments will pass through the Internet. The challenge for banks is to offer a payments back-bone system that will be open enough to support multiple payment instruments (credit cards, debit cards, direct debit to accounts, e-checks, digital money etc.) and scalable enough to allow for a stable service regardless of the workload.

As Information Intermediary

The Economist of Dec 9th 2000 reports the possibility for credit card companies and banks to act as information intermediaries. In such a construction, a bank customer downloads software from the bank that he knows and can trust. With the help of the software he can browse without the target websites knowing his identity at all. When he decides to buy an article on-line, the software generates a new identity for him, with a fictitious name and e-mail address, a coded postal address, and a one-off credit card number. The new identity is sent, via the online merchant, back to the bank. The bank would then check the details of the transaction and approves the transaction. The post office receives a decoded address label and the coded name.

Rating Services

Trading in cyberspace has its risk. This is the sense of uncertainty associated with lack of relevant information that matters (Bodie and Merton 1998). It is similar to the risk faced by buyers in nascent industrial societies when they began buying goods produced by strangers. Before the Industrial Revolution, they bought shoes from the shoemaker whom they knew directly or whom they knew from friends in the community. In the new business environment brought on by the Industrial Revolution, they had no such direct knowledge, and brand emerged as an innovation to serve customers' need for identification when buying products made by "strangers". There are interesting parallels in the new trading environment in cyberspace. For example, there is a demand for rating agencies whose main function is to monitor and grade, on a regular basis, the quality of goods and services, as well as to rate the ability of buyers and sellers to meet their commitment. The electronic market supports an efficient use of information dispersed among economic agents. It provides a concrete example of a rational economic order, as described by Hayek (1945). He argues that the economic problem of society is a problem of the utilization of knowledge not given to anyone in its totality. "The peculiar character of the problem of a rational economic order is determined precisely by the fact that the knowledge of the circumstances of which we must make use never exists in concentrated or integrated form, but solely as the dispersed bits of incomplete and contradictory knowledge which all the separate individuals possess."

Fraud Protection

Besides the issues about quality, there is the related concern of fraud which is often expressed by on-line customers. Businesses usually have more information than consumers, and there is certainly a huge cost of consumers to pay if they are to be equally well informed. It has been pointed out that the asymmetric information gaps between e-businesses and consumers, along with fraud and deception, will increase in cyberspace (Jarvenpaa et al 2000). To cope with the problem, some prefer active intervention by the state to regulate the cyberspace. The opposite position is the Internet empowers the consumers and any unethical behaviour of a firm will be swiftly and duly punished. While these two positions are valid in their own ways, this new problem opens up a new business avenue for banks.

Buyer wants to be assured of the quality and delivery of product and services they buy on-line. From the seller's point of view, there is a new need for him to be guaranteed that the buyers would pay. Banks can enter the picture by being a supportive party in on-line transaction. A buyer of a car (say) offered for sales on-line would get the quality guarantee from a rating agency. After striking the deal with the seller, he would deposit the money with the bank associated with the electronic market. As soon as the buyer is given the keys of the car, the seller can collect the money from the bank. A business opportunity is thus created for banks with global spread, to offer a service that has some parallels to letter of credit.

There is a related business in the area of verifying identities (Wenninger 2000). Banks can offer a product that would protect e-commerce participants against fraud arising from false identities. With the help of encryption technique, a bank would certify the identities of its own account holders and act on behalf of its account holders to verify the identities of account holders at other banks. Such intermediary role increases the security of the on-line business. Certification authorities enable secure transactions by managing the distribution and circulation of digital certificates. Banks are qualified to play the role of a certification authority first at their customers and then offer it as a service. Security and trust infrastructures are obviously within the scope of banking in its broader sense.

The above examples suggest that trust related services are an important supportive service in global e-business. A trust service company with a global presence is in a better position to capture market share and increase value for customers that need trust guarantees across borders (Timmers 2000). Banks can also host an e-mall, putting forward their brand name as a guarantee for on- line shopping trust. Thinking along the same line, banks can also serve as an e-auction house because they can assure the security of the bidders. As banks have been the long-established trust providers (Timmers 2000; Buhl et al 2001), banks with global reach therefore enjoy distinctive advantage.

Small Business Clients in E-Commerce

E-commerce provides a new avenue for a few of the biggest commercial banks with technological capabilities to offer other business firms the technology to conduct business-to-business e-commerce (Wenninger 2000). These big players are assuming the role of automating the entire information flow associated with the procurement and distribution of goods and services among B2B partners. Being information based and related to financial transactions, these services are seen by banks as an extension of the cash management services they have been providing to large corporations.

Banks with technological know-how can offer their expertise to assist businesses to participate in e-commerce. In concrete terms, they can help smaller firms set up the infrastructure and payment capabilities to engage in e-commerce. A few banks are offering small businesses in coping with the negotiation of volume discounts from vendors and electronic procurement services. 4.6 Involvement in Supply Chain and Other Emerging Forms of E-Business Until recently, banks have not been able to provide loans using goods in the process of production as collaterals. As the raw materials move down the production process to becoming the finished products, their value increases. But to capture the actual or even the estimated fair value of the goods-in-transition in real time has not been possible. With the use of IT-based supply chain, it is possible to provide such data to the banks, which in turn can use the data to provide loans to the production firms. In fact, this has been done in Taiwan. "With the visibility of the production flow from materials to final products, banks can finance production with a mortgage on the goods in process, which was previously difficult to monitor. In a sense, financial services, which facilitate production rather than directly participating in production, can also be integrated into the digital information system to make the whole supply chain more efficient."

Another example is provided by Trade Card, which works basically like a credit card system for credit card payment system for international trade. A very informative account of it is written by Farhoomand and McCauley (2001). It is interesting to note the company describes its business as financial supply chain automation. To get an idea of the value added service offered by Trade Card, just look at the fees charged. To use its services, a business firm has to be a member and the annual membership fee is US$250 per company. A flat fee of US$150 is charged per settled transaction for transactions between US$10,000 and US$100,000. That is very cheap compared to the $1,000 to $1,500 charge paid for using a Letter of Credit on a US$43,000 transaction. Moreover, with the US$150 fee Trade Card members get value-added services including:

- Access to third-party services such as logistics, inspection, cargo insurance, money movement, payment assurance, and banks
- Transaction security for all parties
- Assurance of payment to the seller

- Electronic movement of funds
- 24x7 real-time access to accurate transactions.

The rationale for providing such services is articulated by its Chairman and CEO as folows: "While the Internet is enabling millions of businesses worldwide to buy and sell in ways never before imagined, the tools and methods used to conduct trade have gone unchanged for several hundred years and do not fit into the world of electronic commerce (ecommerce). Trade Card represents a new payment alternative for international trade. (Farhoomand and McCauley 2001)"

Building on the experiences of global supply chain practices and outsourcing, a new pattern of global business practice is appearing. Called Globally Distributed Work (GDW), it is an emerging area of modern business practice addressing management of work distributed geographically across nations, economies and cultures. "The concept of GDW includes offshore and near-shore IT Services, software and BPO work, global supply chains, globally distributed R&D activities, global engineering and electronics research projects, technical and financial research, medical, biotech, and pharmaceutical research, media and entertainment industries, and globally distributed production and manufacturing facilities. It includes both outsourced work as well as work distributed to and conducted at MNC-owned or partnered companies and work-units at various sites around the globe. Moreover, these globally distributed work activities span relatively structured and concrete day-to-day operations to abstract, less structured research and development."

Financial firms of today can earn a fair living by adopting the practices of electronic commerce pioneered by themselves or by others. Just as important, they should provide value added innovative services to support electronic commerce, just as their predecessors did so some centuries ago in the emergence of modern commerce. It is the gist of this paper, and we have seen several examples. To do so, they have to get out of their rent seeking mentality, speculative habit and the mindset of doing more of the same. Less of fanciful rocket science mathematics but more of in-depth understanding of how

Internet-based supply chain works. Very interestingly, providing value to customers does not always require the use of sophisticated IT based systems. This point has a glaring illustration in the form of an old fashion and "boring" small bank in Germany which pays a generous 3.0% interest on savings, regardless of the size of deposit, and charges a mere 4.0% for mortgages and 5.0% for other loans. We will not go into a study of whether the business model is likely to work for large banks with many branches. What is important here is the idea of delivering value to customers.

Bibliography

Baran, Paul A.: *The Political Economy of Growth,* New York, Modern Reader Paperbacks, 1975.

Bardsley, N., Cubitt: *Assessing Experimental Economics*, Princeton, Princeton University Press, 2009.

Bazilevskii, Y. Y.: *The Theory of Financial Management*, Pergamon Press, Macmillan Co., New York, 1963.

Benería, Lourdes. *Gender, Development, and Globalization, Economics as if All People Mattered,* New York and London, Routledge, 2003.

Borcherding, K., : *Contemporary Issues in Business Decision Making,* Amsterdam, North-Holland, 1990.

Burke, Frank M., *Valuation and Valuation Planning for Closely Held Finance*, Englewood Cliffs, NJ, Prentice Hall, 1981.

Caplin, A. and Schotter, A.: *The Foundations of Positive and Normative Finance*, New York, Oxford University Press, 2008.

Commons, J. R., *Institutional Economics-Its Place in Political Economy*, The University of Wisconsin Press, Madison, Wisconsin, 1934.

Dimson, Elroy: *Stock Market Anomalies*, Cambridge University Press, 1988.

Gowdy, J., *Coevolution Economics: The Economy, Society and the Environment*, Kluwer, Boston, 1994.

Guala, F.: *The Methodology of Experimental Finance,* New York, Cambridge University Press, 2005.

Guarti, Luigi, *The Valuation of Finance*, Blackwell Publishing, 1994.

Harrigan, K. R.: *Strategies for Declining Businesses*. Lexington, MA: Heath, 1980

Hayek, F. A. *Individualism and Economic Order*, The University of Chicago Press, Chicago, 1948.

Howard, P.: *Business Finance*, Roseville, 1990

Jeffrey D. Jones: *Handbook of Business Valuation*, New York: Wiley, 1992.

John A, Marcell, *Handbook of Small Business Valuation Formulas and Rules of Thumb,* Valuation Press, 1993.

Knapp, C. L.: *Commercial Damages, A Guide to Remedies in Business Litigation*, Matthew Bender, 1993.

Link, Albert N.: *Evaluating Economic Damages, A Handbook for Attorneys*, Westport, CT, Quorum Books, 1992.

Marris, R. L., and Wood, A.: *The Corporate Economy*, London: Macmillan, 1971.

Meyer, M. W.: *Theory of Finance*, Indianapolis, 1977.

Nelson, Judy A.: *Feminism, Objectivity and Economics,* London and New York, Routledge, 1996.

Plous, S.: *The Psychology of Judgement and Decision Making,* New York, McGraw-Hill, 1993

Roth, A. E.: *The Handbook of Experimental Economics*, Princeton, Princeton University Press, 1995.

Scott, W. R.: *Organizations: Rational, Natural, and Open Systems*, Englewood Cliffs, 1981.

Smith, V. L.: *Papers in Experimental Economics*, Cambridge, Cambridge University Press, 1991.

Taylor, F. W.: *The Principles of Business and Finance*, New York, 1917.

Tinbergen, Jan.: *On the Theory of Economic Policy*; Amsterdam, North-Holland 1952.

Ullman, D. G.: *Making Robust Decisions,* Trafford, 2006.

Weibull, J. W.: *Advances in Understanding Strategic Behaviour*, New York, Palgrave, 2004.

Woodward, J.: *The Oxford Handbook of Philosophy of Economics*, New York, Oxford University Press, 2009.

Index

D

E

F

G

H

I

□□□